FOLLOW YOUR DREAMS

JANE McDONALD
Follow Your Dreams

HarperCollins*Entertainment*
An Imprint of HarperCollins*Publishers*

HarperCollins*Entertainment*
An Imprint of HarperCollins*Publishers*
77–85 Fulham Palace Road,
Hammersmith, London W6 8JB

www.**fire**and**water**.com

Published by HarperCollins*Entertainment* 2000
3 5 7 9 8 6 4 2

A catalogue record for this book
is available from the British Library

ISBN 0 00 710741 2

Set in Sabon and Bodoni Classico

Printed and bound in Great Britain by
Omnia Books Ltd, Glasgow

CONTENTS

ACKNOWLEDGMENTS   vii

PROLOGUE   1

BEGINNINGS   7

THE PIANO   27

TEENAGE DREAMS   39

FIRST LOVES   57

CLUBLAND   75

RUNNING AWAY TO SEA   109

THE LOVE OF MY LIFE   135

FLIGHT TO DESTINY   151

THE CRUISE   171

A CORPORATE WIFE   195

GOING BALLISTIC   217

THE WEDDING   241

BREAKING RECORDS   253

FOLLOWING MY DREAMS   281

EPILOGUE   307

CAREER HIGHLIGHTS   311

ACKNOWLEDGMENTS

When I was first asked to write my autobiography, I laughed, then I thought I'd have to make myself sound interesting, but this book is not so much about me, but about experiencing life and meeting wonderful people.

I couldn't have written this without the following people who gave freely of their time in reminding me of stories and events in my life: firstly, my mother – the woman who is everything to me, the nicest woman I know, who has shown me unconditional love and support and always makes sure I eat properly. Secondly I would like to thank Henrik Brixen, my loving husband and soul mate, for his patience, support, whiz-kid business head and for being there during the most important five years of my life – I love him with all my heart.

Thanks also go to Janet Pratt, my big sister who will always be the strong one of the family but whom I will always see as the beauty queen from all those years ago. To Tony McDonald, my big brother, my best friend, my protector and confidant – thank you for so many wonderful memories. To Wendy McDonald – goodness knows where I would be without Wendy, not only the best sister-in-law in the world but also a person with the same sense of humour – thank you for all your hard work and devotion: you are priceless.

Thanks to Janet Ferguson, my grandmother, who is an amazing woman – I am full of love and admiration for her, she is the one who taught me manners, respect and how to be a lady (well two out of three isn't bad is it?)

I am also indebted to Elizabeth Ward, my very first best friend. Our times together were wonderful, she will always remain a special person in my life. To Steve Holbrook, my best friend and advisor for the past thirteen years: my guru, always there and always making me feel wonderful – how do you do it? Heartfelt thanks to Sue Ravey, my backing singer, a heart of gold and a friendship that has grown over the years, a fabulous singer who inspires me just as much as the legends. I am so grateful for your wonderful voice, your support and especially your friendship.

Final thanks go to Nick Fiveash – thank you for giving me wings and letting me fly, for always believing in me and for your constant advice and love – also one of the best cooks I know. To Chris Terrill – a messenger from God – thank you for finding me, believing in me and giving me my big break – I will be eternally grateful to you my friend. Grateful thanks also to Mike Alexander, Caroline Joyce, Michael Mullane and Nicky Asker for their invaluable input into this book.

PROLOGUE

I walk through my new house on the outskirts of Wakefield. It is on part of an ancient farm, surrounded by dry stone walls and shaded by tall beech and chestnut trees. In the surrounding woods, the wild cherry and crab-apples are just coming to the end of their blossoming season, perhaps the last memory of a long-ago orchard planted by monks, for to one side is a small copse of gnarled old yews marking where a ruined abbey once stood.

Gazing out of the window at newly-planted lawns and flower beds, I imagine the hooded men who once walked and prayed there in long-gone cloisters, the sturdy Yorkshire yeomen who made bows perhaps from those same yews and the lumbering oxen that ploughed these fertile acres beside the River Calder.

In all my wildest dreams, growing up from the age of six in a two-up, two-down terraced house on the Peacock Estate in the working class part of Wakefield, I never imagined that some day I would be living here, in this spacious airy house. Every new brick and every timber celebrates my incredible luck, a sea-change in fortune which after years of grinding slog in the music business has brought me to this place.

It is a day in early summer and sunlight gleams on the polished furniture in the music room. I run my hands over the grand piano, smelling the perfume from the cream roses in a crystal bowl placed on the top. Also on the top are family photographs. There's my husband, Henrik, fair-haired and gorgeous, a man I keep pinching myself over, still hardly able to believe that he's all mine. At the moment he is away in our other home in Florida where his marine engineering businesses are based – and I miss him dreadfully.

'Our other home in Florida!'

Did I, Jane McDonald, really write those words? Other people, rich or famous people, have second homes – not me. Only now, somehow, in some miraculous way I have achieved just that, and every morning I wake up with a sense of joy mixed with a very large dose of unreality, wondering if it's all a dream because it's happened so fast I still haven't had time to draw my breath. But no, this morning I awoke, and found my good fortune is still here like a little pot of gold the hobgoblins didn't steal away in the night. If you can live a dream, then I am living this one.

I pick up and almost tenderly hold the faded snap of Dad as a handsome young man, with Mum, pretty in a floral frock that Gran made. I am in the middle between them, also wearing one of Gran's summery cotton dresses. My long, dark hair falls forward in two bunches almost down to my waist, my eyes are scrunched up in the sun as I gaze earnestly into the camera that has captured for ever that long-ago summer holiday at Bridlington.

That was the year that Mum and Dad good-naturedly pushed me into the beauty contest, up there on that stage before a sea of faces at the holiday camp where we rented a caravan for a week every summer. I will always remember how embarrassed I'd felt, parading up and down in my skinny velvet stretch pants and a little white blouse, trying to hide behind my curtain of long hair instead of camping it up like the other girls. To my astonishment, I won, even though I was probably the scrawniest beauty queen in the entire history of pageants. The prize was another week's holiday, which we couldn't take up because we had almost run out of spending money. But still the family all crowded around, Mum and Gran proud, my sister Janet just that tiny bit jealous – which seemed really funny to me because she was the pretty one of the family, like Mum, with her blue eyes, pink and white skin and brown curls whilst, in those days, I was still a very plain Jane indeed. Janet was so striking, she had won the title of 'Miss Wakefield' as a sixteen-year-old schoolgirl and I remember the excitement in our house when her photograph appeared on the front page of the local newspaper.

My brother Tony, five years older than me whom I adored with a deep and abiding love, for whom I would still walk on hot coals to the ends of the earth, grinned cynically at me, his little sister, the beauty queen, as only an older brother can.

'I look just like you,' I said. 'If you were a girl you would have won instead, so stop laughing.'

Then came the contest I really wanted to win – the talent contest. I knew 'Downtown', the song I always thought of as mine, backwards, forwards and sideways, as Gran would say. She held my hand tightly, 'Now, lovey, it's only a summer holiday show,' she said in her soft Scottish voice. 'It doesn't matter if you don't win. You've already won a nice prize.'

'I know, Gran,' I said, 'But I can sing better than I'm pretty.'

Gran laughed, 'You do say some funny things, Jane. Now, off you go and enjoy yourself.'

Lined up with the other contestants in the wings behind the tatty curtain, *enjoyment* was the last thing on my mind as I started to feel sick with my first dose of stage fright. I panted and trembled, willing myself not to throw up or run away and hide. Then my name was called, the pianist struck up the opening chord and Dad urged me on. All fear vanished as I opened my mouth to sing. My voice, big even then and surprising, so everyone said, in a titchy little nine-year-old, poured out as I sang the words I had known since I was a baby, from 'Downtown', sung by Petula Clarke.

Everyone clapped and cheered as I took a bow. The compère walked on. 'Thank you, Jane McDonald!' he said. 'Very nice, dear, very nice.'

I should have guessed from Gran's gentle words of caution that, with her special gift of looking into the future, she already knew what the outcome would be, but I longed to win the singing contest and so had not listened. Well, I didn't win, and was more mortified than I can ever remember being, thinking everyone was laughing at me for making a fool of myself.

'The buggers have all got cloth ears. You were the best,' Dad said.

'Jane won the beauty contest,' Mum, the peace keeper, said. 'She can't win both contests, it wouldn't be fair on the other kids, would it?'

'I didn't want to win the beauty contest!' I protested. 'I wanted to win the one for singing!'

'Right, that's it,' said Dad. 'I'm going to have a word with that so-called judge.'

It was no good Mum trying to grasp Dad's sleeve and drag him back, nothing was going to stop him championing me. When he returned, he looked at Mum and laughed. 'You were

4

right – Jane was the best but they wanted another kid to have a chance,' he said, adding with a wink, 'I don't know why I bother, with all these blooming clairvoyants in the family, you know the news before it's in the papers.'

I pick up Gran's photograph from the piano. Her hair, once gold as spun silk, is now white like candyfloss and her blue eyes that always seemed to look into infinity stare back at me. They're fading in intensity now, those eyes, and a recent operation has left her partially sighted, but at the age of ninety-four she's still alert and deals with post from all around the world from people seeking her advice as a psychic of international renown.

The first glimmerings that my gran, Janet Ferguson, had a rare gift came when she was just six years old. Like me, she'd been a lonely and nervous little girl. Her mother, nanny to a rich family, had left Janet at home in a little village near Dundee, on the banks of the Tay, to be brought up by her grandmother while she travelled the world with the wealthy family that employed her. Then Gran's grandmother died and she was passed around from pillar to post for a while until things settled down a bit. When her other grandmother passed away, Janet – Nettie for short – had been dressed in one of those white smocks that all Edwardian children wore at the turn of the century to keep their clothes clean and sent out to play in the garden while the adults got ready for the funeral. When someone remembered to check on her later they found her playing in the dirt. She was taken back indoors, washed, changed and lectured, then sent outside again with firm orders to sit on the swing and not move.

A long time passed and little Nettie grew bored. Thinking

no one could see her from the house, she was about to jump from the swing when she heard the voice of the recently departed grandmother, after whom she was named. 'Now, Nettie, stay on that swing!' said her granny.

Nettie glanced up and saw her grandmother in the sky looking down at her. 'Yes, Granny,' she said obediently, not thinking that this was an unusual event.

It was a story I never tired of hearing as a child.

'She was in her night-gown, fastened to her chin, and her long black plaits hung down each side of her face, tied with white ribbons,' Gran told me. 'I saw her as clearly as I can see you, Jane,' she said, dreamily gazing back to that long-ago scene in Monifieth.

But then, Gran could always see me clearly, too clearly, I often thought, I was never able to get away with very much – not that I ever wanted to get away with much. All I ever wanted to do was to please Mum and Dad.

I replace the photograph and sit at the piano, my hands running lightly over the keys as a new song begins to take shape in my mind. I marvel that I have such a beautiful instrument, remembering my very first piano, a rickety pub Joanna that cost twenty-five bob. You could still see all the cigarette burns and the rings from beer glasses on the top – but Dad said he'd sand it down and re-varnish it. I smile as I remember the excitement as that old piano was wheeled into the house, and the melody I am picking out on the keys fades, my fingers lie quietly in my lap. I think of my life. More and more memories come, things I thought I'd forgotten…

BEGINNINGS

My pretty, brown-haired mother, Jean Ferguson, met my
father, a dashing, darkly handsome young carpenter from
Fife, named Peter McDonald, at the Palais de Danse in
Coatbridge, a steel town with a high rate of unemployment,
near Glasgow. They were married within a month. By the
time my sister, Janet, was six months old, most of the family
suddenly made up their minds to move south to Wakefield to
find work. My mother had written to my aunt Nancy – who
had already made the move with her bus-driver husband and
was doing well – to say they were thinking of joining her.
Nancy wrote by return: 'Make up your mind quickly, because
I can get you a house in the same street as me.'

Mum read the letter to Dad that evening, and at once he
said, 'Start packing lassie – we're going.'

Jimmy, Mum's younger brother, dropped by at their house
after work that evening and he got swept up in the excitement
as their plans were discussed. 'We'll all go!' he exclaimed.

Everybody in the family knew that Gran, widowed for
some four years, was resistant to change, so Mum laughed.
'You'll never get our mother to agree,' she said. 'But you're
welcome to come with us, Jimmy.'

That evening, when Gran came home from work she was

exhausted and went straight to bed. She had the next day off and was going to get up early to do some decorating, the tin of paint already bought for that purpose. She was dozing lightly when Jimmy dashed back to the house he shared with her and his schoolgirl sister, Barbara. He popped his head around the bedroom door and asked, 'Are you awake?' Not waiting for a reply he said, 'Don't open that tin of paint – we're going to Wakefield.'

Remarkably, my grandmother agreed at once. 'Well then, if we're going, we'd best take the paint with us, it will come in handy,' she said. But, erring on the side of caution, she kept her house.

In Wakefield, the family of six settled into a back-to-back terraced house found for them by Nancy in a run-down area known as Piccadilly, in the shadow of the grim, fortress-like prison and the railway station. It was the kind of crowded housing with earth closets, heaps of coal and dustbins in the grimy back yards, where children played in the street. Dad quickly found work as a coach builder. Life was a constant struggle, but my parents worked hard and saved for their dream of a large house on the outskirts of town in which to bring up their two children – Janet and, within five years, my brother Tony. There was plenty of work down the mines and when Dad heard how much men were paid for the dangerous job at the coal face, he applied at once, despite Mum's anxiety.

But her fears gradually faded and with a steady wage coming in my parents could save hard. Within five or six years of their arrival in Wakefield, the family was able to move into a spacious Victorian house in Eastmoor Road on the posh side of town. The fact that the only way they could afford to live there would be to take in boarders, seemed a very small sacrifice to pay for a better life. Finding boarders was no problem, for just along Eastmoor Road was the famed West Yorkshire Police College, where officers from around the world came to do specialist CID courses and needed accommodation.

All this was before I was born of course – but sometimes a part of your history that you cannot have been aware of becomes yours by a process of osmosis as the stories are told and retold over the years during shared family moments – such as the story of my birth. It was an old-fashioned, gallons-of-hot-water affair, presided over by my grandmother. My father, being merely a man and no longer considered useful to the proceedings, hovered downstairs, listening to the radio with one ear and the busy comings and goings of the midwife and Gran with the other. At the top of the house, where few sounds carried were two policemen from Jordan, in their private sitting room. Normally, there would be six lodgers but, as my mother noted, she felt that she'd arranged it rather well because I was born on a weekend, when most of the policemen had gone home.

It seems my mother had been in labour for hours, with all the attendant fuss, when Gran emerged from the bedroom to find young Janet sitting on the top stair in her dressing gown clenching her fists into little balls and fiercely muttering, 'Come on, Mother, get on with it!'

Gran thought the noise of the gas and air machine and Mum's moans had scared the girl. 'You shouldn't be out here, dearie,' Gran said, 'Away to bed with you.'

'Hasn't the baby come yet, Gran?' Janet asked, in an agony of tension.

'Not yet,' Gran said.

'When?' Janet demanded.

'You'll have a new brother or sister by the morning,' Gran

promised kindly, not understanding Janet's concerns. 'Your mum is doing just fine. Now go and get some sleep, dearie.'

The clock chimed in the hall. Janet counted the hours; eleven o'clock! Nearly midnight! 'I don't want the baby to have my birthday,' she cried.

'Well, dearie, Mother is doing her best. She can't make the baby come any faster,' Gran said. 'It will come in its own sweet time.'

That wasn't what Janet wanted to hear. Reluctantly, she dawdled along to her bedroom and got into bed, where she chanted a mantra to herself as she tried to drift off to sleep: 'Come on, come on, get on with it! Make it *today*!'

The cause of Janet's distress was that it was her ninth birthday the next day – the fifth of April – and she was terrified that Mum would still be in the throes of giving birth, and her presents and the iced birthday cake would go by the board. Equally distressing would be to have the new arrival sharing – and somehow diluting for ever – her special day. Happily, I beat the clock, popping into the world half an hour later on the fourth of April 1963, coinciding with a high-pitched shriek from the kettle coming to the boil on the ancient iron range.

Mistaking the sound of the kettle for a new-born's first cry, Janet sat bolt upright in bed, fervently saying, 'Thank you God, thank you, thank you!' Her birthday was safe, she could finally go to sleep. Perhaps she would not have slept so peacefully had she known that for the next nine years she would be inflicted with me sharing her bedroom, until she escaped by marrying at eighteen and leaving home.

Mum had a more immediate concern, which was what to do with a new baby while she and Gran looked after the boarders? Her solution was to feed and change me first thing in the morning then put me in my pram in our private dining room with the radio playing to keep me company while she hurried to the kitchen to prepare breakfast for the boarders. 'Be a good girl for Mummy,' she'd say and, perfectly happy on my own, I lay in my pram, absorbing the songs I heard – particularly a current hit played to death on the radio, called 'Downtown'. Like a parrot, I absorbed the words as Petula Clark painted a picture of bright city lights, a place where you could forget all your cares.

One day, when Mum came to fetch me after breakfast, I held out my arms to her and quite distinctly said, 'Downtown.'

'What did you say?' Mum asked.

'Downtown,' I gurgled, waving my arms around, 'Downtown!'

Astonished, Mum ran to fetch Gran. 'Come and listen! The bairn's said her first word,' Mum exclaimed. 'Tell me what you think she's saying.'

Obviously pleased with the effect I was having, I chimed, 'Downtown... downtown...!'

'Well, I never!' Gran said. 'It's that song on the radio.'

Mum was alarmed. 'Do you think that bang on her head has anything to do with it?' She was referring to the time when my sister Janet had taken my out in my pram to show me off to some of her school friends and had dropped me on my head. She had run all the way home, terrified that I'd be brain-damaged for life while I, with scarlet face and thrashing limbs, screamed like an express train as we flew by the hedges of Eastmoor Road.

I had a few other tricks up my sleeve, all of them pointers to my future career as a singer. When I was about nine months old, Mum had put me down in my cot in her bedroom for my afternoon nap. Later, when she came to wake me up, I had vanished. Alarmed, Mum shouted up the stairs, 'Mum, have you seen Jane?'

'Aye, she's here. Didn't you bring her up?'

'No, of course not,' Mum said.

Long before I could walk, I had climbed out of the cot and crawled up the steep stairs to Gran's flat in the attic where I sat on the rug and entertained Gran by singing a recognisable version of 'Downtown'.

'She came crawling into my room. I thought you'd set her down on the landing outside my door,' Gran said

Mum was shocked. 'Och, I'd never do such a thing – the wee bairn might have tumbled headlong down the stairs.'

Since there was nobody else in the house, the only answer was that, somehow, I had managed to make it to the top on my own. Mum put me back in my cot and they watched. As soon as I was left on my own, I pulled myself up on the bars of my cot and climbed out. 'She's like a monkey!' Mum exclaimed. 'She has no sense of fear.' After that, Dad fixed the cot sides higher and lowered the base to keep me in it, and everyone was extra vigilant where stairs were concerned.

By the age of three, I was dancing as well as singing. My favourite place was in a pool of rainbow colours on the hall floor where sunlight shone through stained glass in the front door, like a spotlight shining on to a stage. The fairy twirling on a jewellery box, I was oblivious to everyone, locked in my own little world.

Watching me, Gran said, 'Ah well, Jane is just preparing for her destiny.'

Gran could say this with conviction since the move to Wakefield had unexpectedly revealed her own destiny. A woman who rarely made spur-of-the-moment decisions, at first Gran had wondered if she had made a mistake in leaving Scotland so spontaneously. She always felt her home was where her family was, but her teenage daughter, Barbara, was homesick and missed her friends. While Gran was aimlessly wheeling baby Janet up and down the pavement outside the house to get some fresh air, a woman stopped and introduced herself, saying she had noticed Gran in the back yard from the windows of her own house in the street directly behind. 'Are you settling down all right?' she asked.

'Aye, but there's not a lot to do, is there?' Gran replied. 'To be honest, I was thinking about returning to Scotland.'

'Come to a social evening at my church tonight,' the woman urged. 'We're a friendly crowd. I'm the secretary, so I can introduce you to everybody.'

'I'm not really the religious type,' Gran said.

'Oh, you don't have to worry about that,' the neighbour said. She explained that it was a Spiritualist Church and run on very different lines from more conventional churches. So, more out of curiosity than anything else, Gran went with Mum. During the social hour in the big back room of the church, a woman, who turned out to be an elderly medium, came over to Gran and said, 'You're in a turmoil. You're going round and round and don't know what to do. Get rid of your house, because you'll make a lot more friends and you've got a lot of work to do here.'

Gran was surprised because nobody knew that she hadn't yet sold her house in Coatbridge. Following this advice, she stayed and discovered that she had a rare gift as a natural clairvoyant. It wasn't long before she became president of the church and famed as a psychic counsellor and demonstrator. Mum had no gift herself, but she became treasurer. For many years, the two of them ran the church – which meant they were there almost every evening. At first, Mum took me when I was still small and needed looking after; but as I grew older, gradually I became Dad's shadow, his constant companion.

It never occurred to me that we were working class because it never does when you're very young. No furniture had come from Scotland when the family moved down, it being considered too expensive to hire a removal van, so when Mum and Dad came to furnish the big guest house, they went to the second-hand shops in the back streets of Wakefield. You could get good solid stuff in those days, Edwardian furniture going as cheap as chips by a generation who wanted G-plan and studio couches. Without meaning to, we ended up with other people's heirlooms, mahogany sideboards with bevelled mirrors, tables that seated ten and the kind of sofas and chairs that demanded antimacassars. Mum and Gran were energetic housekeepers, so everything was polished and washed until it sparkled, spiders got short shrift and dust wasn't allowed to settled for long. The house had that lived-in, comforting smell of furniture polish, pine disinfectant and, with so many meals constantly being cooked or prepared, I have an abiding memory of good smells drifting up from the kitchen in the basement, of bacon sizzling, toast grilling, bread and cakes baking and meat roasting.

The lodgers always came first. They got the best of everything and we tended to get what was left. If the police-men were having roast chicken, they'd get the breasts and the legs, while we got what was left in a pie or fricasseed on a mound of rice. The trimmings from their grilled lamb chops turned into our Irish stew, thickened with potatoes and suet dumplings. Even at the end of the week when the housekeeping tin was empty, Mum dreamed up nourishing and filling meals almost out of thin air, becoming famed for her tasty casseroles, curries and shepherds pies. She and Gran were wonders at creative cooking, making simple ingredients stretch a mile, and their curries, at first tentative experiments devised in honour of the Indian guests to make them feel at home in the chilly climate of the West Yorkshire moors, became praised as being 'really delicious, just like we get at home!'

'One of the good things about a curry,' Mum always said when meat was in short supply and a visit to the butcher out of the question until the bill was paid, 'is that you can put almost anything in it and you can't go wrong.'

Mum and Gran also started baking cakes and buns for the church's coffee mornings and the odd bring-and-buy sale. I can still remember sitting at one end of the kitchen table watching Mum making pastry, mixing it in Gran's big yellow china bowl, getting a ball of dough, sprinkling a fine sifting of flour over the pastry board and then rolling it out. Back and forth went the pin, round and round she would turn the circle of dough until it was the right size. I'd be given my own little piece of dough but it always ended up grubby and as hard as a rock. Something hot from the oven and a glass of milk was always the high point of the daily baking ritual for me, while Bobby, Janet's scruffy, black-and-white, mostly mongrel collie who lay on the rug before the range, was always humbly grateful for my disasters.

Dad had always promised Mum a large garden of her own, where she could plant flowers but, despite having a respectable front garden, the new house had only a very small yard to the rear. Dad managed to get a large patch on the nearby allotments where he spent the first few weeks in a fury of double-digging and manure-spreading, while the more relaxed gardeners looked on grinning and nudged each other, 'Eh, happen the lad'ull soon slow down when he does 'is back in,' they said, pausing for a roll-up.

Dad's rush was that the garden had to start producing food, vital in helping to stretch the housekeeping money and putting meals on the table. He took it very seriously, striding up to the hill behind the house every day in all weathers after he'd put in a hard shift down the mine. I'd always be ready to go with him in my red duffel coat and little red wellies.

'Come on lassie, up wi' you,' Dad said as he hoisted me on to his broad shoulders and off we'd go, him striding along the road and up the hill with Bobby running ahead. Whatever the weather, it always seemed as if we were walking upwards into the light. The view from the top was expansive, over the whole of the Vale of Wakefield to Emley Moor on the far skyline. I could see steeples and towers and rivers. The sense of space made me want to fly like one of the birds on the winds that seemed to constantly blow across the Pennines.

Some of my favourite times were in the spring when the tender new heads of rhubarb emerged from the dark soil. All three of us children would go up with our little bags of sugar to dip the pale pink stalks in, chewing on the tart-sweetness. There were ruby strawberries nestling on their straw beds, fat golden gooseberries and pea vines twining on spiky sticks cut from the overgrown hawthorn hedge that surrounded the allotments.

Mum said that Dad could grow as many vegetables as he pleased – as long as he grew some flowers for her.

'Don't be daft, lassie, it's a waste of space,' he protested.

'I'd like a nice row of chrysanthemums,' Mum mused, 'the

kind with double heads, bronze and yellow. They'll last a long time and will look lovely in the hall.'

'If you want flowers, you can go up and plant your own,' Dad said.

'And in the spring, you can plant me a row of sweet peas. And leeks,' Mum continued, oblivious.

'Leeks? They're not bloody flowers,' Dad said.

'Every self-respecting Scottish housewife has to have her leeks for the stockpot. You can't make a good Scotch broth without it,' Mum said.

'How many rows?' asked Dad, caving in.

'Well, you have to have a stockpot always on the go,' Mum said. 'Fifty plants a year should be enough.'

I'm sure Dad said 'Bloody hell' or something close, but Mum got her leeks and her flowers as well as sacks of potatoes, beets, carrots, cabbages, cauliflowers, marrows and runner beans and, in the summer, a constant glut of tomatoes. I don't know how or where Dad learned to garden, but it rapidly became a passion with him – possibly because most things he planted were a success, unlike some of the other tasks he undertook. It wasn't that he was a poor craftsman – far from it; but he never had enough money to get the proper materials. No matter what he did, whether it was fixing one of his old vans or installing electric wiring in the house, the job was bodged. Dad became known as 'rusty van man'; but he did his best. He'd stand back, look at his handiwork and, knowing it was almost certainly likely to fall to bits pretty soon, pronounced with more optimism than certainty, 'It'll do'. And sometimes, much to his amazement, it did do, for years on end.

But gardening was another matter – in that direction, at least, nature lent a considerable hand and his garden did grow. I can't remember that any of us actually helped our dad, even with the weeding – and I doubt if he would have let us, but I was very happy running about in the allotment in all weathers. When it was sunny, I would find a patch of grass to curl up in, soaking in the warmth like a cat. Tony's favourite spot was the big field adjoining the allotments which was also the rugby pitch for Pinderfields Hospital, where he let me fly the kites that Dad made, wonderful things with long tails that seemed to touch the clouds.

When I was tired after playing all day, Dad would carry me down the hill on his shoulders. I would look down from that height at what seemed an almost vertical slope ahead of his feet striding in their heavy miner's boots, and I knew that I would never fall, that he would always keep me safe.

But peace of mind is a fragile thing, quickly lost and hard to regain. For a child, fear can be waiting in the wings, closer to hand than is realised.

Built of weathered Yorkshire stone, the Parish School was a long low building within close walking distance on the opposite side of the road from our house. You went in one end as a tot and a few years later emerged from the other end, fully-fledged. Janet had already gone off to the nearby girls' grammar school, but Tony still went to the Parish School and I longed to go with him, my face glued sadly to the front bedroom window each morning, watching him setting off. He would turn at the gate and wave at me, then I watched him walking along the pavement as far as I could until he was out of sight. But I knew that if I waited for a few moments more, he would cross over the road to the school. As soon as he was back in my line of vision, I would wave frantically, shouting,

'Tony! Tony!' Of course he couldn't hear me, but I loved it when he remembered to turn and wave one more time before vanishing inside.

Like a dog who always knows when its owner is returning, I would watch out again at the end of the day to see my big brother exploding out of the school with all the other children and running homewards. At the corner, opposite Clifton's corner shop, he'd catch sight of me and wave, and if he'd been given a few spare coppers that day, he would pantomime that he was going into Clifton's to buy a ton of sweeties and would eat the lot, all to himself. He vanished into the shop, emerging a little later, rubbing his tummy and licking his lips as he ran on home. By the time he got to the front door, I would be waiting downstairs for him, always in a panic of suspense, thinking that perhaps this time he really had eaten all the sweets. But he never had and after a little teasing, I would get a share of the swag – a lolly, a half-penny chew, a gobstopper or, if he was in the money, an entire sherbet lemon.

When it was cold and frosty, Mum would tell me that my nose would be frozen to the window pane and all my skin would peel off, but watching out for Tony delighted me. I don't know when I first realised how dangerous it was out there, beyond our blue-painted front gate and the garden filled with old-fashioned irises and lavender. Odd words from adult conversations sifted into my maturing consciousness and, little by little, I put a picture together of mad creatures lurking very close by, lying in wait to steal me away from the security of my home. Then I found they lived next door.

Known as the Loony Bin, the spacious grounds of Stanley Royd, a rambling, old-fashioned lunatic asylum adjoined our house. Verdant green lawns and shrubberies came down to high dark-green iron railings, with the mansion set amidst tall trees as a backdrop in the distance. When the inmates were let out for their daily walks around the grounds, some of them would come right up to the railings and put out their hands to reach for us if we happened to be passing. My dreams are still haunted by those outstretched hands and those beseeching faces or staring eyes.

'Walk on the far side of the pavement,' Mum would always instruct me when we left the house, as if the mad hands and arms were on elastic, able to grow and grab any unwary child. *They* were there at the back of our house as well and I had to be vigilant, always on my guard, in case they crept over the high fence that divided us from them, into the small yard where Mum had all her washing lines strung out. With six policemen lodging with us at a time, the twin tub was constantly on the go, with tablecloths and sheets and uniform shirts to be washed and starched. Many of the officers came from India and there were always tangled yards of turbans in the laundry. Mum would hang out these narrow lengths of muslin, like banners fluttering in the breeze. When people asked how long the back yard was, Mum would always say, 'It's just right to fit a turban nicely on the line.'

To me, she was just Mum, someone who would cuddle me and soothe away my tears, and sing me songs while she bathed me – but she was also a naturally friendly pretty young woman with a quick wit and a ready smile who loved to mother the lodgers. She'd say that many of them were far from home and a kind word never hurt anyone. But despite his good nature, Dad found himself ridiculously jealous over the attention Mum would pay these men and he resented their easy banter while she served their meals. Perhaps part of the problem was that he was an old-fashioned, macho kind of a man, conscious that for all his hard, dirty work at the coal face, he didn't earn enough to keep us. The resentment that we had to have strangers living under our roof to pay the mortgage also fuelled some friction between him and Mum, and while I don't remember any real argument, there was always an added air of tension when Dad was on night shift. To keep the peace, Mum and Gran split up the chores so Mum would spend less time in direct contact with the lodgers. Mum stayed in the big basement kitchen and Gran served the meals and tidied the policemen's bedrooms.

While Mum cooked or did the laundry and the ironing, I would sit at the kitchen table and listen to the radio, singing along to the Sixties songs, learning all the words, even if I sometimes got them wrong and didn't always understand the meaning. I loved it in the warm, cosy kitchen with rag rugs on the floor and the big old range that gobbled coal. But coal was free to miners, or nearly so, with families getting a couple of tons delivered each winter. In the endless struggle to make ends meet, having enough fuel to burn almost carelessly was the one item of extravagance in our otherwise frugal existence.

I was safe in the kitchen but I would never go outside beyond the back door into the yard, anxiously watching through the window as Mum pegged out the washing on the lines that looped back and forth to give extra drying space. I don't know if I was scared that she would never come back, spirited away by the lunatics whose mad laughter I sometimes heard, whose elusive shapes and shadows I thought I saw silhouetted on the sheets billowing on the line. I don't know what I would have done if I'd seen her grabbed by those dangerous hands and carried off – but one thing I knew: I would never be stolen away like the baby taken by goblins in one of my story books, because no way on earth was I going out there.

Days of freedom, of dipping rhubarb in sugar, of chasing spotted white butterflies through the cabbages and listening to the radio with Mum in the kitchen, soon passed. The time came one damp September day when I had to go to school. But far from being the joyful experience I'd dreamed of since I was a toddler with my nose pressed up close to a window, I was afraid. While I was quite happy going to the allotments which lay to the right, away from the asylum, the terror began when I left the front gate and turned to the left, towards the school. For the first day or so, Mum took me, holding me firmly by my hand as she walked quickly past the high iron fence to the school crossing at the end.

'Never put your hands through the railings,' she darkly warned me. I thrust my free hand in my pocket and pressed tightly against Mum's side under the sheltering umbrella, too petrified to raise my eyes.

Mum was always very busy in the mornings with the policemen's breakfasts, so in a couple of days I was sent to school with Tony. I would skip out of the front door and down our garden path in one of the pretty little print dresses Gran made for me, then I would remember. My legs would freeze so I was glued to the spot and Tony had to drag me out of the gate.

I had visions of being seized and somehow pulled through the narrow spaces between the bars of the asylum railings, to be strangled in the shaded black caverns which lay beneath the rhododendron bushes, and I would tremble with fear and walk on the furthest side of the pavement, crossing over the road to the school as soon as we could. Then Tony left to go to senior school and I was on my own, no longer protected by my older brother.

Sometimes, in the golden light of a late summer's afternoon

as I emerged from school, I would snatch quick glances across at the asylum and through the railings would see pale naked arms and legs waving at me from the daisy-spangled grass, not realising that even there – or perhaps, especially there – lust and sex and passion flowered in that unnatural atmosphere. Soon a couple of uniformed nurses would converge at a run towards those entwined limbs and like dogs in heat they would be torn apart. Not knowing what it was that I had seen, I would shut my eyes against the terror and make a dash for it towards the sanctuary of Clifton's corner shop with the jewel-coloured jars of sweeties in the window.

Resembling a hearse, the black ambulance came to the front door, two uniformed men came up the path and knocked on the door. Tony opened it and stared at them, while I hovered in the background, peeping out from behind the lounge door. 'We've fetched your dad home. Is your mum in?' one of the men asked.

Tony didn't reply. He slammed the door shut and went back into the lounge where we'd been playing a game. I grabbed his hand. 'Who are those men?' I whispered.

Tony shrugged. 'I don't know,' he said, picking up his hand of cards.

'They said they had our dad. What did they mean?' I persisted.

Tony didn't answer. Coming from a mining community, he was of the age where a black ambulance fetching your dad home from the mine was often an ominous sight, something my brother didn't want to confront.

The men knocked on the door again, more loudly this time, and eventually, grumbling because she had been preparing dinner, Mum went to the front door and opened it.

'The lad disappeared and left us standing here,' one of the men said. 'Are you Mrs McDonald?'

'Aye, I am,' Mum said.

'Well, we've got your husband,' they said, 'He's had a bit of an accident down mine.'

'Is he all right?' Mum asked.

'Aye, a bit bruised but he'll live,' they said, returning to the ambulance to help my dad out. Mum rushed to help him up the steps into the house, but he brushed her aside. 'Och, don't fuss,' he said.

That was typical of him, always acting like Superman, never complaining when he was in obvious pain, refusing to take an aspirin or lie down when he was ill. We learned that he'd been down the pit walking towards the face when one of the little bogeys broke loose and careered towards him. He tried to jump out of the way but it picked him up and carried him along until he was thrown free, which saved his life. As it was, he had a badly crushed ankle and several broken ribs. He had been at the hospital all day without letting Mum know.

'No sense in making a fuss,' he said, 'I'm home, and I'm all right. Now, how about a cup of tea?'

Within a month, he was going up to the allotment on crutches because he said we needed the vegetables, adding that the weeds would be running riot. I think he hated being seen as weak. I know his injuries must have been worse than he let on, because when he returned to work, it was as a banksman, a lighter job, where he directed the cages that went up and down the shaft. He earned less money than he had at the coal face and shortly, when the police college opened its own residential facilities, the income from the boarders dried up. I think it was around this time that Dad set up in business as a part-time chimney sweep to earn a little extra money. At least at the mines, he'd had a steaming hot shower and changed into clean clothes before coming home; as a chimney sweep, I remember him coming in 'bright black' as we say in the north. I don't think Mum was so happy when she had to clean that ring around the bathtub! Sometimes he took Janet or Tony with him, and they'd have fun pushing the brushes up the chimney, also returning home bright black. The bags of soot were used in the allotment, where it was supposed to keep slugs away.

Another scheme to give Tony and Janet a little pocket money of their own, was their newspaper round. I was too young at that time – and when I did get a bicycle of my own one Christmas a few years later, Tony and I decided to ride to visit our Aunt Pauline, who lived in a small village a couple of miles away.

Full of excitement, I started off. Soon, I started to feel very sick and stopped. 'Tony!' I shouted, for he'd got ahead of me.

He turned around and came back. 'What is it?'

'I feel bicycle-sick,' I moaned.

'Don't be silly – there's no such thing,' Tony said scornfully. 'Get on your bike or we'll be all day getting there.'

I got on again, but we hadn't gone more than a hundred yards before waves of nausea swept over me and I vomited over the handlebars while Tony stood and laughed his head off. We managed to get to Aunt Pauline's by stopping every few yards but I refused to cycle back and Dad had to fetch us home in his van.

Mum and Dad started to consider other options to make our ever-widening ends meet. They could have taken other paying guests. Mum always said she enjoyed the work and wanted to continue; but there had been a growing resentment in Dad for a long time. He told Mum that he wanted a house that was only just big enough for us, without an inch of space spare for friends, relatives or any Tom, Dick or Harry. He wanted Mum to himself, only his family under his roof, beholden to nobody but himself.

'I want to be able to put my head down and sleep at night without any worries,' he said. 'I want to be able to pay the mortgage without holding out a hat for handouts.'

My mother got a bit annoyed because she had worked very hard to make the boarding house pay its way, but as usual she didn't argue with him. Dad had a dark side; a sulker, sometimes he'd not speak for days on end, something we'd all learned to live with. A year or two earlier, Gran had moved into her own little cottage, so finding space for her as well wasn't a consideration. Eastmoor Road was put on the market and Mum and Gran scoured the ads and estate agents' windows for a suitable house. 'We're looking for something small and inexpensive,' Mum told Gran, 'We're downgrading.'

'Well, if Peter wants to keep his family for himself, let him,' Gran said. 'At least you'll have a rest from all that cooking and cleaning, Jean.'

Mum nodded, 'Perhaps. We'll see.' A wise woman, she kept her own counsel.

THE PIANO

The house was too expensive, but something drew us to look around it anyway. All the furniture had gone, but in one of the rooms a piano had been left behind. It seemed to be quietly waiting there just for me, its surface dusty and uncared for. I ran across to it and, never having touched any instrument before, I lifted the lid and started to play by ear a simple melody. In one accord, Mum and Gran looked at each other and said 'We need a piano!'

We didn't buy that particular house but another more modest one, a two-up two-down terraced house in Silcoates Street on the Peacock Estate close to the centre of town. The word 'estate' has an unfortunate ring to it these days, summoning up images of a run-down council dump with graffiti, damp mattresses and burned out cars. Peacock Estate, while undoubtedly impoverished, was nothing like that. The long red-brick terraces with their minuscule front gardens and slightly larger ones to the rear, where there was an access lane, had been built between the wars to house the workers at a tinned food factory at the heart of the estate. While considered working-class housing, complete with an outside privy and the traditional zinc tub hanging on a nail outside the kitchen door, there was a sense of respectability and community about the street that's not known in many contemporary inner city council projects.

We walked through the house, not finding it too hard to count the two rooms downstairs and the two up plus box-room, with a small kitchen extension to the rear. It was obvious that things were going to be a very tight squeeze. With two girls and a boy, we were one bedroom short.

'We'll be like sardines crammed into a tin,' Mum said, perhaps already missing all the space at Eastmoor Road. If she thought this was a step backwards towards the terraces of Piccadilly they'd struggled hard to pick themselves out of, she kept it to herself.

'Where will I sleep?' I asked.

'You and Janet can share a bedroom,' Dad said. 'Tony can have the box-room. There's just enough room for a bed.'

Janet, who was now fifteen and going through the teenage blues, shouted, 'I'm not sharing with Jane. I hate it here – I hate it, it's a horrible ugly little dump!'

'Now, Janet –' Dad said, getting out his tape measure to see which pieces of our heavy Edwardian furniture would fit into these tiny rooms. It was obvious that with or without the optimistic use of a tape measure, none could be shoehorned in and most of it was sold back to the second-hand shops and the money used to buy new carpets and cream paint to cover the drab, old-fashioned wallpaper that had been there so long you could see dark squares where pictures and mirrors used to hang. The only thing about the move that I regretted was that the enormous doll's house which Dad made for Janet and me out of scrap materials had to be left behind because there was no room for it in Silcoates Street. It was beautifully made, every joint fitting perfectly and filled with little bits of furniture that Mum bought from the market, a few pieces at a time.

Of us all, Janet was the one most disturbed by the change in our fortunes. She was devastated at having to leave the posh side of town where all her friends lived for the other side of the tracks, a world of narrow streets, crowded little rows of terraces and light factories. Looking out of the back door and seeing the cracked concrete path leading straight to the privy, she shuddered like an adolescent drama queen. 'What will my friends say when they see that? A horrible smelly outdoors toilet! I can't have them here.'

'They should accept you for what you are,' Mum said mildly. 'You're a nice girl, Janet, and that's what counts.'

'I won't ask them, and you can't make me,' Janet cried.

'Well, dear, you'll still see them at school,' Mum said. 'If you don't invite them, they won't know what our new house is like and you'll still be able to hold your head up.'

'Your father will soon put in a nice bathroom upstairs. He can cut a wee bit off the back bedroom,' Gran said.

But Janet was inconsolable. 'They'll all know where I've moved to and they'll all laugh at me. I'll die! I'll have to leave school and go to work,' she wept.

'You can't go to work if you're dead,' I said, too young to understand why Janet was so upset. I was as excited as Christmas, thrilled to be moving here.

The house had a lovely atmosphere. To me, it felt warm and friendly, it was just perfect. Janet might have been distraught, but I was ecstatic. I'd already checked all the buildings as we'd walked along the street, and finally I'd slipped my hand into Gran's. 'Is there a loony bin here?' I whispered.

Gran looked down at me with her understanding eyes. 'No, lovey, you'll be safe here.'

Safe. It seemed unbelievable. Years later, I was still calling our little home the 'Safe House', a sanctuary where I returned to lick my wounds and share my successes with Mum.

Dad was a real hands-on dad, always ready to listen and encourage. He taught me to swim at the Old Baths in Wakefield, he'd take us dancing, or perhaps we'd be out there with his van, spanners in hand as he let us tighten nuts and get smothered in oil. He'd buy a tent and we'd be off at a moment's notice during the long summer holidays, camping with Aunt Nancy and Uncle Stan at Chapel St Leonards, in a little farmer's field, where Tony and I would run around like untrammelled colts. Later, we aspired to a caravan at Bridlington, where, when I was six or seven, one whole holiday was spent in the bouncy castle. I loved it so much that I was there, waiting for it to open in the morning and they had to throw me out at night. Mum was frantic because I wouldn't eat anything, and she could see me getting thinner before her very eyes.

Like the Larkin family in *The Darling Buds of May*, every journey was an epic misadventure; only Dad wasn't as cheery as Pop Larkin, even when things didn't go wrong, which invariably they did, he could be a right miserable old git. They had to lie to me when we went on our holidays, telling me that we were just popping out to the shops because I used to get sick on almost any journey longer than a mile. There would always be clues to the mass evacuation that I was too gullible to see. Mum would pack a large picnic basket because she knew that even a journey to the closest seaside camp – a distance of no more than fifty or sixty miles – would always take all day because we'd be constantly breaking down. Dad and Tony would carry our armchairs from the lounge into the back of the old Commer van and lash them in place. We had to have armchairs, because that particular van only had a driver's seat up front, and Mum refused to sit on cushions in the back like a bunch of migrants going potato picking.

As soon as everything was ready, all our cases packed and cardboard boxes of food stowed away (since it was so expensive buying groceries at the site shop) Dad would say, 'Come on Jane, up with you lassie, we're just popping out down the road,' setting me up like the Queen of Sheba right in the front where there'd be less jolting, and not such a stink of petrol from the leaking tank which had an old rag stuffed in it because the cap always seemed to be missing. Off we'd go, travelling perhaps five miles if we were lucky before we broke down – or I chucked up; and heaven help us if it rained because it would be grim, packed in the back of the van, windows steaming up while Dad, grumpy now and sour-faced, stood outside, head under bonnet, getting soaked.

If it was fine, everyone would pile out of the back of the van, the blanket would be spread on the grass verge, Mum would unscrew a flask of tea and unwrap the first sandwiches of the day and Tony and I would run around or stay put, according to where we had broken down. If it was the moors it was deemed safe for us to play; but if it was a farmer's field, Mum said we might get tossed by a bull, and if it was a main road, we might get knocked down by a lorry. Janet was usually above all that. Sometimes she'd mooch off and sulkily pick flowers, but mostly she skulked in an armchair, daydreaming of where she would rather be – and believe me, it wasn't in the back of a rusty old wreck stuck on the side of a road just when her school friends from grammar school were sure to pass by in their dads' posh cars and spot her.

I can see Dad to this day when he had finished repairs, wiping his hands on a bit of rag, taking a gulp of tea, leaving oily smears on the side of the cup and saying, 'It'll do, let's go, then – ' Mum's signal to pack up the picnic basket and get us all aboard.

There was a time when Dad came home with an almost decent Austin A-40 motorcar with only a few patches of rust. He patted it proudly as if it was a horse when he showed it to Mum. 'What do you think?' he said, 'Better than doing your shopping in an old van, eh lassie?'.

'Very nice,' Mum said.

'It'll be nice not to keep breaking down,' Dad said almost wistfully. A few days later when he was waiting at a T-junction to turn, a big pub lorry crashed into him from the rear, shoving him forward into the bigger lorry in front. Far from being annoyed, Dad was positively chirpy when he watched the garage towing his car away. 'That A-40 was a bad'un,' he said, 'Nothing but a pile of junk. I'll get more than it was worth from insurance.'

Mum didn't mind about not having a smart car, she never did care about appearances she said, as long as it got her to the shops and back, she didn't mind what it was.

Tony and I had one of the best holidays we can remember when my grandma and Mum took us up to Monifieth in Scotland, where Gran came from. There was nothing there, just a caravan on a beach with pale golden dunes and a misty blue view that seemed to stretch for ever. Even though it wasn't one of our usual fraught excursions in one of Dad's old vans, the journey still had its share of farce. We went on the train to Dundee and caught a local bus along the coast road towards the North Sea. Gran had one of those round leather hat boxes with a central flat loop handle, packed with puzzles and games for Tony and me, that was put in the luggage space under the stairs along with the rest of our cases. Off we set, down the High Street past Dundee's grey granite buildings, when off the hat box rolled. It gathered speed, moving fast in the opposite direction to the bus. I saw people in the street turning their heads and smiling. I waved and smiled as regal as a princess. A Mini stopped, picked up the hat box and came chasing after us, flashing its lights and sounding its horn.

I jumped up and down, 'What's going on, what's going on?' I said to Tony, 'What are they all looking at?'

Eventually, the bus stopped and a fellow came running, holding out the hat box. Gran cried, 'Oh that's my case!' Tony always believed the man had run all the way, chasing after the bus for two miles.

Once there, you opened the caravan door and you were on the beach. Down the road half a mile away was a hamlet containing a cluster of cottages, a general store and a fish and chip shop. First thing in the morning while we were still asleep, Mum used to go and get fresh baps for breakfast. I can still smell the bacon and egg sandwiches of a morning, a smell that would get me out of bed, ready to start the day. Tony and I were on that beach whether it was rainy, sunny, windy. We'd make up games, flying Tony's kite, playing bat and ball, paddling, digging holes that filled up with the sea when the tide came in, collecting shells and seaweed. We'd have a fish supper of a night when the gas lamps were lit, all cosy against the sound of the waves and the buffeting wind. With the taste of salt and vinegar still in our mouths, we played cards, talked and laughed until our eyelids drooped and Mum made us mugs of hot chocolate from a purple tin.

At the end of the summer came a new school, St Michael's, and a teacher who was to have a big influence on building up my fragile confidence. Yvonne Brearley, my form tutor, was also the school music teacher and for some reason, when I was just seven years old, she noticed that I had some ability. She didn't laugh when shyly I told her that I wanted to sing. Instead she gave me an enormous boost when she said with great kindness, 'If anyone is going to make it, you will,' words that remained with me all through the long years of struggle ahead. Whenever I am at my lowest ebb, Yvonne's voice still echoes from a past now thirty years old. Reminding myself that I can do it, I pick myself up and try that bit harder.

I needed all the encouragement I could get when my first piano teacher, who lived up the road, telephoned Mum to tell her that she was wasting her money on me, that I was lazy and didn't practice hard enough. 'Your daughter doesn't have any talent, she's never going to make a musician,' she said.

Mum bristled with indignation. 'How you can say that of a wee lassie just seven years old, I'll never know,' she said, slamming down the receiver. 'Right,' she said to me, 'we'll find someone else.'

That someone else was Francis Walker, a blind piano teacher. Francis could read Braille and had all the patience in the world. He was the one who developed my ability to play by ear. With him, I blossomed. I wanted to practice and did so, for long hours.

Elizabeth Baxter was my first real friend, a gentle, fair-haired girl who lived in Lincoln Street, just behind us. The fact that her father's name was Peter, like my own, drew us close. Mum used to say we were so alike, when you'd seen one you'd seen the other. Always together, walking around with our arms entwined, people thought we were sisters. Our favourite place was the back doorstep where we'd sit for hours talking about absolutely nothing. Three years later, when we moved to our middle school, St Michael's, we were still out there on the back doorstep, still talking rubbish and giggling like drains over absolutely nothing. Mum used to call out, 'Jane, are you practising the scales?' and I'd start at once, pretending to be a posh lady concert player, nose in the air, until we collapsed again with laughter. We'd walk around the house singing 'The Sound Of Music' like Hilda Ogden from *Coronation Street*, or in my Frank Spencer funny voice, I'd sing 'Supercalifragilisticexpialidocious' from the film *Mary Poppins*.

Both our dreams were starting to crystallise. Liz wanted to be a dancer; but I never veered from wanting to be a singer. We role-played, pretending we were on radio or television. Liz would be the audience, or the interviewer, or whatever I wanted her to be. She still has the old reel-to-reel tape on which she's playing the part of a hot-shot radio interviewer and I'm the pop star.

'Well, Jane, congratulations on reaching the top of the charts. Will you sing your record for us now please?' comes Liz's piping voice down the years. You can hear giggles, and then the very first recording of me using a hairbrush as a mike and belting out 'Teacher's Pet'.

'And now for my next number – ' I say, going into concert mode.

'Thank you, Jane McDonald. What are you going to do when you're famous?' asks Liz, while airily I reply, 'I don't *know*! I'll just be famous.'

Liz's dad passed away when she was twelve. It was such a blow, she started to retreat within herself. I knew him, of course, and was scared that someone I had known could die.

At home, Liz found it very hard to grieve properly because the rest of the family were all locked away in their own pain. She'd come round to our house and spend hours talking about her dad, wanting a friend who'd listen. Gradually her grief numbed and by the time we went to Edinburgh that summer with a school party, she was almost back to normal. I remember feeling so degenerate when I talked the teachers into letting us sit up really late to watch the Eurovision Song Contest, because at home, even when we used to go dancing, Dad was a stickler for early bedtimes. That Christmas, Liz and I helped put on a carol concert to raise money for a Heart Appeal. A painfully sickly child, I suffered so badly from nerves, the doctor said I'd never be able to perform in front of people, but Mum would never accept it. Convinced that all it would take for me to shine was constant encouragement, she developed a range of subtle strategies to draw me out. She'd say, 'I was so looking forward to hearing you sing, Jane, it'll really spoil the evening for me if you don't,' and wanting so hard to please her, I had to face my own fears and make the effort.

Janet left home to get married about four years after we moved to Silcoates Street, when she was eighteen. Her wedding and reception, catered for by Mum and Gran, was held in the spiritualist church, then she was gone, off to Huddersfield and a new life. It was strange to have our crowded little bedroom to myself. Janet had always complained that my half of the room was untidy (it was) while I always complained that she put my things away so I could never find them (she did).

When Janet was getting ready for bed, she'd say, 'Come on, our Jane, you scratch my back and I'll scratch yours.' I fell into the trap every time. I'd scratch away for hours while she closed her eyes and luxuriated in it like a cat having its ears rubbed. Eventually, she'd stretch and yawn lazily. 'I'm so tired,' she'd purr, getting into bed. 'You promised!' I'd cry, but too late, the light was snapped off.

When I complained to Mum and Dad about anything (which I'm sure I very rarely did, though Janet seems to think otherwise), she'd frown crossly, 'I'm always getting the blame because I'm the older.' If pressed, she could only remember two naughty things I was supposed to have done. When I was a toddler, she said, I squirted Fairy washing-up liquid all over the new wallpaper in the hall in Eastmoor Road and scratched the dining table for which, she said, she also got the blame. Equally, I felt I was always a nuisance because she had to baby-sit me. Growing up, sharing a room, I'd love to watch her dress and get made-up for going out on her first dates – to which Dad would escort her, and fetch her home. She was a very pretty girl in her teens, a lovely beauty queen – but I never envied her. Then, in a flurry of white satin and lace, she was gone and the bedroom that we had shared for so many years was all mine.

TEENAGE DREAMS

After three years of piano lessons with Francis Walker, he suggested that I might like to join Wakefield Accordion Band, which he led. I had often seen his accordion which he kept there for lessons; I might have run my fingers over the keys out of curiosity, or asked him if it was hard to play, but when he suggested that I might learn it too, my initial reaction was amazement simply because I was such a tiny ten or eleven year old and the instrument was almost too heavy to lift. Francis picked his up, hung it over my shoulders and carefully adjusted the straps to fit. 'How does it feel?' he asked.

'It's heavy,' I said, thinking that if I moved, I would fall either flat on my face or flat on my back.

'You'll get the hang of it, it's a matter of balance,' Francis encouraged. 'Try the keys, see how your fingers fit.'

After a few trial runs, I did get the hang of it and didn't keel over. Somehow my parents found the money to buy me a full-size silver instrument that was almost as big as I was. Eighteen months later, I'd acquired enough skill to play in public for the first time, at a church concert. Part of a larger group, I wasn't nervous because if I made a mistake they might think it was someone else. Although we didn't do much more than a few charity do's, we were absorbed into the unique world of the now almost extinct Yorkshire colliery bands with its eccentric characters. Many Saturdays, we'd converge in some village or church hall, with family and friends in support, sometimes travelling the length and breadth of the Pennines to play our own special brand of almost Gallic accordion sound – a unique world that has almost vanished like that of the colliery bands.

One evening when I came in for my regular lesson, Francis was playing 'As Time Goes By' on the piano. I stood listening for a moment and without really thinking, started to sing along. I had seen *Casablanca* on the television that Christmas and knew all the words by heart. Soon I was lost in the song, no longer in that large back room with its dusty floorboards where we rehearsed the band, but in Rick's Bar, seeing Ingrid Bergman's beautiful face as she listened emotionally to Sam singing as he played the keys of an ageing piano, his words summing up the nostalgia of lost kisses and sad sighs…

As the last note died away, I opened my eyes. Francis was looking downwards as if at his hands that were still on the piano keys. Then he lifted his head slowly and turned to look in my direction. 'How did you learn to sing like that? he asked.

Without waiting for a reply, he started to play the poignant melody to 'Maria' from *West Side Story*. 'Can you sing this?' he asked.

I'd sung to the LP a thousand times before the mirror in the front room, thanks to Dad's cigarette coupons. The words came without hesitation, flowing out of my mouth.

'And this?' Francis said, 'And this…?' as he segued seamlessly from song to song, with me following without faltering.

Finally he stopped playing and stood up. 'Jane, did you

know you have a beautiful voice?'

I shook my head, forgetting that he couldn't see. 'Have I?'

'Yes, you have,' Francis said. 'It's very rare – and in a girl your age, it's incredible.'

Suddenly embarrassed, I said, 'I just like to sing.'

Francis said, 'You have a wonderful gift. Save the money you spend on piano lessons and spend it on singing lessons instead.'

'Aren't I any good at the piano?' I stammered, remembering how the previous piano teacher had sacked me some years earlier. I wondered if Mum would be angry with me for wasting everybody's time and money when I told her Francis said I should give up playing.

Francis seemed to sense what I was thinking. 'Jane, you've done nothing to be ashamed of,' he said, concern in his voice. 'You are very good at the piano, but lessons are expensive and if you've only got so much to spend, you should definitely spend it on developing your voice.'

When Dad picked me up, I gabbled into speech. 'Francis thinks I should take singing lessons!'

Dad glanced at me as he drove the short distance home, 'Well, lassie, how much is that going to cost me?' he asked.

'I don't know – he said instead of the piano, but not because I'm not any good at piano,' I hastened to explain, 'He says I am good, but I'm better at singing.'

'Well, we'd better look into it, then,' Dad said.

After discussing this with Mum, even more money was found to enable me to continue with the piano, the accordion, and also singing lessons with a classically-trained voice coach, Len Goodwin, who worked me hard for an hour a week for many years, going through the scales until he deemed I was good enough to try a song. He'd make me repeat the same section over and over again until I got it right. I'd arrive at his house full of dread and leave feeling euphoric. Once, I made the mistake of mentioning that I liked the Bay City Rollers. Len shuddered artistically, 'Oh my God, darling, don't ever be a pop singer, don't even think about it. You've got a great classical voice.'

At the age of thirteen, my first public performance as a singer, not long after I'd been working with Len, was with the Wakefield Accordion Band at a small charity concert in the Zion Hall. A little figure standing alone up front, this time I was terrified because I had nobody to hide behind, but the concert went well.

At the same time, I started at secondary school. Thornes House was a grand-sounding name for what turned out to be a hell hole that was eventually closed down because one half of the students were bullying the other half. When I went with Mum for my admission interview, I told the head that I wanted to go on stage when I grew up. Far from putting me down and telling me that I'd never get on with that lax attitude, he nodded enthusiastically, 'You'll enjoy it here,' he said, 'we've got a very good drama department'. I only wish he'd told me about the bullying, because I might have begged Mum to let me go somewhere else.

Every morning, dressed in my new uniform, I'd join Liz and together we'd leave the Peacock Estate to walk across a wide main road to a park on a hill dotted with big trees. It looked as if we were walking up to a mansion, and should have been an uplifting start to the day. If the standard of education was good, the discipline was abysmal. Boisterous, disruptive pupils were sent to the Bad Hut, which was run on concentration camp lines and was supposed to make things easier for the rest of us – but what could the staff do when the Bad Hut was bursting at the seams and there was nowhere left to put the delinquents?

The only thing I can say in Thornes House's favour was that I met Wendy, fair-haired and green-eyed; and Caroline, fair-haired with blue-grey eyes, both of them brimming with all the confidence that I wished I had. We went around in a little gang at school but in those early years rarely saw much of each other in the evenings since the others lived some miles away in the opposite direction. More worldly than me, they gave me one firm instruction: 'Keep your head down and don't look up or you'll get into trouble'. I did as I was told, studied hard and somehow made it through unscathed for a couple of years.

When he was seventeen, Tony left school and started working alongside Dad down the mine, but he found it hard to get up at four o'clock in the morning. To keep the peace, Mum would get him up, then cook breakfast and make sandwiches for all of us. She was shopping in town one day when she saw a postcard in the newsagent's window asking for someone to open the shop in the morning, mark-up the newspapers and generally run the place for half a day. She was up at the crack of dawn anyway, so she thought she would apply. Dad didn't like the idea of Mum working; he was the kind of man who thought his wife should be at home however broke they were. But, after Mum told him that she got off at one-thirty in the afternoon and would be home in plenty of time to make his tea, he relented. When Mum got the job, they'd leave the house together, she'd be dropped off at the shop and Dad and Tony continued on to work.

I didn't always hear them leave because, once my head hit the pillow, I was asleep but sometimes in the summer when dawn came, Mum's quiet movements downstairs woke me.

I'd lie in bed and listen to the first blackbird singing outside my open bedroom window. As the dawn chorus joined in, a sense of restlessness made me get up and sit at the window dreaming a teenage girl's dreams as the rising sun flushed the sky with a pale pink wash.

Strangely secretive in some ways, I used to have premonitions of really bad accidents that scared me, but which I didn't mention to a soul. I'd write down dreams (and still do) to recall later when I had time to think. My mind was like a radio channel, with things always flying about. When I was very young I'd go to sleep only to wake with a jolt when I heard my name called, not just by one person, but by a battery, all shouting, seeking attention. At first I thought I was going mad; in the end I was so used to it I'd tune the noise out, listening only when I wanted to – although fifty people shouting, 'Jane! Jane! Jane!' in my head as I went to sleep was very different to what most other girls got in their heads.

One night, very angry, I sat up and shouted back, 'WHAT?' Taking that as an invitation, the noise increased, grew louder; excitable, babbling, like a telephone exchange. Suddenly, light dawned, I knew about this!

Next morning, when I heard Mum moving about quietly below preparing breakfast, I slipped out of bed and went downstairs. I loved quiet moments alone with her, knowing that she was never in too much of a hurry to ask about my day or to listen to any small problem that I might have

'You're up early, Jane,' she said, pouring me a cup of tea. 'Are you all right?'

I told her what I'd been hearing in my head, how it was driving me to distraction. I asked, 'How do I handle this? I can't get to sleep.'

Without surprise, she said, 'Just ask your guide – she'll stop all that racket.'

'My guide?' I said, blankly.

Mum nodded, 'Yes, the voice in charge, like air traffic control directing planes. Gran will tell you what to do. You must learn how to channel things and become more focused.'

When Dad and Tony came down, she said, 'Ah well, I have newspapers to deliver,' and they left while I went back to bed for a couple of hours' sleep before I had to get ready for school.

Thanks to that little chat with Mum, I did learn how to deal with the voices. Spirits are well-behaved; if one comes to you when you're busy or tired, all you have to say is, 'No, not now, it's not convenient'. And they go, returning at a better time. Now I would only let people in when I needed to, usually just to pass messages on, something I still do. I was very receptive in the beginning, but gradually let it slip and stopped developing my gift when there was a political upheaval at the church that led to Gran and Mum resigning. You have to be dedicated, and I had so many other things I wanted to do. Even a natural psychic doesn't have to let it take over their life. Small children have their secret friends, someone they talk to; grown ups will smile benignly, but who's to say that a child can't see and speak to someone no longer visible to an unimaginative adult? A gift that's not used gradually fades away. When you're not believed, you forget, you grow up, your mind fills with other things. Some very spiritual people, like Gran, get led back into it.

I remember one night Gran came to stay overnight with us when both Janet and Tony had left home. She was given my bed and I was put into Tony's old room, the boxroom next door. Gran was just dropping off to sleep when one of my regular spirits arrived. Quite casually, Gran said, 'Oh, Jane's next door,' – and blow me down if the bugger didn't wake me up.

Dad loved to dance at the local Working Men's Club. Athletic and remarkably light on his feet, he was a powerfully-built, handsome man with olive skin and dark hair, and I was always proud to be seen with him and for people to know he was my dad. Going to the club with my parents in the evenings had long been a regular event in my life. After Dad had come home from the pit and Mum had cleared away and washed up the evening meal, they loved to dress up and unwind at the club, enjoying a drink with their friends. But gradually, the spiritualist church took up more and more of Mum's time and they rarely went out together.

We had dance lessons at middle school, where Liz was my partner. As we grew older, we started going out in a group to Balne Lane Working Men's Club, a low, modern pebble-dash building that resembled a wartime prefab – me and Dad, Liz and her parents – to sequence-dancing sessions which all the local clubs held once a week, alternating with bingo, whist drives or snooker. Becoming almost fanatical, we went to whichever club had dancing that night.

After work, Mum might look at Dad who would be getting ready to go out and say, 'If you hang on a bit, I'll get changed and put on my dancing shoes. I haven't been out for a while.'

Dad would roll his eyes and show pretend alarm. 'No, don't – you're a heavy Scottish lass – and anyway you have to deliver your newspapers in the morning, you'd better get to bed early.'

It was a standing joke because Mum didn't deliver papers.

But after a long day she was far happier putting her tired feet up with a cup of tea and a magazine until it was time to go to church with Gran.

Dressed up in one of my long frocks, with my long hair flowing loose around my shoulders, I looked old-fashioned and demure and far younger than my age, so no boy ever looked at me. But one night, someone did look at me. He was a sixth-form boy from my school whom I knew by sight, but not to talk to. I said nothing when he came and sat next to me at our table. I stared dumbly down at my glass of Coca-Cola, hiding behind my curtain of hair. He didn't speak. I wondered why he was sitting there at all – to me, sixth-formers were like gods and they scared the hell out of me. After a while, he got up and moved away, the bees stopped buzzing around my head and I could breathe again. I didn't realise that other eyes had taken in the scene and made more of it than there was – nor that this apparently insignificant event would lead to months of torment.

The previous week, I had decided to audition for the annual school musical, that year to be *The Wizard of Oz*. Those who'd put their names forward for a part were called out to the front of the hall one at a time and given the words to 'Somewhere Over the Rainbow' while the music teacher played a verse or two through a couple of times on the piano. 'Ready?' he'd say and with much clearing of throats and cracked voices, the pupil would launch into the song. Giggling at everybody's performance seemed to be the thing, and the poor sod who'd just humiliated themselves would scuttle red-faced back to their seat, as the teacher called out another name.

When it was my turn, I felt that familiar panic, but willed myself to walk up to the front. I knew the song backwards and had no problem with standing up facing the piano, my back to the rest of the kids so they wouldn't put me off by making silly faces. The others had done a verse before they'd been stopped, but this time, the piano played right to the end. There was a deathly hush, then a few titters, while embarassed, I returned to my seat.

I had no expectation of getting anything but a very small part in the show so my hopes were not raised when we were all called together for the music teacher to call out his choice of cast. He started at the bottom with small roles and slowly worked his way up through the more important ones, from the Good Witch, the Wicked Witch, the Lion, the Tin Man and so on. Even though I wasn't expecting much, I was still a tiny bit disappointed as role after role came and was handed out elsewhere. Then, right at the end, I heard him say, 'And the role of Dorothy is going to Jane McDonald! Well done Jane, you knocked our socks off at the auditions – and I hope you'll do the same on the night.' He laughed a little at his joke, while I sat there, my mouth hanging open like a goldfish as all the others turned and stared.

When they got over the surprise, my friends crowded around to congratulate me, Overwhelmed by squeals of praise and laughter, I didn't notice the vile expression on the face of a sixth-form girl. Since I don't intend to shame her here by giving her a real name, I'll call her 'Sarah'. She was the leader of a girl gang that hung around the town at nights in studded leather jackets and spike heels.

Later, as I ran out of the school on my way home to break the wonderful news, Sarah and one of her friends, another big girl, stopped me by the school gates. 'Here's Dorothy,' they said.

I tried to pass, but they shoved me. 'Dorothy! Dorothy!' they chanted nastily, pushing me backwards and forwards between the two of them. Small for my age, I felt like a rubber ball in a terrifying game, unable to break free, getting more bruised and battered with every shove.

'Let me go,' I started to cry.

'Oh! Cry-baby Dorothy! Dorothy's a cry-baby!' they taunted.

I don't know how things would have ended on that particular day had not a couple of women approached along the pavement chatting to each other. Clutching my school bag, tears dripping down my cheeks, mixing with snot from my nose, I ran all the way home, across the park and over the busy main road, not even seeing the traffic. I had a key and quietly let myself in, sneaking up to the bathroom to wash my face. I didn't recognise myself as I stared in the mirror, my eyes were dark and blankly staring, my hair a tangled mess and my face red from weeping. I looked like one of those poor mad creatures from the loony bin – and now I knew what some of them must have felt like. Being mad was like losing control, of having things happen to you that didn't make any sense.

In my bedroom, I switched on the radio low and lay on my bed, knowing that I couldn't go downstairs for my tea until I had calmed down and my face wasn't so blotchy because I didn't want Mum or Dad to know what had happened. At the time, I didn't realise that shame was part of the psychology that bullies depended on to stop their victims from talking.

I must have dozed off because Mum came upstairs and opened my door. 'Oh, there you are, Jane. Tea's on the table.'

'Just coming, Mum,' I said, not looking at her.

'Are you all right?' When I didn't answer, she came right into the room. 'Jane? What's upset you?'

'Nothing – I'm okay. Mum, I've got the part of Dorothy!' I blurted out, wanted to divert her from asking why I looked as though I had been crying. I knew she'd be excited because we'd talked about the audition.

'Oh, that's lovely! Come down and tell us all about it.'

I followed Mum downstairs and sat at the table while she went to the kitchen to take my fish and chips out of the oven. 'I'm glad I got in something nice today, we can celebrate,' she said as she put the hot plate on the mat in front of me.

'What are we celebrating?' Dad asked.

'Jane's got the part of Dorothy in the school show,' Mum said proudly. 'Why don't you put the record on, Jane?'

I went into the front room and put the *Wizard of Oz* soundtrack on, cranking it so we would hear it. For once, I didn't feel like singing along, didn't feel like answering Mum and Dad's questions and could barely eat anything.

After tea, Dad went off to the allotment, leaving me with Mum.

'Are you sure everything is all right, Jane?' she asked. She stared hard at me. 'You've not eaten your tea. Something's upset you. Have you had a fight at school?' she asked perceptively.

'No, I'm just tired,' I lied. 'I sat up late last night doing my homework.'

'Now I know you're not well,' Mum said. When I didn't laugh, she said, 'Do you want to cancel your singing lesson this evening?'

I nodded. Usually, I enjoyed singing and never missed a lesson – but still sick to my stomach with fear, all I wanted to do was to go to bed and pull the blankets over my head to block out the world.

Next day, I didn't want to go to school, but forced myself

to dress and join up with my girlfriends to walk across the park. They talked excitedly about the show, but all my pleasure in it had gone. I was even beginning to hate the name of Dorothy and I thought I would never be able to sing 'Somewhere Over the Rainbow' again. Liz had also been given a part in the musical, as a munchkin, her face and teeth all blacked up. The black cape she was given, from the big box of dressing up clothes, was so smelly she felt ill all the way through her performance, but she stuck it out. Another thing she endured was the Victorian hooped skirt she wore. When the curtains were drawn between scenes, still on the stage, her skirt stuck so far out through the gap in the middle that people in the front row could see her drawers!

Yes, I did have moments of fun, when I would forget my troubles – but all day, I was on my guard, watching out for the bullies, trying always to be with a group of my classmates. As the final bell rang, I rushed to leave the building, grateful that the previous day's torment had seemed to be a one-off. My relief was short-lived. Like spiders, the two sixth-formers had lain in wait in a dark corner and sprang out on me as I hurried by. Before I knew it, other girls in their gang joined in and I was surrounded. They knocked my bag to the ground and started pushing and shoving, calling me names.

'Slut! Tramp!' they chanted, tugging my hair and kicking my shins.

'If you talk to my boyfriend again, I'll kill you,' Sarah threatened.

'I didn't! I don't know any boys!' I cried.

'Liar! Liar!'

The others took up the chant, 'Liar! Liar!'

Sarah grabbed my blouse and pulled me up close. Her face inches from mine, she said, 'You made eyes at him at that club you go to with your dad. Everyone saw you!'

'I didn't!' I sobbed. 'I don't even know who he is.'

With one last violent shove against a wall, Sarah said, 'I'll never let you off. You've had it now, McDonald. Watch out – I'll be around every corner waiting for you. And remember – if you tell anyone, we'll really hurt you. And I mean *really* hurt,' she finished with her fist balled up under my nose.

The next two or three weeks passed in a blur. On the one hand, I was in rehearsals for *The Wizard of Oz*, putting my heart and soul into the lovely songs and on the other hand I was living in constant fear, absolutely petrified whenever I saw Sarah and her gang. I couldn't tell anyone, not even my best friends. Finally, I forced myself to see a counsellor at school.

'Come and sit down,' he said kindly, as I hovered in the doorway, torn between staying and taking to my heels. 'I won't bite, Jane,' he said. 'What do you want to talk about?'

I sat down and gazed at the floor, tears brimming my eyes. 'I'm being bullied,' I whispered.

'That won't do at all,' he said. 'Who's behind it?'

Sarah had instilled such fear in me that I realised I couldn't tell him. 'It's no one,' I blurted and stood up. As I left the office I almost died. My tormentor was standing there, waiting to go in. I felt as if she had punched me in the face; I felt as if she could read my mind. Had she followed me there? Wild thoughts swirled around my head as my legs turned to jelly. We gazed at each other and she narrowed her eyes. 'If you say one word, I'll kill you,' she said, her voice like ice.

I gave her a horrified look and found the strength to run. That was it – I never spoke of it again, never went back to the counsellor, and started truanting almost every day.

My fear that someone would see me leaving the school after registration always lasted until I reached the sanctuary of home. My key was on a piece of string around my neck and I had it out ready when I was halfway along the road. I'd open the door quietly and stand listening in case Dad, who might be on night shifts, hadn't yet gone to bed and perhaps was having a cup of tea or watching the TV. If he was there, I'd creep in and go upstairs, walking carefully like a burglar on the sides of the treads where they didn't squeak, safe only when I was in the bedroom that was just mine now that Janet had grown up and left home. I was always scared that Dad might have heard me, constantly expecting him to come up and open my door, but he never did.

On those days when he was at home, I'd have to keep as quiet as a mouse. I'd lie on the bed and read for hours, losing myself in different worlds. I didn't go hungry because I had my packed lunch in my school bag, which usually included a drink. It was easy when Dad was on the day shift. I could make tea and toast, have a bath, watch TV, listen to the radio, loving the peace of mind, the freedom, safe from Sarah and her cronies. Sometimes I dreamed that I was grown up and married to a pop star. What we actually did was very sketchy, it was just enough to dream that he adored me and I was at home waiting for him to return to my arms from a world tour. I'd listen to the radio and when I heard one of his songs, I imagined that he was singing just to me.

Sometimes out of a sense of virtue – or maybe guilt that I was missing so many lessons at school – I would practice the piano when I knew the neighbours were out. I was quite good at playing by ear melodies that I loved and avoiding the scales I should be practising diligently. If I knew the neighbours were in and might mention the phantom pianist to Mum, I'd play my records softly, singing along to them while practising my 'look' in front of a mirror.

Lots of teenage girls are quite narcissistic in this way, but for me posing in front of a mirror was serious because music was so important to me. Instinctively, I knew I was preparing myself for a career though I hadn't really defined exactly what shape that career would take as yet. If anything, I just dreamed I was a star like Barbra Streisand, without working out how a nobody like me got from A to B. It wasn't just pop songs I was interested in; I knew the songs from all the big shows. Dad used to collect the coupons from inside the packs of Embassy cigarettes he smoked, sending off for free LPs of the soundtracks from musicals like *Showboat* and *The Student Prince*. As soon as a new record came in the post, I'd shut myself in the front room, put it on the record player and sing right through from beginning to end in front of the mirror until I was word perfect. I wasn't the only one who was word perfect. The whole family knew all the songs because I played them continually – which is why Mum can always tell me when I get the words wrong.

Things did get better gradually and I did have moments of fun in some classes, such as art and French where the teachers were good sports, but my real life was lived out of school, where I was happiest. I'd go dancing with Liz down the Mecca on a Monday night, where we were both very good at jive and back flips. There were two pubs inside, Nocturne, which was lit with a blue light; and Bali-hi upstairs, where we'd get a big plate of chips and coke while waiting for my dad to come and pick us up.

Sometimes, Dad would take me, and Wendy went with her family, (we were both about sixteen then) to Alverthorpe Working Men's Club, where he'd take turns to dance with us, even though Wendy infuriated him because at school she'd always been 'the man' when she danced with Caroline, and she couldn't break the habit. My dad never said anything to her, but it was funny watching her push and him struggle. One evening, Tony dropped into the club and was dancing with me when Wendy arrived. She came over when the dance ended, and I noticed her fluttering her eyelashes at him. When Tony went off to the bar to get drinks, she said, 'Trust you to have the only man in here with his own teeth.'

I said, 'Who do you mean?'

'Tony, he's smashing,' she said. 'You're so lucky, Jane, I wish I'd seen him first.'

The penny dropped. 'He's not my boyfriend – he's my brother. You can have him!' I said.

By the end of the evening, Wendy was in love and Tony had asked her out. Loyal to my brother, I didn't tell her that he was seeing another girl. After a while, when it was obvious that they were becoming an item, Tony did get around to confessing. Wendy said, 'I already know, Caroline told me.'

Tony wasn't aware of how popular he was with the girls. His role as DJ at the local youth club was where his fan club really started. He had a big collection of the latest hits, and would spin them with not much chat, but looking really cool and 'Fonzish' in his blue jeans and black leather jacket. Liz's little sister, Audra, developed such a massive crush on Tony that when Liz used to come over to our house, Audra started tagging along. She'd sit quietly in a corner, not saying a word, waiting for Tony to come in. When he did, she froze, like a rabbit in the headlights of a car.

Liz and I decided we'd get Tony to telephone Audra at home as a surprise. One night, when Tony came in I handed him the phone and dialled the number. Audra, who was sitting in her dressing gown, watching TV with Liz, picked it up.

'Hello?' she said.

Tony said, 'Do you know who this is?'

Puzzled, she said, 'No.'

He said, 'It's Tony.'

Audra went bright red, dropped the phone and screamed on Liz's neck. Tony looked completely mystified. 'What was all that about, then?' he said.

I shook my head, 'Just girls being girls,' I said.

FIRST LOVES

Despite the fun I sometimes had, my schooldays had been spoilt by bullying. I left with a handful of 'O' levels, glad to be gone. There are not many jobs you can do at the age of sixteen, so I thought I was lucky when I managed to get work in a big furniture shop in the centre of town as a junior clerk in the office, typing and filing. With the job came a steady wage, new clothes – and my first boyfriend. I was what they call a 'late developer'. Small and skinny until well into my teens, I didn't start to bloom until I left school; but, as Mum said, I wasn't bad once I got going.

Richard was a nineteen-year-old lad from Huddersfield, whom I met through Janet, who worked with his sister. A carpenter by trade like my dad, Richard was tall, dark and handsome, with chiselled features and a heart-breaking smile. He was also a divine disco dancer with the pick of all the girls, so I was stunned when he chose me. There and then I decided I was going to marry him, the second boy I'd chosen for that honour. The first was Richard Tinker at St Michael's school, who never guessed my secret passion for him.

I knew my Richard loved me when he put the words JAN-RIK on the windscreen of his precious Volkswagen van. I thought it was so cool and was the proudest girl in Yorkshire up there on the front bench seat – along with all his sisters' kids. No matter where we went, whether it was swimming at the local baths, taking a picnic up on the moors or trying to smooch in the back row of the cinema, Richard and I always had our little gang in tow. My dad was delighted by this high degree of chaperonage – but most of all, he crowed that his genius would be a great asset to the family after Richard built him a magnificent shed – as sheds go – up at the allotments. Had I married Richard, I'd have been the girl who went down in Yorkshire folklore as having been given away by her father at the altar for a shed. That's not such a bad thing – at least the shed is still standing.

I felt quite at home with Richard's extended family, a large and boisterous clan who were always doing something new. When they asked me to go to Majorca with them, I was over the moon.

'Nay sixteen year-old daughter of mine is going with her boyfriend to Majorca,' my dad growled, his eyebrows meeting in a deep frown. 'Nay lassie, you're staying at home.'

'I'm nearly seventeen,' I protested. 'All his family is going. There'll be lots of people there.'

'I dinna care if the King of Siam is going,' said my dad. 'I'm not having you drinking that sangria muck and getting into trouble. The answer is no and that's an end to it.'

Convinced that I would die of a broken heart, I went into a moody decline until Janet – who could always wrap our dad around her little finger – came to my rescue. She said she would accompany me to Spain and keep an eye on me. Well, mostly she did, until she got into the sangria at the disco one night. A little tipsy, she was talking away on the way home to our hotel when she stumbled on some steps and fell headfirst into a bush. One moment my chaperone was with us, the next, all we could see in the moonlight were her feet sticking out through a garland of hibiscus blossom. Janet had been a wonderful gymnast at school, and I fully expected to see her spring up with a backwards somersault, but she remained in the bush, her legs doing semaphore. When we stopped laughing, we hauled her out.

Richard and I did have a lot of fun, but in the end I drove him away with my jealousy. I used to ring him constantly when we were apart, asking, 'What are you doing, where have you been?' I was a pain in the backside and got on his nerves. Dad said he was a good bloke and I should stop giving him such a hard time, but my degree of insecurity wouldn't allow any common sense to shine through, and we eventually split up.

'Darn it, I was about to ask him to build me a new lean-to out back,' Dad complained, pointing to the large pile of old doors and windows filling the yard. He'd taken several trips in his old van to Pinderfields Hospital where they were doing some renovations, each time returning with a stack of junk until he had enough to build a patchwork extension. Mum had long yearned for a 'conservatory' where she could grow a few flowers, and Dad had long promised her one. When she saw the finished haphazard edifice, she shook her head in disbelief. In his defence, Dad said, 'Jane should've hung on to that lad, he was a good carpenter.'

While I was still sixteen, in my first year at the furniture store, I saw an advertisement in the local paper for a female singer in the Brian Gordon Sound, a well known band in the North, one which played the kind of music made famous by Joe Loss or Glen Miller, heavy on the brass. I stared at the advert until my head spun. They were auditioning in Ossett in Wakefield. I have no idea why I thought I would get the job, why I even bothered to go. Things were going well with the accordion band and perhaps that gave a boost to my confidence. Suddenly making up my mind, I went on my own, not telling a soul.

'What are you going to sing for us, Jane?' Alan Cobett, the compère, who was also the trumpet player, asked.

I'd done my homework and quaking, I said that I would sing 'You Light Up My Life,' a bluesy number with deep emotion and a wide range that I knew was in their repertoire. They counted me in and I started. As the final note soared into the dusty hall where the auditions were held, Alan came forward and said, 'Where did you learn to sing like that?' Familiar words, that I'd heard before, from Francis Walker.

'I've always been able to sing,' I said, still quaking from the strain of standing up there with so many experienced musicians.

'How old did you say you were?' Alan asked.

I didn't know whether to fib – would he turn me away if I told the truth? But I've always found it hard to lie, so I took a deep breath and said, 'I'm nearly seventeen.'

'Still sixteen, then?' Alan said.

'Yes, but I've left school and I go to work,' I blurted. 'I'm legal age.'

That made them all laugh. The job was mine.

Dad only let me do the job because I was collected and returned home afterwards. Every evening after work, I'd dash home, get ready and someone in the band would call for me. It was a very popular orchestra, always fully booked, especially at weekends. We travelled all over the north-east, mostly in Yorkshire, never staying away overnight because the musicians were all middle-aged married men who would rather have been at home. This suited my dad's notion of curfew and fitted in with my day job.

After a while, I gained in confidence and was ready to take on new challenges. One night, I was on stage at Burmantoff's Working Men's Club in Leeds, where you had to climb up eight flights of stairs to get to the stage. Alan Cobbert and I were larking about a bit, back-chatting and cracking jokes, when I picked up his trumpet, put it to my lips and, after a couple of false starts, pretended to play along with the band. I don't know who was the most surprised – me or Alan.

He turned to the audience and said, 'Blimey, isn't there anything she can't do? She'll be wanting my job next.' The audience loved it and raised the roof, obviously believing that it was all rehearsed. Afterwards, Alan said, 'You never said you could play the trumpet.'

'I can't,' I admitted, 'I was pretending. That's the first time I've ever touched one.' To this day, I'm sure he didn't believe me.

I stayed with the band for almost two years but, although I was very grateful for the experience, I didn't want to get locked into a groove with them. Besides, I was only being paid about £5 a night and I knew I could earn more elsewhere, so I handed in my notice.

With Dad and Richard's help, I had learned to drive quite well. Dad agreed that I'd be safer in a car instead of walking home in the dark of an evening and we found a snazzy gold Vauxhall Viva that I thought was IT. It cost about £400 and needed some work done on it – but for Mr Fix-it, it was no problem. Soon, I was zooming off to work in my car instead of waiting for the bus. Despite all Dad's efforts, my new car was basically knackered and broke down yet again, leaving me without transport. When I heard that Tony and Wendy were going abroad on holiday, I asked my brother if I could borrow his car for a week.

'Of course you can. If it rains, wipe the spots off,' he said.

I laughed, since it was a standing joke that Tony polished his red Vauxhall Viva three times a day. 'Don't worry, you'll have it back in perfect condition,' I assured him confidently.

When Tony and Wendy returned a week later, as they rounded the corner at the end of their street Tony beamed, pleased at the sight of his beloved red car sitting in the kerb outside their house as I'd promised. But something was not right.

'My God,' said Tony in shock, 'T'bloody boot's blue!'

After he recovered, Tony telephoned me and, deeply embarrassed, I had to confess that I had reversed into a lorry and caved in the rear. Knowing how much Tony loved his car, I'd nearly had hysterics. But Dad came to my rescue. After towing the car home he'd checked out the damage and said, 'Dinna worry lassie, it looks worse than it is. I'll have it sorted in no time.'

True to his word he got in his van, went round to a scrap yard and got a replacement part that – thanks to his experience as a coach builder – fitted perfectly and closed with a satisfying clunk by the time he'd finished. Standing back to admire another job well done, he said with pride, 'Aye, lassie, it'll do.'

'But, Dad, it's *blue*!' I'd exclaimed, unable to believe my eyes.

'Aye – but it fits lovely,' Dad said, opening and closing it, a satisfied smile on his face. 'A lick o' paint and our Tony'll never know any different.'

Despite my reservations, Dad was proved right. By the time

Tony had resprayed the blue boot red, it was as good as new. However, I still needed a reliable car. Dad had managed to get my gold Viva back on the road, but it was so old I knew it would always be breaking down. We'd had it drummed into us since childhood that if you needed anything, you worked for it, so daringly, after work, I walked into Pussycat's, a ravers' paradise run by a couple of very camp gays, where big acts like Lulu booked in.

I recognised one of the owners and went up to him. 'Any evening jobs going?' I asked.

'Have you ever worked in a bar before?' he asked.

'No, but I'm a quick learner,' I said.

To my surprise, he agreed to try me at 7.30 that evening. He told me what I'd be paid, adding, 'We don't like to take advantage of the customers, so tips are a maximum of ten pence. When you reach a pound, you don't take any more tips.'

'A whole pound!' I pretended to gasp, 'I can't wait!'

He laughed. 'Oh, I can see you'll fit right in, darling,' he said. 'Wear shorts.'

Luckily, I had a pair of old shorts which were very tight now that I was starting to fill out nicely, so I dug them out, wriggled into them, slapped on a ton of make-up and admired myself in the mirror. 'That'll do,' I said, echoing Dad's trademark comment. In those days I didn't have much money to spend on clothes – a far cry from the time when, many years later I would have so many lavish stage outfits, they overflowed my room in a torrent of sequins and I had to knock a hole through into Tony's boxroom to accommodate them.

I saved my big news up until I was gulping down my tea, in a hurry to be out. 'I've got a night job,' I announced.

'Hang on,' Dad said, 'What kind of a job?'

'It's at Pussycat's,' I said, 'Behind the bar. Tips are good,' I improvised.

'The fun club? I think I'll have a look at this,' said my Dad in a tone that broached no argument.

I didn't mind. I wasn't one of those girls who never tell their parents anything and keep half their lives a secret. 'Thanks, Dad,' I said, giving Mum a kiss. 'See you later.'

'What time will you be back?'

'Around midnight,' I said, fingers crossed.

'If you're not, catch will be on the door,' Dad warned.

'So nothing different, then,' I said cheekily. Dad didn't care how old you were; when you were under his roof, you followed his rules. Right up until the time that Tony left home to marry Wendy at the age of twenty-five, the catch was put up if he came in after Dad's idea of parental control and curfew.

After he'd dropped me off at Pussycat's and poked his nose inside the door to give the place a once-over, Dad told me that he would be back to collect me on the dot of midnight – almost as if I was Cinderella. Then he drove off in a cloud of smoke. I watched the fumes disappear into the distance and knew he would be out there tinkering with it next evening after work, the story of Dad's life.

Of course I wasn't through by midnight. Normally, I worked on Thursday, Friday and Saturday until two-thirty in the morning, staggered back home, slept for a few hours and was at my day job by nine a.m. Because I was so fast on my feet and had a good line in chat, I got my maximum tips very fast and was soon promoted to the famous centre bar, where the female staff danced on the top as the evening wore on and the fun heated up. To the words and music of 'Having a Gang Bang' and shimmering back and forth in unison, we'd soon get the whole place rocking and rolling. I had an affinity with gays, got friendly with the owners, and went to many parties at their homes. I thought I was really living.

By saving hard, I was able to buy a fast little black TR7 – but now I had the savings bug so I could buy fashionable clothes and go to somewhere other than Bridlington for my holidays, and I decided that I could manage three jobs. Next to Pussycat's was another club, Casanova's, whose owner, Michael Craig, I knew by sight because he would often pop into Pussycat's to check out the competition. Not really expecting to get more than a flea in my ear for my cheek, I dropped into Casanova's on one of my free nights and asked for a job there.

Mike looked me up and down and laughed. 'You've got a cheek,' he said. 'OK, I've seen you work, Jane – you're good. Monday, Tuesday and Wednesday then?'

How the hell I fitted it all in, I'll never know. To keep going, I'd spend my half-hour dinner break from the furniture store getting a tan in the sun-bed shop – my power nap, I called it – and it seemed to work, almost as if I'd been plugged into a battery and re-charged. I was a live wire, always tanned and looked great. My tops got tighter, my shorts got shorter and my legs got longer. The boys were flocking up at the centre bar to ask me out. Mike noticed how quick and popular I was and asked if I would like to work full-time for him as bar manager of the exclusive new VIP lounge for business-men that he was thinking of opening inside Casanova's.

I jumped at the chance, handed in my notice at the furniture store and at Pussycat's and started drumming up business for the VIP lounge, handing out cards, signing businessmen up for membership at £100 a year and even seeing how to book the acts. One thing I admired about Mike was that he was always ready to listen to new ideas, even from an eighteen-year-old like me. When I suggested that I could organise a team of girls to dance on podiums around the club, he thought it was a great idea.

'I'll call them Panther,' I improvised, imagining slinky girls on little stages like something out of the Follies Bergere.

'Right, get on with it,' Mike said. Full of confidence, having spent years one way or another dancing in every club around Wakefield, even if was mostly ballroom dancing with my dad, I advertised for dancers and models, rehearsed them and launched them with a fanfare. They were very good and new members flocked in to sign up for the VIP lounge. Word went round and one of the top agents in the North, who I'd known from the big acts he'd booked into Pussycat's, said he wanted to sign my dancers on his books provided that I joined them. I got scared. I told myself that I wasn't really a trained dancer and was only playing at this: 'It's not real!' I exclaimed to Mum. 'What shall I do?'

'Whatever you're comfortable with, Jane. You're doing a lot already, plenty more than most girls your age,' Mum said.

Feeling I was being loyal to Mike, I turned the agent down. When one of my girls got an audition in York to join another dance troupe, she asked if I would go with her for a bit of moral support. I'm not sure how it happened, but she went for the audition, and I ended up getting the job with her. Suddenly, I was a proper dancer in a proper dance troupe – in Italy.

When I added that I was going to be an exotic dancer, whose outfits would consist of little more than a sequinned G-string and a bunch of feathers, Mum and Dad had a fit, but I convinced them that I would be in good hands and would be very well-chaperoned, which, as it turned out, was truer than I thought.

In Italy, all the men were beautiful and all the women were elegant stick insects. The scenery was beautiful as well, but soon I had more pressing things on my mind.

In Castelleone, where we were staying in an all-girls' pensione, we rehearsed new dance routines. I picked them up really quickly and enjoyed myself until the troupe manager looked at me critically. 'Jane, you're too fat, we're putting you on a diet,' he said. I'd been skinny most of my life and was pleased when I started to get curves, but he made me feel big. I was put on a very strict diet which didn't supply me with enough calories to sustain the hours we spent stretching and warming up before going to work in the clubs, and I was perpetually hungry. It was impossible for me to cheat since we were given no money at all and were delivered door to door in the back of a big van as if we were cattle, guarded by a big Alsatian dog. That dog – who was trained to eat men – even slept outside our rooms. We were not allowed out, not allowed to mix – and in my case, not allowed to eat. I was so hungry, I would even have eaten the dog's dinner had he not wolfed it down so fast himself.

In desperation, I stole boxes of All-Bran from the dining room and ate it dry, out of the packet. Admittedly, the cereal was on my diet, but I was allowed only a small portion with skimmed milk with it for breakfast. Anyone who has over-indulged in this cereal will know that it plays havoc with the digestive system: in one end and straight out the other. I got terrible piles, and if you've ever experienced the excruciating pain of sharp, glittery little sequins on a G-string sticking into your arse, you'll know exactly about the pain I mean. I still won't wear those instruments of torture – with or without sequins – to this day.

By now, my Italian wasn't bad and I got the gist when the

singer in an Italian rock band in one of the clubs asked me to write out the English lyrics to the Michael Jackson song 'Thriller'. 'Grazie, Jane,' he said, slipping me a thousand lira note. Quick as a flash I stuffed it into my G-string and started dreaming of the big plate of pasta I now had the money to buy, if not the opportunity. Images of rich Bolognaise sauce and heaps of Parmesan cheese filled my head. My stomach rumbled so hard I could hardly dance, but fortunately the music was so loud that the men leering at me as I shook my feathers and shimmied my beads couldn't hear the volcano within. That night after the show, I climbed out of the second floor window of the pensione, down the drainpipe and went in search of paradise in a trattoria. Unable to wait, I slunk furtively into the newsagents next door and bought a large Mars bar, which I crammed into my mouth as fast as I could.

'Merde! You want another one?' asked the razor-thin woman behind the counter, eyeing my bulging cheeks.

But no sooner had I gulped down the last chocolatey mouthful, than the terrible guilty conscience I was born with kicked in and I turned tail and hared back to the pensione. It's one thing to slide down a drainpipe – it's another matter to climb back up it. I stood under my window and thought, 'Flipping heck! How am I going to get up there?' But I did it, shinning up like a cat burglar. As I tumbled through the window, I waited for the axe to fall, for a voice to boom, 'McDonald! Is that chocolate around your mouth?'

Lying in my hard little bed I wept with homesickness. I wanted to go home so badly it hurt, but it wasn't easy to break out with no money and no return ticket. The next day, with the change from the thousand lira, I called home and spoke to Dad.

'I'm so hungry!' I wailed. I was explaining how I was living, begging him to rescue me, when the money ran out. I stared at the phone in despair. I hadn't been able to give him my number because it wasn't on the box, Suddenly a miracle happened. The phone rang. I snatched it up and it was Dad.

I asked, 'How did you do that?'

He sounded puzzled. 'I don't know. I picked up the phone to ask the operator if she could trace your number and before I even dialled, I heard the ringing tone and you answered.'

What had happened was impossible. Some things are beyond explanation and you just have to accept them. Dad got me a ticket, paid back the money the troupe said they'd spent on my training and expenses, and I flew home to Gatwick. Carrying a packet of sandwiches, Dad came all the way down from Yorkshire on a train and across London on the underground for the first time in his life, to fetch me. When he handed me the sandwiches, tears filled my eyes. I thought, 'my dad is the best in the world.' If nothing else, the experience taught me that I wasn't yet ready to go into the wide world.

Casanova's welcomed be back with open arms. Mike even gave me the prestigious DJ slot, which I did from seven till ten; after which, I'd open the VIP lounge. As soon as I was back on my feet and had some money saved, the subject of our annual family holiday came up. I said to Dad, 'Why don't we go somewhere really special? If I go to Bridlington once more I'll scream.'

'And what's wrong with Bridlington?' Dad asked.

I said, 'We've gone there every single year and we know it better than we know Wakefield. Come on, Dad let's give Mum a decent holiday.'

I decided on Jersey. It was the first time we had been that far afield as a family, the first time Mum had ever flown. We had a lovely hotel in St Heliers, another first. We'd always had a caravan, which meant no holiday for Mum, who was one of those women who had to clean from top to bottom when we arrived because you never knew who'd been there; and from top to bottom when we left because she didn't want people saying she was lazy. In Jersey, Dad, who with his olive skin only had to pass a window to get a tan, and I were on the beach every day while Mum went shopping. We got to see shows on a night, ate every meal out and Mum didn't have to wash up once.

It was the best holiday ever. Everything, the weather, the hotel, the food, was perfect. I can remember sitting in a restaurant on the front and Dad saying, 'I don't know why we haven't done this before'.

'Och, I could get used to this,' Mum said almost wistfully.

'Well, get used to it,' I said, 'because this is just the start.'

'You're a good lassie, Jane,' Mum said. 'You should be on holiday with your friends, having fun.'

'I am having fun. You know I love being with you,' I said. 'You're my best friends.' I meant it. The three of us got on so well, I couldn't imagine it ever being any different.

On my return from holiday, Mike asked if I knew any good bands for the club. Immediately I thought of a young drummer named Paul whom I had first met when he and his group played at Pussycat's. I'd always admired them, so they were booked.

Perhaps I was looking at everything through rose-tinted glasses, or it could have been that my hormones, repressed for so long in Italy, were running rampant. Whatever the reason, I decided to fall in love with Paul. He had plenty going for him; he was good-looking, a good musician, had a lovely personality – it all added up to an overdose of infatuation on both sides and we started an affair that culminated with me moving to Sheffield and into his flat. It was only twenty miles away from home, down the M1, close enough for me to commute to work – or so I thought. I was concerned when Paul said he didn't like me working in a club.

'But it's a wonderful job and the pay is good,' I argued.

He went into a macho mode about 'his' woman and late nights and other men ogling me. Well, I could understand that only too well, because Dad was like that with Mum, and I thought it was quite endearing, if smothering. In my mind it was what all men were like, so I agreed to give up the night life and get a normal nine-to-five while Paul continued with his music. I knew it was that or lose him, and I wasn't ready for that.

Most of my friends, and all the women in my family, had married young and I was now twenty-one. Telling myself that it was time I settled down before I was left on the shelf, I went job-hunting in Sheffield. The only work I could find was temping as a typist at Nixdorf's, a big computer company on Parkway. When a vacancy came up on the computer floor, I applied at once, even though I hadn't the faintest idea what I would be doing. I was given a demonstration and then was told that I had the job. I was there for two years – I even enjoyed it.

Sometimes when Paul and I discussed the future, I would say wistfully that what I really wanted was to sing. Bizarre as it might sound, Paul had never heard me, and had no idea that I had any ability. When he met me, I'd been managing a club, not singing. I never bragged about the two years I had spent with the Brian Gordon Sound because I didn't want him to think I was putting his own band down. My secret didn't come out until our wedding in 1986, when Paul and I sang together – a big shock for his family.

They sat there, stunned, and said, 'We didn't know you could sing.'

I shrugged. 'I don't think of myself as a singer,' I said.

It was true. Other people were professional singers, other people cut records and performed on stage at the London Palladium, never someone like me. I had such a low sense of self-esteem that in my mind I was always just a Yorkshire lass who happened to have a big voice, unable to make that mental connection between progressing from being an amateur to being professional. Shirley Bassey, Barbra Streisand were real singers, but I didn't know by what alchemy they had come to be so. It seemed impossible for an ordinary girl like me to rise to that level. It was as if I thought there were regulations, a diploma I had to have that said: 'Jane McDonald you are a entitled to sing professionally', without which I would be called a fake. I do know that I was the despair of my mother. For years she had tried to encourage me, tried to make me see that I had a gift, a destiny to follow. But lacking confidence, I couldn't see this.

After everyone's reaction, Paul looked at me in an entirely different way. 'I'll leave the group, we'll start our own,' he said, making plans. It's true that I had given up working in the clubs to stay at home in the evenings, but this way, I wouldn't be out there doing my own thing; I would be working with him.

Paul was a drummer, and a good one. We found a lead guitarist but still needed a bass guitarist. With no money and no gigs to offer, it wasn't easy. In the end, I said, 'I'll play bass.'

After keeping my voice under a bushel for so long, Paul

didn't know what to expect. 'Can you play?' he asked.

I said, 'No, but put one in my hands and I'll give it a go.' It was like the piano and the computers, I knew I could do it, and I did. Not very well, I admit, but well enough to get by.

We did some small gigs, then dear old Mike Craig offered us a job at a new club he was opening. Now we were able to take on a real bass guitarist. The job lasted a few months but our marriage started to flounder. Paul had meant it when he said he wanted a wife at home – but I wasn't that woman and realised that I never could be. Even though we were out there working together in the clubs, it wasn't the same as cooking dinner and being there when he came in. Gradually, we drifted apart. Six months after we had married, with a sense of sadness, yet great relief, we agreed to a divorce, which was finalised the following year. Ultimately, I was grateful to Paul because he brought me back to singing. He showed me that I didn't need a diploma. I was a pro. After we split up, I never looked back.

CLUBLAND

Tony was always ready to come at a moment's notice when I needed him. As he drove me away from Sheffield, he said little, the perfect listener. When I finished letting it all out, he simply said, 'If it wasn't meant to be, it wasn't meant to be. What will you do now?'

I stared out of the window at the grand sweep of the moors on either side of the motorway. 'I don't know. First thing is, get a job.' I knew I would get one at once. I'm a grafter and finding work – any work – has never been a problem for me. I'll always say, 'yes, I can do it,' then work out how.

At home, as we usually did when there was something to sort out, we sat down and had a family conference. 'Right, you're staying are you?' Dad said.

'Yes, I'm not going back, chapter's closed,' I replied.

Mum said, 'What are you going to do?'

'I'm going to be a singer,' I said with quiet conviction, looking at her to see her reaction. She'd been after me for a long time to get focused. She'd always believed in me, so why hadn't I?

She nodded. 'Good, very good. You know what I thought of that computer job of yours, all that time wasted.'

I had enjoyed the job and made some good friends, but I

knew what Mum meant. I was lazy in creative ways; I had the talent but I just didn't use it enough, that's what my mother used to say. She'd yell, frustrated that she couldn't get me to see, 'You're so lazy. You have to achieve your potential. For God's sake, Jane, you've been given a gift, how can you waste it?' Previously, I'd blocked my ears, but now I was listening at last, full of enthusiasm for the future.

'Come on, I'll be your roadie,' Dad said, banging the table.

'Are you really up for it?' I asked.

'When do we start?' he said, taking a gulp of tea from his mug. 'Life's too short to sit around on your arse dreaming.'

I gave him a quick look. Dad never said much, never showed his inner feelings – had his life not been all that he wanted it to be? He was such a powerful man, such a doer, who recently had taken voluntary redundancy. Retirement can sometimes catch a strong man unawares, bringing him up against the relentless passage of time and his own mortality. I caught a swift flash of something, then it was gone.

Excitement started to build in our crowded little living room. Mum made numerous pots of tea and put plates of sandwiches on the table while we discussed all the pros and cons. By the end of the conference, Dad had offered to buy a PA system with some of his redundancy money and I said I'd find an agent who would get me work in the clubs. First priority, though, was a day job to get me back on my feet.

I decided that my appearance was important if I was to be taken seriously at an audition. An act is more than just a good voice, it's the whole thing: looks, clothes, presentation, attitude. A good tan always made me feel my best but I was skint, so I walked into a big shop in Leeds that sold sunbeds. 'Any chance of a job?' I asked. They said yes at once and I was in there the next day, selling hard. I got the best sales because

I was always so tanned, people would come to me because they thought I must know what I was talking about. We were on individual commission, but with me getting it all, the other staff insisted on pooling it, which upset me as I knew that I would need every penny to finance my career as a singer until I found my feet.

Next on the list was the agent. I already knew quite a lot about how the system operated. The Northern clubs and agents worked together in a very incestuous way. Each of the top agents had a group of clubs he serviced with his acts and they all swapped with each other, keeping the business going round in a circle. Because it was a closed shop, you had to get your toe through the door. This was achieved by Dad driving me to an agents' audition in Leeds, that showcased hopeful artist's talents. Looking good, with a new hairdo, new outfit and new tan, I went in front of the three leading agents and did my bit, with a bit of chat, a joke and a song.

One of them said, 'Stop talking.'

'Stop talking?' I repeated.

'You don't need to talk in between, you're a good enough singer, forget the chat, just get on and sing,' he said.

I gathered that he wanted me, but I didn't agree with what he was saying. There are plenty of good singers around but I have always considered that what makes me a little bit different, gives me that advantage, is my relationship with my audience. I could never be a toffee-nose who comes on, sings, bows three times and then walks off, not having connected with the audience.

Les Parker, one of the other agents at that audition, said he liked the way I communicated and signed me up as a 'personality vocalist'. I already knew him because he owned a pub in Wakefield where he threw private parties for his performers, great evenings, where the cream of northern talent gathered and swapped gossip. We sorted out a programme and he said he'd let me have my dates as soon as possible. I rushed home to tell Mum.

The old blue van was given a fine tuning, I got my backing tapes laid down in case there wasn't a band and sorted out my music in case there was. I had three different sets of sheet music; 'Great' for a really hot band that could read music *and* play it; 'Mediocre' for a so-so band; and 'Easy' in case they were hopeless, which occasionally they were. Dad loaded in my PA system, I put jumbo rollers in my hair, packed a sequinned frock, gold shoes and my make-up and we were off. I might have had butterflies in my stomach about getting up there on stage for the first time on my own, but I knew I was in familiar territory because I'd grown up in working men's clubs. These were my type of people, I could talk to them on their terms in language we understood.

I'd talk mostly to the women, discussing shared interests and topics they could relate to, usually gossip about the Soaps, in a chatty way: 'Hey girls, what do you think of Ken Barlow, blimey, what's he up to, eh?' I'd also crack jokes about ordinary, everyday life: 'When I was a baby, me mum used to bath me in the sink – and after Sunday lunch, there'd always be a fork left in with its prongs facing up'. I would nick a few jokes from the comedians – we all did.

The people in clubs are very vocal. If I sang something they didn't like or want, they'd shout, 'Sing us sommat we know!' I soon learned that I couldn't experiment. Very rarely, I'd slide something different in, just to see how it went down. Mostly, however, I stuck to what the audience wanted, which was probably why I rapidly gained a big following. There was a generality in what the audience wanted. They'd accept a *Top of the Pops* number if the song was catchy, and they enjoyed medleys that they could sing along to, but more often than not, they wanted standards, big songs like 'The Power of Love' or 'You're My World'.

I remember once a young rock and roller cheekily asked me why I sang crap, like 'Blanket on the Ground'. I got very annoyed. 'These songs are standards because they've passed the test of time. They're not just good – they're great,' I replied.

I used to make a joke about that particular song in my club days: 'Now if you don't shut up, I'll sing "Blanket on the Ground"!' I'd threaten. As soon as I struck up that first note, everybody was clapping and singing and swaying. It was a crowd pleaser every time, despite being done to death. The audiences loved the happy songs, the heart wrenching songs. A piece of music is like a memory trigger – you can always remember where you were when you heard it. I wanted to put in all the emotion that made a song special to someone out there in the audience, especially towards the end of the evening when things were winding down and their mood was mellow. Invariably the mood would be broken by the club secretary yelling, 'Time please! We're closing!'

As I got established, I gave up the sun-bed job and started working full time as a performer. At last I was becoming what to me had always seemed an elusive dream, a proper singer. My week consisted of going to the clubs at night and during the day I'd work very hard at home on the music side of my act, making sure it was always current with the big hits as well as the evergreens. Most people in clubland have got families to keep and every penny they get goes on buying their kids shoes, whereas I was able to put most of my money back into my act. I had the best sound system, a large wardrobe of sparkly frocks that everyone looked out for – and I knew when people liked what I was wearing, or not, because they'd tell me. I didn't let on that I got my 'Jane McDonalds' as they came to be known, really cheap from boutiques here and there because no one else would buy them!

When I started, I thought I knew how performing would be, but I'd only seen it from the floor, never from the stage, behind the tattered red curtain. Those first weeks, I had a crash course in being a club singer on the Northern circuit – a very hard school where you are in constant competition with bingo, the bar and even the snooker table. It is said that if you can win over an audience there, you can win one anywhere. Over the course of the years, I learned my trade and discovered what people wanted, in front of an audience who were the real backbone of England. There's nothing like a Northern audience, even at their worst. And believe me, it could get very grim.

I remember one disastrous night in Leeds when I was using an expensive new lighting system. I always improved my act as much as I could because, so I was assured, I'd be paid more money. But I never was. I did my act, everything went well; the comedian went on, he was brilliant. There was a lengthy interval and we put on the second act. It was pay-day for most of the club members, which meant that the drink had been flowing for some time. What I didn't know was that this was Hatfield and McCoy territory. Two hard clans were there in force in the audience that night, with eighteen pints each under their belts and a long ongoing feud to settle.

I started to sense that all was not well, possibly because both tribes were getting restless and exchanging insults with each other, like bare-knuckle fighters getting primed, their women egging them on.

'Go on, Jock, 'it 'im!' screamed one blonde bombshell in a studded denim jacket.

'He's insulted me, Billy, do 'im!' screamed a redhead in thigh-high patent plastic boots.

Steel toecaps pawed the floor, snooker cues were snapped in two, bottles were clenched ready in massive fists – and the biggest scrap I'd ever seen exploded from one end of the big room to the other. The entire place was heaving with the speed of a tidal wave sweeping across it. My expensive new lights keeled over and Dad grabbed me, 'Get off, Jane!' he yelled above the din and the sound of breaking glass, hauling me along to the dressing room, where he locked me in until it was all over. The police rushed in and broke up the fight. The walking wounded were arrested and taken down the nick, ambulances carted off the unconscious. When I eventually emerged, everything was trashed. I looked at my wrecked lights and said bitterly, 'Why do I bother?'

From Burnley to Grimsby and back, across the length and breadth of the Pennines, most weekends, there were fights and feuds, mayhem and madness in some club or pub. Luckily, it didn't happen to me very often, but on the times when it did, Dad was always there to sense when the powder keg was about to blow and the words: 'Get off, Jane!' would be my cue as, yet again, I'd be locked in the dressing room, my expensive, hard-earned equipment crashing with a bang in the thick of the fighting.

It got so bad that I eventually wouldn't sing in pubs any more because the tiny stages were so close to the drinkers, and I felt too vulnerable. Fights weren't the only problem. At one club in Manchester, when I came out to get my gear, the car windows were smashed through, and everything inside had been nicked. There were some clubs, no matter who was on, where the audience just didn't want to listen. It's difficult to stand up there, singing your heart out when all hell is breaking loose around you. There were lots of other times when I thought, 'Why am I doing this?' as we'd be driving across the Pennines in the snow, a blizzard blowing in the dark and unable to see where the road ended and the bog began, with an ominous rattle starting in the engine.

However hard I tried, it was never very easy competing against the main entertainment of the evening: bingo. In one club, I was told that I had to be offstage before the bingo started. I was putting my all into Barbra Streisand's 'Evergreen' when the audience started tittering. Out of the corner of my eye, I saw the two curtains swishing towards me. At the very last moment, I thought, 'Right you buggers, you're not going to do this to me!' I jumped to the front and carried on singing. The audience loved it and gave me a big cheer – before clearing the decks for their precious bingo.

In a club in Doncaster, I learned how important it is not to brush the audience up the wrong way, though thankfully it wasn't me they turned against. The comedian, who was a bit of a lost cause, asked if he could borrow my equipment after I'd done my first set. Reluctantly, I agreed. For some reason, they didn't like his act and started yelling out loud remarks. Suddenly he said, 'If you lot don't shut up, I'll bring back the girl singer.'

My blood ran cold. Dad said, 'Cheeky bugger, I'll sort him out.' He was about to go up on the stage to snatch back my microphone, when I realised that the audience were booing. They gave that comedian a terrible time of it – and when it was my turn to go back on again, they raised the roof.

Northern audiences might treat you badly but they don't like it when somebody else does.

The calibre of the band was another problem, because often until you got to a club, you never knew whether the house band was going to be good or bad – and no matter how good you are, a poor band can kill you. I could tell at once by the equipment what the band was like. A good band would have a stack of keyboards and a good drum kit; but my heart would sink when there was nothing on the stage but an old organ and a little bass drum with a snare and a cymbal. I'd say to myself, 'Jane, this is not going to be good.' I used to pray for Albion Road, a club in Rotherham, where there was a fantastic backing called Gary and Nigel, so good they sounded like a full orchestra.

I've shown some of the downside; but it wasn't all bad. I loved clubland, or I wouldn't have kept on working there for so long. I liked the excitement and the bustle, the cameraderie, the backchat, the good laughs and the exceptionally close friendships I formed with women like Sue Ravey, a terrific singer in her own right, who was eventually to become my backing singer when fame struck out of the blue. Like all live performers, I needed an audience to keep the rapport and the buzz going. I really appreciated and loved the audiences in the clubs, getting to recognise faces and names, and enjoying a chat and a drink with them between sets or afterwards before it was time to hit the road home. When I won the Clubland Female Vocalist of the Year award two years running, to me it was like winning an Oscar. It was a real award, because it came from the hearts of real people, the salt of the earth and, to me, twenty fans are equally as important as twenty thousand fans. When I look out, I don't see a sea of people but individual faces.

It was while I was singing in a club in Wakefield that an old friend, Vicky Calvert, dropped in to catch the show. I hadn't seen Vicky for a while, having heard through the grapevine that she was singing on cruise liners, from all accounts having a great time. We caught up on news during the interval. Suddenly she asked, 'Do you fancy working on the ships?'

At once I said, 'Yes! – not half!' I was always up for a challenge and it seemed a great idea.

'Right, I'll put your name in at my agent in London, he's casting at the moment,' Vicky said. 'You'll like him, his name is Al Radcliffe.'

My head was buzzing with this unexpected turn of events. There was no question in my mind that I wouldn't get the job. I don't remember where Dad was that night, but I think he was at home and hadn't been out with me. As soon as I got in, I woke Mum and him up and said, 'I'm going on the ships! I'm going down to London to audition with a new agent.'

As usual, they got up and Mum put the kettle on and we talked it over. I had been doing the clubs for a while and, much as I enjoyed them, I felt I needed a change, I was ambitious and thought that a wider venue would be a step in the right direction to being discovered.

Mum nodded. 'You've been a bit low recently – perhaps it will do you good to get away.'

Dad said, 'Remember Italy – come back at once if it doesn't work out.'

I went down to audition with Al Radcliffe at Matrix Entertainment, an agency that exclusively produced shows for cruise liners. As Vicky had predicted, we got on famously. When Al said, 'When can you start?' I replied 'Today?' We both laughed and he said he'd try me out with a short-term contract on the *Black Prince*, a relatively small ship that was used by the agency as a training ship to assess how new recruits handled life at sea.

Al elaborated: 'A ship is what you make it. You can either go on board and have an absolute ball or you can be a misery, unable to cope. It's a world of its own, for both crew and passengers. For the passengers, it is a romantic interlude – for the crews it can be hell. Crews are there sometimes for months on end, crammed in tiny cabins. Tempers and passions can run very high. It can be an incestuous little world and you have to get on with all types – because once you're afloat, there's no getting off. Think you can handle it, Jane?'

With my usual breezy self-confidence, I said, 'There's not much I can't handle.'

Al laughed. 'I can see that.'

I wasn't to know that the comedy *Doctor At Sea* would be tame compared with the realities of the cruise ship world. Quite amazed at the speed with which I'd been accepted, I rushed home to tell Mum and Dad the good news.

When Tony heard, he roared with laughter. 'Our Jane on a ship?' he hooted. 'I can remember the time when you were bicycle-sick.'

'That were a long time ago, I don't get travel sick these days,' I said, fingers crossed behind my back.

Once a week, I would go down to the Maida Vale flat of Sam Jones, a former member of the Vernon Girls, whose job it was to coach me in the new shows and ensure that I could reach the high notes. Sam would say, 'Right, sing this bit.' When I sang it word-perfect first time, she'd laugh. 'Yes, you know it – now how about a cup of tea?' We'd spend the rest of the day chatting until it was time for my session with Peter Gordino, who was the choreographer for the shows. (Peter now lives near us in Florida, and we visit – but I'm leaping years ahead!)

I was always very excited on the train down to London, thinking I had finally hit the big time, and still buzzing on the return journey. It was only gradually that doubts began to creep in. Was I doing the right thing? I would be entirely on my own, afloat on a ship, unable to leave. I remembered the loneliness of my time in Italy. I knew how much I would miss Mum and Dad, the family and all my friends in Wakefield. Excited as I was, I felt like the kid in the fairy story with a red-spotted handkerchief over his shoulder containing all his worldly goods, going off into the great blue yonder to seek his fortune on his own.

I flew to Tenerife to join the *Black Prince*, feeling very apprehensive. For the third time, I was striking out on my own into the wide world beyond Wakefield. The first time had been Italy, the second had been Sheffield and an unsuccessful marriage. From being the small girl who was terrified of leaving the house, feeling very excited and grown up, I was now setting off on travels that would take me even further afield than I'd been before: was it to be third time lucky?

My biggest fear was that I would be seasick – and I was, but only once or twice to start with; as soon as I got my sea legs I was fine, except in the worst of storms. From the first day, I teamed with Vicky Calvert, who'd suggested the job in the first place. During those twelve weeks cruising through the dramatic volcanic islands of Grand Canaria, we crammed in every experience like two girls in the sweet shop, having our pick of anything. We went on the tourist trail, visiting every volcano, every cave, every grotto and tasted everything on the menu. Confronted with smoked salmon, tiger prawns and caviar every day with exotic fruits I had never seen before, let alone knew how to pronounce, I came to realise that I was definitely not a stew and dumplings type. There's a common joke in the cruising world that people go on as passengers and come off as cargo; in my case I went up from a dress size ten to fourteen in those twelve weeks.

It wasn't just the food that was over-indulged in: Bacchanalian nights played out under a silvery moon in a phosphorescent sea gave way to oiled bodies entwined on sunbaked, secluded beaches. For a strictly brought up girl who had never been in that sexually free and easy world before, it was quite a shock – but I soon got over it and jumped in feet first. By the time I'd moved on to the bigger ships in the Caribbean, I was sated, even bored, with what was politely termed: 'all that sun, sea and sail'. Whenever I was invited to a party, I would yawn, 'Thanks, but I'd rather go back to my cabin and read my book.' However, it wasn't all play on the *Black Prince*. A small ship with little room for crew, when we weren't singing, we had to help look after the passengers, who tended to be better behaved and far easier to please than on the huge floating palaces I was soon to join.

On the *Black Prince* the entertainment was very much like that in a night-club, with four singers of equal importance and no dancers. The system was entirely different on the bigger ships, where passengers expected lavish shows along Broadway lines, with big names headlining. The rest of us, the anonymous mass of the good but the unknown, were lumped together in a team category known as 'production performers'. Coming from being quite famous in Yorkshire, where I'd won various awards, it was hard for me to accept that 'Jane McDonald' had all but vanished. Still, I consoled myself that it was an upward career move, not appreciating for a long time that, like all production performers, I was a small fish in a very big pond; a little sardine swimming in all innocence into the Sargasso Sea, where I would remain becalmed for some years.

When I flew to the States to join the *Horizon*, a big ship in a fleet of big ships, owned by Celebrity Cruises, based in Fort Lauderdale, I met Debbie Wells. Small, dark haired and vivacious, she was a joy to be around. Quickly we became best friends, sharing a cabin, clothes, money, life stories – everything. Our bond was forged from our shared sense of humour and urge to rebel. I used to sit back in awe, amazed at Deb's vitality, especially the shows she put on when she had drunk too much and danced on the tables. Of the two rules we had to obey on the Celebrity line, we broke both. The first was the curfew. Because dancers helped look after the passengers, they were considered as crew – so for health and safety reasons, they had to go to bed before us. We were singers, and therefore officer class, whose curfew was later, at 2 a.m.

When we were read the regulations by the staff captain, I said to Debs, 'Hang on, I haven't been told what time to go to bed since I was about seventeen'.

Her eyes sparkled. 'Something must be done,' she agreed at once.

The second rule was that we weren't allowed to drink in public areas where the passengers were. Egged on by Debs, I broke both rules simultaneously. At 3 a.m., I was wallowing up on deck under the stars in the Jacuzzi, with a bottle of Champagne on ice, reading the *Financial Times*. It was a glorious night just off Bermuda and I was just thinking, 'This is luxury,' when the staff captain's voice boomed in my ear. Planting his white uniformed bulk right in my face, blocking out my view of the velvety sky, he bawled, 'McDonald, what do you think you're doing?'

I said, 'I'm sat in the Jacuzzi with a glass of Champagne, reading the *Financial Times*. Would you like to join me?' I gave him a sultry wink.

Trying to sound authoritative he snapped, 'No, I wouldn't!' The effect was ruined when he started to laugh as he walked off.

I thought, 'That's one up to me – I haven't been fired.'

After our stint on the *Horizon*, Debs – now Debbie Moore – married a snooker player who worked in the casino, had two lovely children and left the sea. When my contract ended, I flew home and almost immediately, in the early summer of 1993, got the offer of my first season at the Maid Marion Club in the Robin Hood holiday camp just outside Skegness. Much as I had enjoyed life afloat, I had missed everyone at home and snapped up the offer at once.

I came to think of the Maid Marion almost as my spiritual home – and certainly it was a great proving ground for my performance, as well as being one of the best experiences of my whole career. The season was long – twenty-eight weeks – but it was a good place and I always enjoyed it. There was something very special about the audience there; they were supportive, good-hearted and a joy to sing for. In return, they called me their very own Maid Marion and some of them would have banners with my name on, which they waved to show their appreciation. It was like looking out at a good-natured football crowd, everyone having a great time.

Many of the holiday-makers at the camp had their own caravans that they'd return to season after season, often staying for the entire twenty-eight weeks. These regulars adopted me, treating me like a daughter, even inviting me around for Sunday lunch. June and Albert Mulligan, a lovely couple in their early sixties, really took me under their wing, making sure I ate, leaving me cakes at my caravan door. Bill and Betty Johnson were another wonderful couple in their fifties, who also left me treats and snacks. When I sang, they would sit at a table right up front, huge grins illuminating their faces, showing me just how much they valued my performance. Our love for each other was a two-way street; I emanated with love for them, and could feel their love in return. It was like being bathed in a cloud of warmth and goodwill.

As usual, it was a live-in job, so I didn't need Dad to act as my roadie, but I told him we'd be off again on the road in October. The Maid Marion club room was massive. It was a social club very much like the working man's clubs I was used to, seating people around tables where they could have a drink and a chat and watch the show in a relaxed atmosphere. It was always busy with constant movement, drinks coming from the long bars at the back and children running around. It was hard on a performer and if you didn't grab the audience from the start, it was an uphill struggle all the way.

One night I ran into Alan Cobbet, the trumpet player from the Brian Gordon Sound, who was there as a guest artist. As I complained that it was hard to put emotion into a big song with a constant hum of background chat, he gave me some really good advice that I've never forgotten. He said, 'Always remember that a clap is a bonus. If they listen, that's enough – but if they clap, that's a bonus.'

This relaxed me and I settled down for the summer with a good entertainment team, many of whom were old friends. I learned how to host, learned how to talk to an audience properly, especially when our Musical Director used to say,

'Jane, I'm running short ten minutes – go out and fill.'

At first I panicked, faced with two thousand people who were just as likely to stamp their feet when things didn't go right as clap when things did. Sometimes, if I judged the mood was right, I'd fill in time by trying something different. One night, I tried Dolly Parton's incredibly atmospheric and moving song, 'I Will Always Love You', something you would never normally think of doing in a club because your voice has to rise above the constant background hubbub. But you sometimes wonder if maybe this time they'll listen to some vocal acrobatics. That night, they did listen. In fact, the entire crowd was silent. For a split second the place went deathly quiet while that very first haunting a cappella note soared up over the heads of the audience to the ceiling rafters.

There was a crescendo of cheers and the crowd went wild. Oh my God, what have I done?' I thought. The cheers seemed to rebound from the walls as I continued with that wonderful 'I' – a single, one-letter word which in that song has a million depths of meaning and seems to bend sound itself: 'I Will Always Love You'.

At the end, I glanced at the table directly in front of me and everyone was openly weeping. Suddenly, they were all on their feet, clapping and screaming. That was when I learnt that people will respond if you reach out to them with sincerity. I had two thousand people there I could entertain, who wanted to listen to me, who respected me.

I had my own caravan at the camp which, as usual, I made as homely as possible. I had Wednesday nights off and usually made the long drive home, returning to Skegness the following day. At the end of the season, I arranged to go home that final Wednesday night with my car and swap it for Dad's van so I could bring all my stuff back home on the last night when the camp closed at the end of September.

The cruise ships have a turn-around season, when the ships leave the potential tropical storms and hurricanes of the Caribbean, to sail mostly in the Mediterranean or through the stunning scenery of Alaska, past ice-blue glaciers. Therefore, at the end of that first Maid Marion season, I could have returned to sea; but something held me back. I decided to stay at home and go back on the road, to my old stamping ground, the clubs, with Dad. Although he didn't show much emotion, I could tell he was pleased. Over dinner, he told me that he had worked out my itinerary and all the maps for my bookings that coming winter.

Mum laughed. 'Thank goodness you'll be home soon, Jane. He's been like a bear with a sore head since you've been gone,' she said. 'You're the only person who can do anything with him.'

The main reason for Dad's early retirement had been ill health, although he didn't say too much about his illness, brushing aside any questions. 'I'm fit enough to go on road with you,' he growled. Before I'd gone to sea, I had noticed that he'd started to be really picky about the clubs I was booked in at, refusing to travel too far, turning down all clubs with stairs. At the time, I just thought it was Dad being Dad, living up to his reputation as a 'character'.

'We're not doing that,' he sometimes said brusquely when he looked at my schedule and he'd get on the phone and argue with the agent. One of the clubs he refused was Burmantoff's with its killing eight flights of stairs and another was the Harehills, also in Leeds, where the way to the stage door was up an old metal fire escape. One winter, when the steps were covered in ice, he'd slipped while carrying my amps and fell down about ten steps, twisting his back rather badly.

It got to the point where Dad had started demanding all kinds of terms from the agent: no stairs, help in moving my gear from club secretaries, and not much travelling. The furthest he would go would be Burnley, a round journey of some eighty miles. Amazingly, they let him get away with it because he amused them. I can remember people mimicking him, never in malice, finishing off with a laugh, adding, 'That Peter McDonald, he's a one!'

As I left the house the following morning to drive back to Skegness for the final week, Dad saw me to the garden gate.

'God, I can't wait for you to come home. I'm bored out of my head,' he said.

'Well it won't be long,' I said. 'I'll see you in a few days.'

I was walking towards the van when something made me turn and look at him standing forlornly at the gate. I walked back and said, 'I do love you – but you know that.' It was the last thing I ever said to him.

He simply said, 'Yes.' before I turned away again and left.

Even as I joked and chatted to the large audience of sunburned, happy holidaymakers during my last few days at the Maid Marion, I had a sense of urgency, as if my getting to the end of September was a race against time. Some evenings as I applied my make-up before the show, I found myself whispering, 'Hang on, Dad, I'll be home soon, then we'll be out, back on road'.

They had a big party the last night but I told everybody, 'I'm not very good at goodbyes and all that, so I'll just sneak out and go'.

'See you next year,' they said.

'No,' I replied, 'I'll be doing something different next year.'

Prophetic words; I had no idea what I'd be doing, nor how different my life would be.

I'd packed most of my stuff and loaded the van, the caravan was tidy. As soon as I'd done the show, I added the last items to the van and left, leaving the lights of Skegness behind. I recalled the years that Dad and I had been on the road together. He was such a strong, magnetic personality that when you walked into a room you were always drawn to him. He was also quite a joker of the deadpan variety. I remembered one night at a club in Derby, I was singing 'The Power of Love' to a backing track, putting all my heart and soul into the emotional words, when everyone started to laugh. It was stifled little giggles at first, then it grew to full-bellied, raucous laughter.

I always spent as much as I could afford on quite lavish evening outfits because that was what the people expected, but often they were 'all show and no knickers', as a miner would say to describe something that was superficially glamorous but poorly made. Had a seam split? Was I trailing bugle beads and sequins in my wake? Casting a quick glance over the stage, out of the corner of my eye, I spotted Dad on the edge of the stage at the back. In fact, he wasn't that much on the edge – more plumb centre, really, where everyone could see him.

Oblivious to the effect he was having on the audience, he sat on a stool right behind me, eating his sandwiches, unscrewing his flask and pouring out his tea. 'Aye, that were nice,' you could almost hear him sigh in satisfaction as he swallowed.

I stopped the backing tape, turned around and arms akimbo said, 'Dad, what the hell are you doing?'

'I'm fine, don't mind me, lassie,' he said.

'Dad –'

'Get on with it, lass, you can't stop singing in the middle of a song,' he said, picking up his western and thumbing through the pages to find his page.

Shaking my head, I said to the audience, 'He's me dad – but I can't take him anywhere.' They laughed and perhaps many of them thought it was set up, part of the act. Hard to explain that Dad was a natural comedian, he didn't give a toss.

My eyes were blurry with a mixture of present tears and remembered laughter and I wiped them with one hand, keeping my eye on the road. It was late, well after midnight, and there was little traffic across the flat Lincolnshire landscape. I knew the route backwards but no quick, direct route could ever be magicked up from the fat bulge of the Lincolnshire coast to Wakefield, which lay almost exactly in the middle of England. All the motorways went in the wrong direction and I was stuck on narrow roads that all seemed to wind nowhere in a van that chugged along at a snail's pace.

'Come on! Come on!' I cried, hitting the steering wheel in frustration, feeling that I should be at home. I found myself talking to Dad's van as if it could hear me, 'Can't you move any faster you daft bugger? What have you got – lead in your tanks?'

I thought again of the years with Dad. It had been a damned hard graft and I knew that without him behind me from the start, I wouldn't have bothered to strike out on my own. He was the one who showed me what I could do, he developed the faith I had in myself. Sometimes I wished he'd complimented me when I felt I'd done well but, although he never said I was brilliant, never said, 'Well done lassie,' you could tell he was proud. He'd give a nod and there'd be the hint of a smile in his eyes.

I had long passed the outskirts of Lincoln with its old castle walls and medieval cathedral when the van broke down in the middle of nowhere. It sort of stopped with a last gasp kind of hiccup. I was furious. It was 2 a.m. and I thought I'd be spending the rest of the night at the side of the road. But after a moment or two, the engine started again and I drove on. I got all the way back to Wakefield and the van died, in the back lane right behind the house.

Dad had been to his club that night as usual, where he'd said to all his mates, 'Our Jane's coming home tonight, you won't see me next week because I'll be out with her again'. On his return, as they were getting ready for bed, he said to Mum, 'Shall we get up when Jane comes in?'

Mum agreed because there was no point in waiting up for me, and they went to sleep. Mum heard me come in at about 3 a.m. and switched on the light. Dad – who slept on the edge of the bed, half on a chair to aid his breathing – didn't move. Thinking he'd had a pint too many, she slipped out of the room and had a cup of tea with me.

The next morning, at about 9 o'clock, Mum knocked on my door and said, 'Jane, I'm really sorry to bother you, but come and have a look at your dad. I think he's dead.'

How do you react to something like that? I always sleep in the nude. I sprang out of bed, and ran around the house like a headless chicken trying to escape the axe that had already fallen. I didn't want to see him, didn't know what to do, what to think. As my wits returned I said, 'Just calm down, Mum, come downstairs.' Then I realised I was the one who was running about frantically, stark naked, and went back up and put a dressing gown on.

I rang Wendy, who said, 'Oh my God, how am I going to tell our Tony?' She drove to the mine to get him out of the pit – a drama in itself, smothered in coal dust as he was. After she had broken the news, he sobbed all the way home.

Then I rang Janet, who was on holiday in Tenerife. 'I'm coming back at once,' she said.

Not once did it occur to me that Dad might not be dead. Mum asked again if I should look at him to make sure, but I couldn't handle it at that time. In the end, a friend went in and confirmed it.

Knowing how important it was to the grieving and acceptance process, Mum pleaded again, 'Jane, please go in and have a look at him'.

I forced myself to go in and stood by the bed, looking down at him. I'm glad I went in and saw him as he was, peaceful, but I knew he wasn't there any more; that wasn't my Dad, just his shell. I had never had the faith of my mother and my grandmother, but looking at my dad, knowing he wasn't there, yet was surely somewhere, brought me to a realisation of what spiritualism was about. People didn't die; they simply passed over into another dimension, to a place from which they could communicate with those who were tuned into that dimension.

I went down to the doctor's and played holy hell because Dad had been with her two days before and she'd signed him off. I said: 'How dare you! My Dad's dead! You signed him off, said he was fine.'

She looked at me and said quietly, 'Of course he wasn't fine. Your dad knew he was dying.'

That stopped me in my tracks. We knew that he was ill, but we didn't know he was going to pop his clogs as quickly as he did.

'Why didn't you tell us?' I demanded.

She said, 'I'm not allowed to. But your Dad knew for a long time that he was on his way out. I couldn't do any more to help him because he wouldn't stop smoking.'

With a shock, I visualised Dad's chair in the living room. The wall behind it had to be constantly redecorated because it was so darkly stained with nicotine. Suddenly, everything else made terrible sense, Dad's bad temper, his refusal to go to clubs upstairs, his refusal to travel were all part of his illness.

When I went back and told the family that Dad had known for eight years that he had a bad heart yet hadn't told any of us, Mum became angry because he hadn't sorted anything out. 'He could have thought of me,' she said. 'He had plenty of time to make proper arrangements.'

There was no money, just bills. Then within a few days everything broke down. The electrics blew and the fire grate, main source of heat and hot water, cracked. It was as if when Dad died half the house stopped working, like he had been keeping it all together – which he had. But we had no idea then of the lengths he had gone to patch up and bodge.

'What about the van? Shall we sell it?' Tony suggested.

I'd almost forgotten about it, sitting out there with all my stuff still in it. We unloaded it and the garage came and towed it away to their premises around the corner. 'How much will you give us for it?' we asked.

They laughed. 'Big ends are gone. Engine's seized solid. It's not even worth scrap.'

'But I drove it back from Lincoln,' I argued. 'It broke down once, then it was okay.' I described the hiccups and they shook their heads in disbelief.

'Ee, lass, that weren't no hiccups: that were the big ends going. Are you sure you didn't get out and push it home?' they laughed, grinning at each other as if to say, this lass is touched.

When we talked it through afterwards, we came to realise that Dad had died at about that time, at 2 a.m. It reminded me of that old song about a grandfather clock, that was seventy years old, the same age as its owner, and tells how it stopped short, never to go again, when the old man died.

I felt that once my big sister was there everything would be all right because Janet by now had run her own business for years and was very organised. Funnily enough, she looked straight to me for support, as they all did, because despite my initial headless chicken reaction, in the end I was the only one strong enough to handle everything that had to be taken care of.

Firstly, we got a man in to have a look at the blown wiring. He was downstairs in the cellar while we sat upstairs in the living room discussing immediate problems. 'What am I going to live on?' Mum asked, being realistic. She had a small pension, but it wasn't enough. She looked about her, 'This is like Jack Duckworth from *Coronation Street*'s house. Just look at the state of it. It needs a fortune spending on it.'

We looked around, seeing it for the first time as if through outsiders' eyes and knew she was right. It needed redecorating, the furniture was shabby and worn. The back door didn't shut, the porch door didn't shut: burglars could have just walked in. We joked that they probably had done, before walking out again because there wasn't anything to nick. 'They'd have felt sorry for us and left us their swag,' I said.

Dad just wouldn't spend the money. In truth, he had very little to spend. Life had been really hard for him and Mum, but they'd brought us up well and that counted for a great deal.

While we'd been talking, we'd heard nothing else but the words: 'Bloody hell!' coming from the cellar. When the electrician came up, he said, 'My mate'll never believe it. Can

I bring him down to have a look?' He picked up the phone and said, 'You've got to come over and see this!' so dramatically that Mum's eyes widened apprehensively.

'What's wrong with it?' she asked.

'How the hell you haven't gone up in flames, I'll never know,' he said with feeling.

When his mate came, we all trooped down into the cellar while he pointed out the unbelievable confusion in the electrics. Old wires were twisted into new wires that shot off on unknown tangents like tangled knitting wool; adaptors were plugged into adaptors, eight and nine deep; the fuse boxes looked like something out of the Ark.

Sucking on his teeth he said, 'I don't know how he made things work with this little lot – it's nigh impossible. It's a time bomb waiting to go off.'

'Most illegal wiring I've ever seen,' agreed his mate.

'That's our dad – he always were a dangerous bugger,' said Tony. 'Do you remember the time he drove about with petrol cans in back of van seat, rubber hose going straight to carburettor?' Tony was talking about the time when a leak sprang in the petrol tank of one of Dad's more rusty vans. As a short-term remedy, he'd put a couple of gallon tins of petrol right behind the front seat, the tubing snaking past us, through the dashboard and into the engine.

'And he never stopped smoking,' I said. 'Driving along surrounded by petrol fumes, he'd be striking matches without a care in the world.'

We shook our heads in disbelief.

'Do you remember that time the throttle went?' Tony said. 'He tied a yard of string to the carburettor arm, through the dashboard and, instead of using the accelerator pedal, he'd yank on bit of string.'

'You have to admit he tried,' I said. 'Look at wiring for the telly.' We'd noticed for some time that our tellies always used to be a bit fuzzy and thought it was because the aerial was dodgy – but no, it was because my dad had put every television in the house on one aerial. 'At least,' I said, 'when this lot's sorted, we'll be able to watch the soaps without Lux flakes all over screen.'

When Mum said, 'How much is putting this lot right going to cost then?' the electrician said, 'I'd go back upstairs and sit down if I were you, Mrs Mac. You're going to have to remortgage house.'

Back upstairs, Janet said, 'What are you going to do, Mum? You can't afford all this. How will you manage?'

Mum said, simply, 'Jane's going to buy the house, she'll sort it out.'

I said, 'Yes, I am.' Just like that. Then I thought, that's not a bad idea. Being a cautious Yorkshire lass, I'd set up a small pension fund for myself when I'd first started to earn money. I had a car, no debts, I could afford it. Pointing to the old lean-to that Dad had made from old doors and windows, I said, 'The first thing that's going is that flipping outhouse.'

But when it came time to demolish it, it wouldn't budge. It looked haphazard but proved to be as strong as hell with perfect dove-tailed joints and coach bolts holding the whole edifice together. The builders said, 'Whoever built this bugger meant it to last.'

'That's my dad,' I said. 'He were such a good craftsman and had such crap to work with.'

After Dad's cremation, we went to the allotments to scatter his ashes. It had been so long since any of us had been there that, as we opened the gate leading up, Mum said, 'I hope we don't scatter the ashes on somebody else's allotment'.

Wendy and I looked at each other and we were gone: absolute hysterics. We've always had the same sense of humour, often it's our way of coping. Once we'd started there was no stopping us.

My mother was disgusted. 'Will you two shut up!' The more we laughed, the more my mother hissed, 'Shut up! Be serious will you!'

Trying not to look at each other, we sorted ourselves out and continued. Mum looked around. She asked, 'Do you know which allotment it is?'

I said, 'I don't know – I think it's the one back by the shed.' This was the famous shed that Richard had built – it was still there.

'Well, we can't scatter your dad's ashes on somebody else's cabbages, they wouldn't like it,' Mum said. That started me and Wendy off again. Our shoulders started going first, then it was hands stuffed into mouths, eyes streaming, bodies heaving; we clutched each other and collapsed in an undignified heap.

The more Mum hissed, 'Will you two girls stop it!' the more we howled.

At Dad's wake, talk turned to the past as it always does on such occasions. We had some good memories and sad ones, too. At one point, I said to Mum, 'You must have had a time, your whole life with Dad was a struggle.'

She said, 'No, I've been very happy with my life.'

Looking at her, I saw she looked very serene, her face youthful, her eyes clear and her laugh still girlish. But I couldn't help remembering how she had knocked on my door the day he had died and said hesitantly, 'I'm sorry to bother you –' It troubled me that she had waited for some time rather than wake me up, that she had put my tiredness after a long drive home so far ahead of her own fears. I wanted her to put herself first for a change. My mother is such a lady, she deserved the best, I wanted her life to be easier. I vowed then that I would look after her and try to make things as easy as I could.

But Mum was also keeping an eye on me, wondering when I would break. Everyone knew how close I was to Dad and they'd all expected me to go to pieces when he had died, but I hadn't cried, really cried – except with laughter. She knew something would go wrong if I couldn't come to terms with my grief. I took four weeks off because I couldn't face singing, then plunged back into work. Dad wasn't there as a roadie for me, but his maps and schedules were. I asked various boyfriends to help out with my equipment and thought I was carrying on as normal, not realising that my grief was turning inwards. The pressure started to build when every time I walked into a different club, they'd say, 'Where's your dad, then?'

The trouble was that we had practically been a double act, and he was so much a character, so much a part of the club scene, that everyone expected to see him when they saw me. In the end I wanted to scream, 'He's died – now stop asking me.'

I was on stage singing at my favourite club, Albion Road, when in the middle of a note my voice went. A small strangled sound emerged, I tried again – nothing. I made my apologies and rushed off stage to the dressing room, where I sat shaking. After a week, I still couldn't sing a note. The doctor said she thought it was an emotional problem, I needed a psychiatrist, but I refused to believe her. I was convinced it was cancer. A few weeks later, I suddenly started weeping uncontrollably. My mother said, 'Thank God for that!' She knew I would be all right.

For the first time I was able to think about my father without then blanking the thoughts out. I recalled the times we'd been stuck up on the moors in the middle of the Pennines, having to knock on somebody's door for water for a leaking radiator. We'd been towed by the RAC so many times the regular patrolmen came to recognise us. They sent us postcards when they went on holiday, saying 'hang on, we'll be back soon'. The first thing I did when Dad died was buy a new car, a solid Volvo estate, wondering why I hadn't done it before. But I knew why – it was Dad always saying, 'It'll do,' that got us into so much trouble.

I felt angry. I thought of the times we had huddled in the cold in the snow, walked through rainstorms to find a phone. Then I remembered the good times. One memory was when we drove down to London in the rusty old van to the Rifles Club, after I'd won Clubland of the Year Award as Female Vocalist of the Year for the second year running, which was quite a big achievement. When we arrived, we parked the van next to the Porsches and the Mercedes and Dad went off to introduce himself to the management. He returned looking very pleased. 'Your name is upfront,' he said. 'It says, "The Rifles Club presents Jane McDonald, Female Vocalist of the Year!" – and it costs twenty-five quid to get in.'

I said, 'Oh my God! I'd better be good.'

It was a very posh venue, with dinner and a cabaret – I was the cabaret. Usually Dad went everywhere looking scruffy but this time he had made a real effort, looking dapper dressed up in his suit. I was so proud of him that night. That was the first night I really felt like a star because not only was I in London – but after everyone had eaten their dinner they were giving the stage their full attention, not chatting or playing dominoes or waiting for the bingo to come on. To me it was unbelievable that people actually came out to be entertained: it seemed so sophisticated and civilised. No broken beer bottles and smashed lights, no leaping through the curtains as they closed before I'd finished, no being locked in the dressing room as all hell broke loose.

At the end of the show, I got a standing ovation and was promptly booked back in. They said they had rooms for that night and we could stay over, but Dad would never stay away from home unless we'd broken down and he also had no choice, because Mum would have worried.

Inevitably, given the distance the old van had travelled, we broke down at about one o'clock in the morning just outside London on the M25. It was summer, but cold. Dad went off to find a telephone and call the RAC. Hours seemed to pass and I started to shiver with cold. Dad put his coat around me and we huddled together. He had never been very touchy-feely and this was quite unusual. We laughed, told stories to each other and talked and we bonded for the first time as adults. It was a very special moment. I felt very honoured that the last thing I'd ever said to him was 'I love you,' because although we were so close it was something that we simply had never articulated before.

My crying jag cleared my mind, and my voice started to return. I knew I had to change direction, I'd had plenty of offers, including one to return to the Caribbean with a big cruise liner. I thought about Mum – how would she manage without me now that Dad was gone? Which offer should I accept?

I was still perplexed and weighing up my future when Mum asked if I would like to go to Rotherham with her, where Steve Holbrook, a protégé of Gran's, was holding a psychic demonstration. I had known Steve for years, although I hadn't seen him for ages. He lived in Wakefield and had a hairdressing salon in Leeds, where I would occasionally have my hair done. Curiosity drew him to the spiritualist church when Gran was president. Expecting a dark, spooky atmosphere with a great deal of mumbo-jumbo, he was pleasantly surprised by the spacious, bright room full of quite ordinary people. He asked if he could join the development circle. The very first time he went, he was so scared he ran out of the church. He said it was like being in a giant receiving station, a one-man Jodrell Bank, with signals streaming in from all over the Galaxy. When he settled down and got over the shock, he came to accept that he was a natural, fully developed clairvoyant, that what he had experienced happened to only a few.

Oddly enough, long before he connected me with the church, if I was singing in Leeds, Steve would sometimes drop into the club after work, standing at the back, listening intently. I came to recognise his face and we became casual friends. One evening when I had a night off, I popped into the church with Mum and Gran as I often did – and Steve walked in.

'What are you doing here?' he said in surprise.

'I was practically born here,' I said, pointing, 'That's my Gran and that's my mum.' It was remarkable that we had never bumped into each other there before.

Steve was such an astonishing medium that his demonstrations were always full. When we arrived at Rotherham, there was a queue of some two hundred people waiting outside the hall, unable to get in. I said to Mum, 'We might as well go, we're never going to get in tonight.'

On the way to where we had parked the car, we passed the

back door just as Steve popped out for a quick smoke. Simultaneously, we exclaimed, 'Jane McDonald!' – 'Steve Holbrook!'

'Are you coming to demonstration?' he asked.

I shook my head. 'No, place is packed, we can't get in.'

He opened the back door wide, 'Come on, I'll get you seats.'

When we found that there were just two seats left in that crowded auditorium, we knew it was meant to be. During the course of the evening, the other psychic on with Steve, a woman I didn't know, said, 'I'm coming to someone who's just lost their father –'

In the seat next to me, Mum nudged me to put my hand up. I whispered, 'No it's not me.'

Several others put their hands up. The psychic said, 'No it's not any of you.' She paused and concentrated: 'You came in the front door as he went out the back door. Does that make any sense?'

Mum whispered, 'It is you! You came in the front door when your dad died. Put your hand up.'

But still I wouldn't. Pointing at me, the psychic said, 'It's you, in the red coat... your dad's here... he says there's nothing wrong with your throat... you're so emotional...'

I sat up in my seat, gobsmacked, as she continued, 'You've just been offered a ship... go on it and stop thinking of everyone else around you.'

RUNNING AWAY TO SEA

When I accepted the offer to sing on the *Horizon*'s sister ship, the *Zenith*, I jokingly told everybody that I was running away to sea, because that's what it felt like. I thought I was escaping the reality of my father's death and the pain of all the constant reminders that he was no longer there. Often, I wished that I hadn't left the *Horizon*, and wondered if I would ever find another ship like it. It had been such a happy ship with a great atmosphere. In time, I was to realise that a ship is like a Christmas tree, a triangular shape, with the captain as the star on top. If that star is just a little bit tarnished, the knock-on effect trickles down through the staff and crew, until everybody is miserable and resentful. In bad ships, tempers run high and nothing seems to work.

Fortunately, the *Zenith* proved to be another happy ship. I started working with another Matrix singer, Mick Mullane, who was the best male vocalist I have worked with. Together, we made an impressive team, fronting the loosely themed shows that the audiences loved, invariably clocking up the highest scores in the ratings year after year for the four years that we worked together. I have to say that the Matrix shows were really fantastic, very well received by the audiences night after night, which is not always the case with other shipping lines.

If I haven't mentioned the show ratings before, it's because they were a terrifying ordeal, an instrument of torture for performers that all of us would rather pretend didn't exist. Forms would be left in the passengers' cabins for them to fill in, awarding points and commenting on our individual performances. Anyone getting less than 7.6 out of ten points three times on the trot was sacked, a ruthless cull that caused a great deal of heartache. To be thrown off a ship can be a very humbling experience, and the poor devil who knows they are due for the chop, either walks around full of bravado, saying 'I don't give a toss, I'm glad I'm leaving, I hated it anyway' – or they slink around, shame-faced, with nobody meeting their gaze until they can disembark. Fortunately, Mick and I always achieved unheard of ratings, 9.6 or 9.7, making us, as he said, 'fireproof'. It didn't stop me feeling sick in the pit of my stomach each time the ratings were added up, because I couldn't believe that we would continue to sustain such high scores – but we did until something happened a couple of years ahead that was to destroy both our record and our confidence.

Because I could be depended on to always give a spotless performance, I was the one they called on for 'special duties'. At that time the Celebrity line was owned by a very wealthy Greek family, who were very kind to me – ultimately, a few years down the line, giving me the chance of a lifetime which led to me being 'discovered'. But now I'm jumping ahead! The family enjoyed coming aboard from time to time for a week's cruising with a large party of their friends who, of course, were always given the best attention. At night, after I had done the show, often some senior member of the family might approach me with: 'Jane, do you fancy coming up for a drink?' I always knew this meant, 'Would you sing for us?'

But I never minded because the family was so pleasant. I also knew I might be called upon quite late at night to perform for the VIP guests, so I would go to my cabin and sit up fully dressed, to wait for the inevitable words at my door from a waiter: 'Jane, they want you upstairs'.

I would follow the waiter to the family's luxurious private suite, where a large party would be in progress. The owner of the line himself would come up to me and say, 'Jane, do you mind singing?'

'I'm delighted to be asked,' I'd reply.

Many of the faces were famous or would look vaguely familiar from the pages of celebrity magazines, but I never really knew who any of them were. I'd sing two or three songs, be thanked profusely and then leave. Most of the guests were courteous in the extreme, though of course there was the odd one or two who drank too much and made the inevitable offers that I'd learned skilfully to avoid without giving too much offence. The family always behaved impeccably – like the Greek officers, who always treated me with respect and behaved correctly to me – once I'd made it clear that I wasn't interested!

Many of the officers looked like gods, muscular and handsome in their spotless white uniforms, so it was no surprise when young stylists and casino workers fresh from England rushed headlong into steamy affairs. I was the one the girls turned to for comfort when things went wrong, as they inevitably did. I'd long gone through that giddy phase, that crazy sense of freedom that everyone seems to experience when they first go to sea. I was now den mother, the shoulder to cry on in the cabin I always tried to make as homely as possible, however cramped it was. I'd have cushions, a rug, and a tea tray with my own kettle. For the homesick, there'd be a big stack of video soaps (*Coronation Street, Emmerdale Farm, East Enders*) sent faithfully week after week by my mother.

Many nationalities are isolated on board a ship, crammed in tiny accommodation, their lives often hell, and passions can run high. Signing on, sometimes for years, they are the bread winners for their extended families. Very poorly paid, every penny they get is sent home – but a pittance on a ship is a fortune in India or the Philippines. Sometimes, I would come across a young galley girl – whose workload was not so very different from a galley slave from ancient Rome – cleaning the cabins, and sobbing because she missed the baby she hadn't seen for a year, unable to fully express herself because her English was so poor. Nevertheless, I would feel her despair as she tried to communicate that if she lost her job, her family would probably starve.

One night, when I was off duty, someone knocked loudly on my cabin door. I opened it and one of the waiters was standing there. In his hesitant English, he said, 'Come quickly!'

'What's the matter?' I asked.

He looked frantic and wouldn't come in, repeating that I had to go with him at once. 'Quickly,' he urged. 'Please come quickly. I think she will die.'

'Who?' I asked.

'One of the girls, she has thrown herself off the ship,' he said.

'Is she still in the water?' I exclaimed, wondering what on earth one did in those circumstances – stop the engines? Turn the ship around?

'No, no, we jumped in and saved her,' he said, not explaining how this miracle had been achieved. 'She is very sick. It is a sackable offence to drown, we can't bring the doctor,' he said perfectly seriously. 'We cover for her, she is not missed yet. Please come, there is no one else to help, just you.'

'I might have to call the doctor,' I warned, quickly closing the door of my cabin and following the young waiter. All kinds of thoughts raced through my mind as I hurried down to the crew quarters and stepped through the door that divides the luxurious and romantic world that most passengers see from the area we called 'the Third World' that the staff and crew inhabit far below decks. Down there, in the bowels of the ship, to coin a crude expression I once heard from an Australian, it stinks like an old croc's gizzards: a pungent mix of bilge water, hot engine oil, garlic, boiled vegetables and dirty socks.

But I had no time to dwell on the stench as the waiter hurried me along. We reached a tiny cabin, and he opened the door. 'She is there,' he said, watching as I went across to the narrow bunk where a pathetic looking little Russian girl lay; a small wet bundle.

Like a stranded mermaid, she had seaweed in her mouth and in her hair. I touched her; her skin was icy cold. 'My God, she's dead!' I said.

'No, no, she is alive. She is breathing,' the waiter said more in hope than certainty.

I sat her up. She smelled of the sea, the skin around her eyes and mouth was blue. I fished the weed out of her mouth and banged her on the back. At once, she vomited a salty stream of sea water and alcohol and started to groan.

'I think she'll be all right, leave her with me,' I said with far more confidence than I felt. I undressed her and put her under a warm shower. As the warmth crept through her body, the colour returned to her skin. I dried and dressed her in a T-shirt and quite literally carried her back to the bed, where I sat next to her, stroking her hand while she fell into a peaceful sleep.

When Celebrity commissioned the construction of two gigantic new cruise ships, a strong selling point was that they would have the best shows in the world. Part of the plan was to appoint a former musician as the Entertainments Director, so cutting out any agents. Mick and I got such a good reputation as a top duo that the Entertainments Director approached us with an offer of a lot more money and headline status, which included passenger cabins – this latter being a strong inducement, as anyone who has slept in a crew cabin will testify. The only drawback was that we had to sign on directly with Celebrity, cutting ties with our long-term agency. Mick pointed out that our contract with Al Radcliffe said we couldn't work for a line he'd signed us up with unless there was a complete break of six months.

'Then go and do something else for six months,' the Entertainments Director said. 'The ship is still being built in Germany.'

So we told Al Radcliffe that we were leaving Matrix because they hadn't progressed our careers in terms of money and star ratings. At once he got his skates on and came up with work heading up the production cast on a fabulous round-the-world line, something I had longed for. 'It's the Rolls Royce of cruising, and the pay is exceptional,' Al promised.

Now we were in a dilemma. I wanted to go with Al, and I also wanted what the Entertainments Director had to offer. In the end, we decided to see which offer would be finalised first.

It seemed that we were in an enviable position with two people vying for us, and we were happy to milk the situation as much as we could. When I look back, I am amazed that we were so naive.

While we waited out the six months, Mick commuted between his lovely home, a sixteenth-century water mill near Toulouse, France, and a record company in Hong Kong, working on karaoke backing tracks. I returned to England and signed up for the summer season at my old stamping ground, the Maid Marion Club in Skegness. It was strange to be back there, especially on the first week when I watched a comedy act do the 'sandwich' routine Dad had invented. My father had not staged it – it was just him being himself; now here it was, part of a comic's repertoire.

Mum and I dropped in on my gran for a cup of tea and a nice long natter. I was full of the wonderful round-the-world shipping line and as Gran poured out the tea, enthusiastically I described the exotic locations the ship would call at, from Hawaii to Tahiti, Cape Town to Sydney, all places I longed to see. 'And the money is marvellous, I'll be treated like a real star,' I finished.

Gran had poured Mum's tea but the teapot was poised above my favourite mug, when she got a strange, almost haunted look on her face and her hand was – well, it was sort of 'arrested' in mid air as if someone were holding it back. Then she put the teapot down, and stared at me.

My excited babble petered out. 'What is it, Gran?' I asked.

'No, you're not going on that one,' she said in a very matter of fact tone of voice.

I have always listened to Gran, but this time, I laughed and said, 'Come on, it's a wonderful opportunity, I've worked six years for this.'

But when Gran says something she means it. She looked at me, saying nothing. Then I knew she'd had one of her visions and I said, 'Oh no, don't do this to me – you can't do this to me!'

'You're going on a big blue ship with a white cross,' she said, describing it as if she could actually see it. 'It's not as good a job as the world cruise, but it will change your life. Your destiny lies on this ship, Jane.' She looked straight at me with her clear blue eyes, 'And you will meet a man called Henry.'

For some reason that rather old-fashioned name struck a funny chord and Mum and I began to giggle. 'Henry!' I said. 'Someone with slippers and a pipe! Come on, Gran, can't I meet someone else? I don't want to be stuck with a Henry! How about another name?'

'No, it's Henry,' Gran said.

That got us going, howling with laughter. Mum and I would calm down, then we'd look at each other and be set off again. We laughed until our eyes were streaming and I got a stitch in my side.

'Drink your tea before it gets cold,' Gran finally said.

I recovered a little and took a sip from my mug. 'So you think I should turn down the cruise of a lifetime for some old geezer named Henry?' I asked.

'Lovey, you must go where destiny leads you,' Gran said.

Destiny, it seemed, wanted us to accept the Entertainments Director's offer, even though we still didn't have a signed contract. Al Radcliffe couldn't finalise the round-the-world deal and the Celebrity Entertainments Director had sent us our tickets to New York, where we were to rehearse. We had still been negotiating hard with Celebrity right up to the time we were due to leave and when they telephoned to say that they were going to have to reduce our money, alarm bells rang. But we believed that this job would be the making of us and Mick was delighted that he'd got his stunningly beautiful girlfriend, Jenni, a dancer for another shipping line, included in our package. We accepted the lower rate of pay, packed our bags and flew to New York.

Our fears subsided in New York when we saw the high level of investment in the shows. We were put up in a good hotel just off Broadway and started work with a top choreographer, who had a Disney show running on Broadway. After the first week, the choreographer called me over as we were leaving the rehearsal room and said, 'You're going to make it, Jane. I'll see you on the big screen some day.'

Feeling good, I rushed back to the hotel for a cast costume fitting. My face when I looked at the way-out, punky costumes for the finale, was a picture. They were like Gilbert and Sullivan's 'things of shreds and patches' in the most ghastly, clashing colours. Picking up two of the worst, I said, 'Oh, my God, who designed these, then?'

The designer, another famous person with costumes in a Broadway show smiled, 'Oh, I did, aren't they great?'

I couldn't help myself. 'I'd like to see your house,' I said.

'Thank you,' she simpered.

My comment went straight over her head, but the dancers were all over the floor. Two of them, Nicky Asker and Charlotte Revell, quickly joined forces with me, and we became known as the Slappers' Club. We were best friends during what was to be one of the worst years of our lives, when, without the support of our shared sense of humour, all three of us would probably have thrown ourselves off the side of the ship we were shortly to join, like that Russian galley girl.

Despite the frantic pace, we enjoyed the hard work of rehearsals. Just off Broadway, living in the heart of a great city, we were filled with boundless energy and enthusiasm, particularly when we were told repeatedly that we were the ones who had been chosen by Celebrity to take Broadway to the high seas. The Music Director – yet another talent with a show on Broadway – led us through incredibly complicated harmonies. Part of the problem was that the arrangements were so complex it was almost impossible to learn them. I'm a session singer so I can just read the music and sing; but Mick worked differently. He was such a perfectionist that when he didn't get it right first time, he got angry with himself and worked even harder. When we had finished for the day, he would be in his hotel room, headphones on, learning all night. Once he had it, he never faltered, every performance was perfect. But the more we did, the more they wanted; and when the Music Director threw in even more unnecessarily complicated parts for us to learn, Mick exploded.

He had every reason to be angry. Before he had become a cruise singer, he'd been a member of Stutz Bearcats, a very successful group. Masters of harmony, they'd been known as the London Manhattan Transfer. The previous night, we had been to see Manhattan Transfer perform at the theatre right next to our hotel, and this had reminded Mick of where he'd come from and how good he was; he saw how he was now being systematically drained of confidence.

'I understand harmonies, and I know what turns people on,' he told the Music Director. 'Most people watching these shows on ships don't care about sevenths or thirds! We're wasting too much time.'

But there was no let up, the complex harmonies stayed in. Mick and I continued to learn them until we were note perfect. Then we found that two Americans were to join us; Mick Mullane and Jane McDonald had been seamlessly absorbed into the newly created Celebrity Singers.

Only the week before, I had called Miami and spoken to the Entertainments Director's secretary. ' I still haven't got our agreement in writing,' I reminded her.

She said, 'We'll look into it.'

The dancers were in the same situation. The choreographer seemed to be in competition with the music side to make things as complicated as possible. She wanted everybody to know everyone else's routines, regardless of whether they'd be doing them or not. She was so obsessed with minute detail, she'd even rehearsed facial expressions for hours on end.

Nicky was laughing when she told me that she had a solo Ginger Rogers routine – but all the other fourteen dancers were also rehearsed in her solo until they had it off pat, even though they didn't need to be involved. We were laughing, comparing notes – but it came as a shock when we had finished in New York and were ready to fly to Germany to join the ship to be told that in a month we had learned only one show of three when usually it took two weeks to learn an entire season's repertoire.

From a distance, as we drove up to Bremen Docks, the ship looked spectacular. It was as big as a skyscraper, painted blue with broad white bands. High up, the central funnel was painted with a white cross, the Celebrity emblem. Climbing up the gangway, we entered a megalithic builders' yard full of scaffolding and workmen.

'My God!' I said, as we stumbled past towering internal scaffolding and workmen with ladders, 'They're still building the boat!'

Because the *Century* was already seriously behind schedule, we were confronted right from the start with all the problems entailed with launching a brand-new ship. Exhaustion was to push us to the brink as tempers grew more fraught with each passing day – as days gave way to weeks, and then to months. But, despite everything, from the very first day we all knew that it was up to us to make the shows work, so that put even more pressure on us.

The *Century* was the biggest ship of the line but they had squeezed in extra space for hundreds more passengers by cutting out space for staff. My cabin was the smallest I'd ever had – and Mick was worse off because he was sharing his sardine tin with Jenni and a mobile studio. I found the Entertainments Director, who'd flown in with us, and said, 'Where's our cabins, the ones we were promised?'

With a weak smile, he said, 'We had to give them to the doctors. Anyway, you can't have a passenger cabin and leave all your colleagues in crew cabins.'

I said, 'Oh yes I can!'

We laughed when someone found out that they were so badly organised there was no storage space for even the toilet rolls. Some 100,000 were piled in passenger cabins. Our amusement faded when we found that the theatre wasn't finished; we had to practice in gangways, in the gym where workmen criss-crossed with swinging ladders and tannoys crackled out messages in German for the fitters, drowning the band. We practised in a freezing loading bay in the bowels of the ship, where meat and vegetables would eventually be stored. As it was, there was no heat, no food and no cooks.

Me at 6 months old.

At Skegness. Enjoying
the beach with Mum.

On a picnic with Dad
at Thornes Park,
aged 18 months.

Above left: Christmas at Eastmoor Road 1965. I'm sat between my sister Janet and brother Tony (who was wearing his favourite penguin cardigan!)

Left: Aged 8, with Mum and Dad on holiday at Withernsey.

Above: Our house at Eastmoor Road, with two of our policeman boarders standing in front.

Right: Me with Liz Baxter, my first great friend.

Aged 14, with Mum and Dad at Blackpool.

In a pub in Bridlington, aged 16. Mum would coax me to get up and sing with the organist whenever we were there.

Jersey – the best holiday we ever had! The weather was fabulous, we were finally staying in a proper hotel and, as I was working, we could afford to see a show every night.

My first cruise in 1989, on the *Black Prince*. After this picture was taken, I went up two dress sizes during my time there!

On the *Horizon* in 1990. Mum had never been on a proper flight before yet flew all the way to America on her own to see me.

Summer season 1993 at the Maid Marion Club, Skegness. This is where I really perfected my trade as a compère and singer.

During a short break from cruising, we got together for a family reunion. Clockwise from front: Mum, Wendy (my sister-in-law), Tony, Janet, me and Garry (my brother-in-law).

In 1995 – at last – I got my own show, although I still performed in the production show and got no extra money. I now worked seven-day weeks on the *Century* but I didn't care.

Me with Mick Mullane, one of the best male vocalists I've ever worked with.

The cast of the *Century*.

High jinks on the high seas.

The show on the *Century* was incredibly difficult to perform. You can just about make me out here – I'm the one at the back, balancing the ball on my head!

We shared what was available, including, to my disgust, fishheads. I felt like *Top Cat*, raiding the dustbins. After two months, so many of us were ill that rehearsals resembled a war zone with bodies keeling over from sickness and fatigue. We were permanently hungry and unable to go out to buy a meal until our wages – which were delayed for weeks – turned up from the States. As soon as they came, we escaped like jailbirds breaking out, to find something to eat and a great deal of alcohol.

By now, Nicky, Charlotte and I had progressed from being 'The Slappers' to calling ourselves 'The Singles Club', determined that we would not get involved with a shipboard romance. Every night, we'd go out in a taxi, a tight little threesome, and get trashed in Bremen, particularly in one bar, the Take It Easy which was adopted by the crew as our local. How the hell we got home some nights I'll never know – but we needed to drink.

Dying to get away to drown our sorrows after some eighteen hours of rehearsing all that day and most of the night, we rushed down the gangway as we were, old clothes, sweaty, caps pulled over our dirty hair, no make-up. One night, after a few drinks, one of the guys from our band, asked the resident keyboard player in the hopeless house band if he could play instead. I jumped up and grabbed the mike to launch into 'The *Century* Blues'. I have always loved the blues; now I sang them with real feeling. I sang of all our woes, of how bad the ship was, how everything was going wrong. I named names and didn't care. The Entertainments Director was there, as drunk as all the rest. He joined in the laughter, and even stood up and clapped, loudly calling out, 'Encore! Encore!' I should have punched his lights out, but laughed instead. It was a good night, our frustrations and tensions were released, we slept well and hungover or not, felt able to continue the next day.

It didn't last. They told us we had to rehearse two more full shows – making the equivalent of five full Broadway musicals which we were expected to alternate throughout the week so the passengers would have a new show every day, two shows a night. When we complained, we were told it was in the sales literature, we had to do it. We felt duped, stitched up and left without an option. Mick was very depressed because he felt he couldn't leave after having fought so hard to get the job in the first place.

By now, the fantastic stage was nearing completion and we could start rehearsals there. Tons of state-of-the-art equipment, from trap doors to turntables, was being flown in and installed every day over our heads and around us while we worked. The more expensive and lavish the equipment was, the faster it broke down. When the rock band Pink Floyd toured the world, they had massive banks of lights – we had more. Unfortunately, workmen dropped oil all over the stage. Dancers were going flying. Unbelievably, we had to mop the stage before we started and, halfway through, had to mop it again. The stage was supposed to revolve like *Sunday Night at the London Palladium*, but in the whole nine months of my contract it worked twice; once when they started it up and the second time when they sent technicians on to see what the problem was. Ludicrously, we had to shuffle around on the stage as if we were revolving merrily away, crazed grins glued to our faces. All the special effects were computer controlled from a space-age cockpit three storeys up. When anything went wrong, someone had to sprint a mile up this Everest to fiddle with the computer since there seemed to be no direct means of communication.

The dance captain was beside herself as one thing after another, intrinsic to the complicated choreography, collapsed. She established Plan A, Plan B and Plan C. When something jammed, she'd cry 'Plan B!' and we'd all go into another routine that we'd hurriedly learned. When something else broke, she sobbed, 'Plan C!' and like frantic marionettes, we jerked into a different dance, working our way through the alphabet to Plans X, Y and Z. It wasn't just learning the shows – we had to learn our get-out plans for everything else; if something didn't work we had to dance around it, make out we were meant to do that, however silly it appeared. Dancers were bumping into each other, props weren't where they were supposed to be – it was like 'Springtime for Hitler' from the Mel Brooks film *The Producers*.

The final straw, where equipment was concerned, was the magic show that was designed to last for fifty minutes – and we, who had never done a magic trick in our lives, were to be the chief wizards. There were eleven props that cost a quarter of a million dollars, one of which was so heavy, a forklift truck was used to get it aboard.

In awe at their stupidity, Mick shook his head: 'How the hell are we going to move it for the show?'

Those eleven props were cut down to three as we struggled to get to grips with them. We spent a month and a half rehearsing the magic shows alone, until it was realised there was no room to store the props and we didn't have enough people to shift them anyway. Then there was the pipe cleaner incident.

From the time we had started rehearsing, everything was choreographed with the intention of having hand-free microphones on our heads, like Madonna. These still hadn't arrived in our last days in Bremen, before we were due to leave on the first leg of the Atlantic crossing. Instead, someone rushed us a batch of small Lavaliere conference mikes, the kind that clip to your lapel; they didn't work, swamped by the loud music and the amount of feedback on stage. While we were struggling with them, the Entertainments Director turned up with a large box of pipe cleaners and handed them out to the cast.

I took the one he was offering me and stared bemusedly at it. 'What am I supposed to do with this?' I asked.

Enthusiastically, he demonstrated. 'Twist it like this and stick it around your ear,' he said. 'Pretend it's a head mike.'

Our mouths fell open with shock as we stared at him with a pipe cleaner dangling from his ear, wondering if it was us or him who had finally flipped. Here was the Entertainments Director of a show costing millions – reduced to using pipe cleaners. It was unbelievable. Even more unbelievable was the fact that we actually did it – we spent two or three days with pipe cleaners wrapped around our ears as if it was a perfectly normal way to carry on.

A few days later, the *Century* was officially launched and we travelled to Southampton, where we were to dock for a couple of nights for a big preview show, to be attended by dignitaries and the media flown in specially for the occasion. Obviously, we couldn't perform with pipe cleaners a-dangling, so the Entertainments Director rushed us hand-held mikes which would be fine for a static singer but, to give an example, in one scene we had to pick up suitcases as if we were travelling. Somehow, Mick and I managed, although the microphones picked up every clunk and bump of the cases we struggled to hold. The other two singers found it impossible and kept fumbling and dropping their mikes. 'What are we supposed to do – hold them in our teeth?' one of the Americans screamed, throwing down the microphone and suitcases and storming off.

Ultimately, we had no choice; the show had to go on. Having rehearsed for months with the intention of using head mikes, we spent the entire season with hand-held ones, so exhausted that we didn't see how ridiculous it was. We forgot our sane identities, our own needs and requirements and somehow accepted this as normal, getting very run down in the process. By the end of the contract, the doctors were treating several stressed out, exhausted performers.

The five-day Atlantic crossing was made towards the end of November, into the teeth of a force eight gale – the same gale that hit the *Queen Elizabeth* with a hundred-foot wave, causing so much damage that she had to return to port. The weather was so bad that we couldn't stand up; yet we were ordered to continue with rehearsals even though it was so dangerous that people were injured the whole time. I think we stood upright for ten minutes in the whole five days of the crossing. In the rehearsal room where the main stage was, the ship was coming down with such force, you couldn't hear yourself speak. All the equipment, on casters for quick scene changes, was careering back and forth all over the stage, falling off into the auditorium in splinters.

The male dancers and scene shifters played around by sitting in the audience seats in a row and, when the ship crashed down, they would fly up and land in the seats in front. On stage, we got the same effect by shooting up towards the ceiling as if we were on a trampoline. The ship would crash into a trough – and we'd still be in the same position in the air, our heads hitting the ceiling. A kind of hysterical storm frenzy took over, everyone competing to do the most crazy and dangerous things imaginable.

My cabin, which was towards the centre of the ship, wasn't too bad. But the dancers, in the bows, took the full brunt of the massive waves. Scared that the sides would cave in, Nicky and Charlotte moved to my cabin, where we lay heaving, drinking water and nibbling on crackers to stop the nausea. In more rational moments we'd look at each other and say, 'What on earth are we doing here?'

While waves as high as a six-storey block of flats continued to crash over the ship, we were still expected to rehearse. Finally, Mick and I had it out with the Entertainments Director. 'It's too dangerous to continue,' Mick said. 'Somebody is going to be seriously hurt.'

We could see that it was no good arguing with the little man, his attitude was fixed in stone. I suppose it wasn't all his fault – he had to answer to head office and his neck was on the block if we failed to deliver the expected entertainment. Waves of nausea hit me. I lurched off to my tiny cabin, where I lay on my bed and threw up into a bowl. Several decks down, in the centre of a potential *Poseidon Adventure*, I was too ill to care.

Meanwhile, Michael called an officer as a witness and insisted that the Entertainments Director accompanied him to the theatre where the cast was gamely trying to work in those awful conditions. The ship was veering from standing on its bow to standing on the stern as it staggered through the gigantic seas with hundreds of tons of water falling on the decks, chucking everyone all over the place.

'We're not doing it – we'll be brained,' Michael yelled above the roar of the wind and waves.

'Very well, but you'll have to catch up later,' the Entertainments Director said, stomping off in a huff.

A brand new opening show was pulled out of the bag when we arrived in New York, still staggering after the storm. It was unheard of to rehearse solidly, eighteen hours a day for five months on a nine-month contract and still be faced with new material to learn. When we saw the content – which we thought exceptionally weak – Mick refused to get involved and naturally, I felt I had to support him, but by calming him down and trying to diffuse the situation. Every time he threatened to go to the Entertainments Director's cabin and kill him, I advised Mick to chill out, spend time on his music.

Exhausted by living with a madman, Jenni would come to my cabin next door to escape and I'd put the music on, make a cup of tea, and we'd talk. Eventually though, tempers got so heated that the Entertainments Director came down to my cabin for a meeting with us where the others wouldn't hear the row. We started the conversation on an even keel, went through the history of the endless rehearsals, the terrible time at Bremen, the Atlantic crossing and so on and so on. It was a long list. I don't think the Entertainments Director listened to one word.

He said, 'It's part of the plan, you have to do these extra shows. The new show has been created by the best talent in New York,' he added, stiffly.

'Yes, and we've just spent the past five months seeing at first hand what the best in New York has to offer,' Mick said. 'After twenty years on ships all over the world, I know what people want.'

The conversation got heated. The Entertainments Director

told Mick that he wasn't a team player. That sparked Mick's rockets. He started screaming at the man, 'Get out of the cabin, I'm leaving the show!'

'You're fired!' the Entertainments Director yelled.

'Sack me, then,' Mick yelled back in his face.

To cap it all, the Entertainments Director thought I was the gang leader. He turned around where I was sitting on the edge of my bed, and, 'You're behind this, McDonald'.

'You silly man,' I said, 'if I was, everyone would have walked off by now. I've tried to diffuse the situation. But Mick's right – the shows just don't work.'

The Entertainments Director consulted everyone else involved, including everyone in New York, and without exception, they said he couldn't get rid of Mick, they couldn't pull off the shows without him. Mick and I ended up with more money, I got a better cabin and the offer of my own occasional cabaret act – but in return, we had agreed to do the shows we despised so much.

We docked off Puerto Rico just before Christmas; but there was to be no shore leave for any of us. Disgusted to learn that we were expected to rehearse even on Christmas Day, my usually even temper deserted me and I had a massive tantrum.

'Look, it's Christmas Day. This is ridiculous!' I said.

'Are you refusing to work?' the Entertainments Director asked.

'YES!' I screamed. 'We bloody well are.'

That worked; we got the day off, but what really hurt was that they didn't even arrange a Christmas dinner for us. We organised our own slap-up dinner in a restaurant in San Juan. In place of turkey, roast potatoes and Brussels sprouts, they served us chicken fajitas and salad, washed down with a large amount of potent Mexican wine. It was different, but it was a case of when in Rome, and we made the best of it, ending up by having a great time.

Boxing Day brought us down to earth with a bump. Nursing hangovers, we were ordered back to rehearsals. I marched up to the Entertainments Director, who was quite short – not that much taller than me – and, right in his face, I snarled, 'It's Boxing Day, you horrible little man.'

'What's Boxing Day?' he asked, leaping back a full yard.

'It's a very important festival in England,' I said, knowing that as an American he had probably never heard of it. 'We have to wear boxes.'

For a moment doubt flickered in his eyes. 'Boxes?' he croaked uncertainly.

'Boxes,' I said firmly, trying to keep a straight face.

'Very well,' he muttered and skulked off.

For the rest of the morning we walked about with boxes on our heads, camping it up like crazy. That afternoon we went ashore for another great meal and drank enough vodka to float a battleship. 'To boxes!' we toasted, laughing like drains.

But, despite such moments of fun, I longed to be at home with the family. Knowing my family would all be crowded around the table at Mum's as usual, I completely lost it, breaking down and sobbing my heart out in front of everybody. Once I started, I couldn't stop. All the pent-up frustration and anger of the past few weeks – perhaps even of years – reached bursting point and like a broken dam, it all flooded out. I howled on and on, my head in one of the dancer's laps.

People came and stared, they patted me awkwardly, a few took me in their arms and hugged me, but I was oblivious. My misery even made them feel better. At some funerals in the old days in places like Ireland and Wales they used to pay a 'sin eater' to come along, someone who took on all the burdens of the dead so they'd be spared purgatory. Other cultures have official mourners. That dismal Christmas, I was the sin eater and mourner all wrapped in one. I was 'Grief' in a Greek drama, the figure who was chosen to absorb the burdens and pain of the cast.

I wept so hard and for so long that the question travelled around the ship – 'Is Jane still crying?' The door at the back of the auditorium kept opening, people would peep in, see that I was still howling and gently they'd close the door and creep off.

I can remember saying to the officers, 'I swear I will never set foot on another ship after this unless it's as a headliner.' At his lowest ebb, Mick was so desperate that he even contemplated hurting himself so he'd be airlifted off.

A week later, still totally unprepared, we were moored off Fort Lauderdale, a band playing, flags flying, sickly smiles pinned to our faces, welcoming the first passengers for the *Century*'s gala maiden cruise. Within a few hours, with 1800 passengers aboard and 800 crew, looking forward to a wonderful holiday, we steamed towards the Western Caribbean.

Now that the passengers were on board and rehearsals – so we believed – had come to an end, we thought we'd have more time to ourselves. During the previous months we hadn't seen the sun; we had barely seen daylight, trapped in the bowels of the ship, going from our windowless cabins to rehearsal areas, to the canteen – with the result that we were as sickly as we looked. Many of the dancers said they had never had so many spots and cold sores in their life. Now we snatched every spare moment to lie in the warm January sun in the Gulf of Mexico and soak up some much-needed vitamin D.

However, we were still under great pressure because, despite all our hard work, the shows were a disaster due to their insensitive content. They had been created for a sophisticated New York audience by slick, trendy New York writers – while the majority of our customers were elderly, many of them very overweight. They didn't want to be greeted by an opening 'Fit and Fat' medley rammed home by lithe young dancers on the first night of their cruise. They didn't want to be told: 'keep young and beautiful, it's a sin to be old and fat.'

Mick came on in an inflated costume, singing about a man who weighed 250 pounds and had a stroke; then I came out, rollers in my hair, padded hips and bosom to say if they listened to me, they didn't have to look so disgusting. We'd both go off and come back glammed up to the hilt. 'Now you can be young and beautiful like us,' we repeated – watching our audience get up and walk out.

As if that wasn't enough, the next act, the last remnants of the bizarre magic show, infuriated the elderly Jewish people, many of whom had come through the Holocaust. The theme was good versus evil, not too bad on its own, but the special magic effects involved torture, stakes through hearts and exploding coffins containing skeletons that got up and danced and had dancers dressed in striped concentration camp-style suits. By the time we'd finished we had an audience of about three young honeymoon couples, oblivious in the back row.

The final straw was when for the first time ever, I started to get scores as low as six and seven. It was no good Mick telling me that the passengers weren't keen on the shows, not us; that we had to ignore the ratings and rise above it. The only thing that rose to the surface was my insecurity. Night after night, I'd get terrible stage fright waiting in the wings to do the despised shows to a half-empty auditorium. I was deeply humiliated and demoralised, as were all the cast. I'd do ridiculous things to cheer us up, such as play a serious scene with a weird accent and a stuffed parrot on my shoulder. Nobody seemed to notice the parrot, or the fact that half the dancers were reeling all over the stage laughing. We carried on in this deranged way until some shows were dropped, new shows were thrashed out and things got better.

The letters from home, especially the packages from my mum twice a week with my favourite magazines and videos kept me going. I'd put the soaps on, the dancers would all pile in and we'd have girlie nights down in my cabin. We were all so low on morale, we'd sit with a bottle of wine and watch *Coronation Street* for three hours. I tried to cheer the girls up with a glass of wine, a pot of Earl Grey tea, and a shoulder to cry on. I was more valuable on the ship as a counsellor and den mother to the crew than ever I was as a singer.

One thing many people, usually the girls, asked me for was a tarot reading. Some of them thought I was a bit of a mystery because they felt I could almost read their minds. The truth is, like my grandmother, I use the cards as a tool rather than being able to mind-read. I believe that, when I read the cards, I get communications from another dimension; a slight vibration, more a psychic voice in my ear, and I go from there, interpreting the cards in my own way using that information. Sometimes, the inner voice takes over, and I start talking very loudly, which scares people. When the girls used to come to my cabin, I would say, 'I'm going to find a lot out about you – do you want this?' I don't think anyone said no, but most of them only did it for the fun and didn't believe a word of it, which didn't worry me – I knew they often just wanted to talk.

During one of our lowest times on the *Century*, a dancer came in for a laugh, egged on by her friends. I was sitting on the floor, shuffling the cards when I got this voice in my ear: 'She doesn't believe a word you're saying'.

I looked up at her – she was smiling away as I laid the cards out, telling her what I was seeing. 'Yeah, yeah, yeah,' she went, not listening. Then I heard a little voice in my ear saying, 'That's my auntie.' I ignored it. The voice repeated, more insistently, 'That's my auntie.' In my head, I replied, 'Oh is it?' – 'Yes,' said the voice, 'she's got my picture in her wallet. I'm wearing a red jumper.'

I looked up and said in a very matter of fact way, 'There's this little boy – he's passed away. He says you're his auntie, you have his photograph in your wallet, with him in a red jumper.'

She broke down, showed me the picture and sobbed her heart out. It wasn't only the nephew she was crying over but also everything else in her life, including the nightmare ship we were on. She'd reached breaking point and, although she didn't believe in the tarot, she wanted to talk. She must have told her friends what had happened, because soon all the dancers were lining up to have a reading from me.

One dancer was really upset because she'd just lost someone close to her. She came to find someone to say to her, it's OK, you can cry. I used to have boxes of tissues because, almost invariably, every time I did a reading, people would burst into tears. It was like therapy: they wanted to talk, needed someone to listen. With this dancer, straight away I laid out the death card. Her eyes widened and she started to panic. I laid out a second card; it was Death again. Then it was me who was panicking, though remaining outwardly calm. I said, 'Is someone else ill around you?' She replied, 'No.' I glossed over it, 'Oh, it's just confirming the first…' at which she promptly burst into tears, pouring out her grief for the next hour while I kept the tissues going. The next day, she learned that one of her best friends had committed suicide: the second death card had shown its role.

I decided that I would give up the readings; they were too emotionally draining.

THE LOVE OF MY LIFE

St Valentine's Day 1996 felt like the worst day of my life. Watching the joy of honeymooners who had booked a special cruise, I'd had enough misery and loneliness to last a lifetime. Bawling my eyes out that night alone in my cabin, I whispered a heartfelt prayer for happiness and for a love of my own. Overwhelmed, I stood up and, raising my hands towards heaven, I cried aloud, 'I can't fight any more. If there is a divine intervention, you'd better take over now. Whatever it is that I am on this ship for, if it doesn't come soon, I'm out of here!' Then I sat down and wrote a letter of resignation which I put in a drawer, intending to hand it in when the ship docked back in Fort Lauderdale at the end of the week.

The following day, the captain granted us a full day off. For the first time in months, the weather was perfect. I had joined forces with Jeffery, one of the dancers, who had become a good friend but we were so worn out that we didn't really want to go out to explore the sights, and decided to spend the day sunbathing with the dancers on one of those tropical beaches fringed with palm trees that made our slave-driven existence bearable. By evening we felt almost human again, our skin sun-kissed and golden as we packed our swim suits and bikinis to return to the ship.

'Hey, kids, we've got to go out tonight, show these tans off,' Jeffery said as he flexed his muscles against a backdrop of the sun setting into a dark blue sea.

I yawned, and ran my fingers through my hair. It was spiky and thick with salt and I felt lazily tired, wanting only to sit in the downstairs crew bar where I didn't have to make an effort or dress up and where the beer was cheap, but Jeffery was a natural cheer-leader and got us to agree we'd meet up later in Tastings, one of the smart bars aboard the *Century*.

After a long, refreshing shower in my cramped little cabin to rinse off all the salt, I dressed in a pair of beautifully-cut white jeans, a brown silk shirt and white boots, leaving my hair long and loose. I felt a sudden stir of excitement. Lightly brushing on the merest whisper of blusher and some lip gloss, I smiled into the mirror. My glance fell on the drawer where my letter of resignation waited in a crisp white envelope and I shrugged. All that could wait – tonight, I was going to have fun. The words of 'I Will Survive' by Gloria Gaynor, one of my favourite songs, went through my mind, and uncon-sciously, as I walked along the long passageway below decks and made my way up the crew stairs towards the top, I started to hum the words that so expressed my mood.

My route had taken me into Tastings from above, so I had to walk down the sweeping circular staircase into the bar. As I descended like some kind of Hollywood movie star, I knew I looked good. Every woman will recognise what I mean. You have a kind of sexual aura about you, you glow. It's like one of those days when you wake up and you feel a sense of expectation, knowing that something magical is going to happen, but not knowing what.

I spotted Günter Boodenstein, the German guarantee engineer, at the bar and smiled. Then I looked at his companion and at once, time stood still. It was as instantaneous and as certain as that. This man with broad shoulders and blond hair stared up at me, our gazes locked and there seemed to be some blue flash like electricity between us. The moment passed, time unlocked, and I continued down the stairs thinking, 'Mmm, he's nice'.

The further I got down the stairs, the nicer he got. As I reached the bottom, they both stood up.

Even before Günter introduced us, the man put his hand out and I took it. That elusive blue flame of electricity flashed again, I could feel my heart racing. I thought, 'My goodness he's arrived at last!'

Günter said, 'Jane, this is Henrik Brixen. He's here to trouble-shoot a little problem we have with the boilers.'

I know Henrik said something but I didn't hear a word. His handshake seemed to pierce my soul. I looked straight into his eyes and I thought, 'I'm going to marry this man'. That's how strong it was.

Coming down to earth, I heard Günter say, 'Jane, can you stay and have a drink with us?'

I shook my head and explained that I was meeting Jeffery and the others. Then, not caring how forward it might seem, I said, 'I shall have a drink with you later if you're going upstairs at midnight for the party.' I addressed my remarks at Günter, but I looked at Henrik while I spoke. 'I'll meet you there,' I repeated brazenly. A Yorkshire lass would never have asked a bloke out but at that moment it seemed the most natural thing in the world to do.

'Sure, we'll see you then,' Henrik said. I realised my hand was still clasped in his.

From the time we met again at midnight, to the time Henrik left the ship, we spent every second when we weren't working, together. Naturally, he had his technical work to do – words such as 'boilers', 'main engines', 'evaporators', vaguely penetrated my consciousness – then he would try to get some sleep in my cabin, waiting for me while I did the show – which is why he never saw me sing at that time. I have to say that I kept him up until dawn; and while I slept the morning away, he was back with the boilers, main engines and evaporators, putting in twelve-hour days. When I look at the photographs taken then, he looks exhausted, his eyes like slits.

I tore up my letter of resignation and tossed it like a stream of confetti out of my porthole. Relationships between crew and passengers was banned; runaway romances were rare (although a lot of the crew did jump ship and never came back) – and sharing cabins was strictly forbidden. The efforts the big Dane and I made not to be discovered, flitting like Inspector Clouseau in and out of doors, was comical. However, everybody noticed my delirium and gave me knowing smiles, but I didn't care; fun and joy was back in my life again. Henrik extended his workload from a week to ten days, until he ran out of excuses to stay when the ship docked at Puerto Rico.

'Jane, I have to leave tonight, but we'll keep in touch,' he said on our last morning together. 'But first, I've planned a little surprise,' he continued.

He had booked a room in the wildly romantic Old San Juan Hotel. It was stunning, like a pre-war casino going back to colonial days. The reception area and casino had the biggest, glitziest chandelier I have ever seen over a big central bar. It had its own beach front surrounded by palm trees, where you could sun yourself on old rattan recliners, or lie in the shade, drinking Margaritas from tall, dewy glasses.

It was our first real date. I was excited because for the first time in months I could have a real bath where I could wallow and stretch out luxuriously instead of squeezing into a cramped shower where you couldn't even bend down if you dropped the soap. In the lovely old-fashioned suite, I rushed to turn on the taps in the big tub. 'This bath is the only reason I'm here!' I exclaimed, watching the water gush out.

Henrik roared with laughter. 'Well, you can spend the day there if you want, but I thought later we might have drinks on the beach and in the evening, a very nice dinner.'

Later that evening, with me dressed in tight black jeans and high-heeled black boots, and Henrik wearing a jacket, we went to dinner like a proper couple, walking over a little bridge that crossed a stream filled with goldfish into the hotel's Chinese restaurant, Backstreet Hong Kong, which is designed like an old wooden sailing ship. I felt so proud when we walked in, noting that Henrik had a certain presence; women turned to look and four waiters flapped around him. I ordered a vodka and cranberry – no ice just chilled – and Henrik had a gin and tonic: it was so James Bond, cocktails before dinner, hedonistic luxury after the life I'd been leading.

Henrik ordered a really good bottle of wine to go with Chinese vegetable curry, one of his favourite dishes, and my Szechuan Phoenix, which is chicken and steak done in a spicy Szechuan sauce; I can still taste it, that's how good it was.

I looked at Henrik and raised my glass with a satisfied sigh. 'This is the life for me!' I said, wondering if I would ever see him again. He seemed to read my mind.

'I'll fax you. When the ship docks at Fort Lauderdale next Saturday, I'll be waiting for you,' he promised.

That night, when he left from Puerto Rico to fly back to

Florida on the last plane, I thought my heart had been ripped out. I went back on the ship, where Nicky and Charlotte were waiting in the bar, and said to them 'Come on, let's get drunk.'

'Cheers!' they said. 'Here's to men.'

I laughed, hiding my sadness. Perhaps it had been just a brief romance, like a holiday fling, something to remember. Henrik had told me he'd see me the next Saturday – but I was a realist; if he turns up, I thought, I'll be delighted, but if he doesn't, it was a great two weeks. 'Well, at least he gave me his telephone number – that's always a good sign!' I told the girls.

One of the first things I always did when coming ashore at whatever port it happened to be, was to telephone Mum. The first time I called her after meeting Henrik, I couldn't wait to tell her all about this good-looking, hunky Dane I had fallen head over heels in love with.

'Mum, he's gorgeous!' I burbled happily down the phone. 'You'd love Henrik. I do! I'm madly in love. He's tall, blond and handsome. I call him my great Dane…'

'What did you say, Jane?' Mum interrupted.

'The bit about him being gorgeous?' I laughed.

'No, his name. What did you say his name was?'

'Henrik – with a k,' I said.

Mum gasped. 'Jane! Don't you remember what your gran said? About meeting a man called Henry?'

I clutched the telephone. 'Oh my God!' I said, going completely cold, feeling the hair at the back of my neck prickle.

Mum said, 'So you got the blue ship with a white cross – and now you've met your ideal man – and he's called Henry, just as Gran predicted.'

That first Saturday at Fort Lauderdale, Henrik was there as he'd promised, leaning against a Ford Mustang parked on the quayside. Nicky was near a window on the dock side of the ship and saw him before I did. She rushed along to my cabin and came banging on the door screaming, 'He's here!'

I was so excited, I rushed up on deck and waved frantically, never so glad to see anyone in my life. I kept on saying, 'Oh my God, he's here! He's here!' But I couldn't get off the ship until we'd done boat drill for the benefit of the US Coastguard. Everybody had to line up behind a white line and, one after the other, step forward and be questioned at length from an official manual that was almost as long as the Old Testament itself. Sometimes this could take hours because everyone has to be able to recite the routine, and half the Filipinos and Indians couldn't speak a word of English. I was wild to be off and couldn't hang around because we had to be back on the ship by 3.30 p.m. Fortunately, I have a very good memory and had learned the entire drill off by heart.

Brazenly, I said to the staff captain, 'If you want to get off early, come and ask me, because I know it all.'

Usually no one volunteers because everyone is petrified of the Coastguard – but I was desperate and threw caution to the wind. The staff captain grinned, 'Okay, McDonald – you're on,' he said.

As soon as the gangway was down and the Coastguard came aboard, the staff captain beckoned me over. I think he thought he was calling my bluff – but he'd met his match. I said, 'Look, that man…,' pointing to a Filipino standing behind the white line, 'he'd be in my charge, I would tell him what to do, so don't bother asking him because he doesn't speak a word of English – he doesn't know what you're talking about. Ask me.'

The coastguard officer ran me through my paces and, turning to the staff captain, said, 'This girl knows what she's doing. OK – you can leave.'

I almost kissed him as I dashed off the ship to cheers and whistles. After that, I was always called and we got off in record time. I was so eager to get off that ship because we had so little free time. It was change-over day for the passengers, four thousand people moved on or off in different directions, with mountains of luggage colliding under the care of the 'Third World' crew. Change-over days were the worst for the poorly paid crew, as they worked so hard they looked like the walking dead, with bloodshot eyes, week in, week out. Saturday was a nightmare for them, which was why the luggage ended up getting battered to pieces.

However, that world was always left behind me whenever I left the ship and raced across the tarmac to where my fair-haired Dane waited in the sun. After a wonderful, romantic day spent with Henrik, usually at his apartment where we would swim, followed by a lingering lunch, I'd be driven back to the ship for another week. Those days were my saviour during the last two months of my contract, the reason I stayed and didn't resign, because I could see this man I was falling in love with more deeply each moment every Saturday in Florida.

The only drawback was that we could never spend the night together because I had to be back on board. 'My mum would be proud of me,' I told the girls. 'This is a real courtship.'

Frequently, Henrik came on the ship because something always seemed to be going wrong with the engines or boilers. The technology was so new and competition to sell it to shipping lines so fierce that major equipment hadn't had time to undergo proper trials and tests before being installed. The diesel engines failed one after another, as well as the boilers, the pumps, the air conditioning units. Once, the ship barely made it to port with equipment that was costing hundreds of thousands of dollars to replace.

I knew when Henrik would be flown in before anyone else did. I'd watch for the white smoke swirling up from the big funnel and say to Nicky and Charlotte, 'Oh, God! Henrik is going to be out soon because the boiler's gone again'. To me, it was like the Pope coming on, white smoke and a great celebration. I'd say to myself, 'Hey-up, girl, he's on again!'

An officer would mention casually to a crew member, perhaps in the bar, that the boilers had gone, and they would say, 'Yes I know – Jane told me'. The officer would look up in amazement. 'How the hell does she know?' When they asked me, I'd tell them in broad Yorkshire, 'Ee lads, I could see smoke out of chimney.'

For nearly four months, Henrik and I had a real courtship, meeting once a week for those few precious hours. The *Century* had a seven-day cruising cycle to most of the exotic tropical islands in the West or East Caribbean, docking at Fort Lauderdale each Saturday. I could never sleep on a Friday night, knowing that I would be with Henrik the next day. Those brief interludes got me through to the end of the contract and boosted my spirits so much that I was walking on air most of the time.

Nicky was happy because she was in the throes of a romance of her own with the manager of the casino, which I had predicted as long ago as New York when we first became friends. When Nicky had discovered that I always carried a pack of tarot cards with me, she had asked for a reading. In my hotel room, I had laid the cards out; the first card was a ship – and we laughed over that one. 'Tell me something I don't know!' she said. The second was a pentacle, indicating money – while the third was the King of Pentacles.

I explained; 'You will meet a man who is surrounded by money or works in money, probably on a ship.'

'Oh, great,' Nicky said, 'I could do with a multi-millionaire or a Wall Street tycoon who'll take me away from all this.'

When she fell for the manager of the casino, she said to me, somewhat ruefully, 'Well, you were right – he's certainly surrounded by money – only none of it is his!'

I always used this as an example of how shipboard romances can sometimes work; but as a sad postscript, the relationship was to break up after some four-and-a-half years.

With a hot romance of my own on the cards, the terrible winter of my discontent now just a bad dream, I started throwing myself into the fun of the Caribbean. Activities that most people would give anything to experience, costing thousands of dollars for the paying passengers, were ours for the taking. We'd explore tropical islands, shop in Kingston or Nassau, sunbathe on the golden beaches of Mexico, dive with dolphins off Cozumel. We enjoyed the latter so much that Nicky and I decided to take our diving certificates, known as PADI. Each week when the ship moored off Cozumel, we would be in the launch, speeding across an azure sea to spend the day in scuba gear. By now we were having such a good time that we didn't always have enough time to study for the exam needed. On the day we took our practical tests, we took the official manual into the sea-water pool with us and kept sneaking glances – it was no help because before the test we dropped it in the water! The instructor walked by and said, 'I hope I'm not seeing what I think I am.'

Like a couple of schoolgirls we chorused, 'No, Miss!'

That night we celebrated passing the test by going to the ship's 'Straight To Bed Club', also known as the staff bar. This wasn't quite as bad as it sounded. We were living life to the hilt, so when exhaustion caught up with me, I might say, 'Well girls, I'm going straight to bed tonight'. Nicky would agree, 'Sure, me too, I'll have an early night.' Then Charlotte would say, 'How about a quick one first?'

'A quick one – then we'll go straight to bed,' we'd agree. Hours later, we'd be found still partying in the bar, usually the last to leave. As Nicky put it, 'We always took a very long detour straight to bed via the bar.'

She and Charlotte were very proud of a written warning they had got after breaking curfew; three times and it was instant dismissal, but on this occasion, I think the staff captain saw the funny side as well. They were having such a good time in the disco that they decided to stay an extra twenty minutes and carry on dancing, first breaking yet another rule by ordering drinks direct from the bar (waiters had to serve members of staff at the table) but often we'd get fed up with waiting and risk it.

The next day Nicky and Charlotte got hauled up before the staff captain. While they stood to attention like two naughty schoolgirls, the staff captain read them out the formal warning: 'You are on report for breaking curfew and standing in the vicinity of a bar stool'.

They looked at each other and collapsed into fits of giggles. 'Honestly, Jane, we couldn't believe it,' Nicky told me. 'We asked if we could have the warning so we could frame it. He said if we continued in that manner, we would be sacked.'

'Well, I want to be sacked,' I said. 'I can't wait to spend an entire night with Henrik. At least I'd die happy.'

We all laughed, but I meant it. I started to take chances after our Saturday trysts, strolling up the gangway long after the passengers had been herded aboard, as if I had all the time in the world at four, then four-thirty – then at five as the gangway went up, moments before the ship set sail.

I dared the staff captain to sack me, looking him straight in the eye. 'Go on, fire me, make my day,' I'd say.

He'd say, 'I hope he's worth it.'

'He is,' I'd say with a pert toss of my head.

'Go on, McDonald – get on the ship,' was the usual response.

Maybe if I'd been abjectly apologetic, red-faced and looking scared, they might have sacked me; but they could tell I didn't give a toss and I think that saved me – not that I wanted to be saved. I really wanted to be pushed right off the ship; but all I was doing was pushing the limits and getting away with it. It's all about attitude.

Our last day was June 7th. For weeks beforehand, I'd be on stage singing my own lyrics to the show's theme tune. 'Seventh of June, seventh of June… di-di-da…' The audience didn't catch on – but the rest of the cast did. Soon I had them all at it, clapping and chanting, 'Seventh of June, seventh of June… di-di-di-di – di-di-di-di – da-da-da-dah…'

I might have been very cavalier about it all, but in my heart I knew that the magic date was looming ever closer, and still Henrik had never told me he loved me, never really hinted at how he felt. I was madly, head-over-heels in love – I think I would have walked on hot coals for him – but did he love me back? If he didn't give me a hint, I'd be heading back to England within a few days, my four-month holiday romance over.

Henrik and I usually had lunch at an elegant restaurant on

Las Olas Boulevard in Fort Lauderdale, a wide lovely avenue shaded by palm trees and filled with designer shops and fancy restaurants. On that last Saturday, I sat in the window and gazed across the street at Suite Suzanne's, one of the most beautiful boutiques on the boulevard. Often, while Henrik parked his Mustang, I would walk across and stare longingly at the acres of satin and lace on display in the window, exactly in the same way as I used to look at the sweetie jars in Clifton's corner shop all those years ago as a child. The sensuous clothes in Suite Suzanne's seemed wildly expensive and way beyond my means so I never went in. Some day, I dreamed, I would buy my trousseau there – only I needed to get married for that and, still, Henrik hadn't asked me!

Now, seated in the window of the restaurant opposite, I miserably thought to myself that this was my last day and that all I had left were dreams. I fought hard to keep the tears from welling up.

Henrik took my hand and my heart leaped. *Now*! He was about to propose! I had my acceptance all ready, a great big cheerleader's Y-E-S! Instead, he said, 'Jane, would you like to stay a week in the apartment for a holiday when you leave the ship next Saturday?'

'I'd love to,' I said, keeping my disappointment hidden. As usual, the comedian in me came to the front and I couldn't resist adding, 'Ee, love, I thought you'd never ask.'

'Can you get a cab to the apartment?' he asked. 'I have to go away next week, but I'll leave the key under the mat. I'll be back that night and we can have dinner somewhere nice.'

Reprieved! A girl could achieve a lot in a week, there was still time to work on that proposal. Later, as we left the restaurant for Henrik to drive me back to the ship, I glanced across at my favourite boutique and whispered, 'I'll be back,

Miss Suzanne – save that wedding gown for me'.

Those final few days on the ship passed painfully slowly. Even though I was bathed in a golden glow of happiness, looking forward to my vacation, I thought my servitude would never come to an end. I was packed and waiting from about Wednesday, looking at my watch every ten minutes, as if that would somehow make the moments pass faster until I was with my lover. On Friday night we had a party and I made my farewells – I was going to be off that ship next morning like a greyhound at the starting gate. Finally Saturday dawned, the ship docked and I rented a car to take me and my luggage to Henrik's modern apartment block.

'Are you sure you don't mind settling in on your own?' he had asked.

'Don't worry about a thing,' I'd assured him. 'I love my own company.' I wasn't placating Henrik: it was the truth. I have never craved company nor attention, which is something many people don't understand. They think that if you're in show business, you must have crowds around you all the time. I love an audience – but when I'm on my own I am truly at peace.

That first day was the most happy day I have ever had. At the apartment I let myself in and stood there, surrounded by my cases and thought: 'Oh my God, this is like real life now.' In a way I can't describe, everything was falling into place. It felt so right, as if I had arrived at a destination towards which I had been travelling all my life, as if everything else until then had been some kind of a dream.

I unpacked the things I needed and got to know the apartment. You walked straight in at the front door and entered a sort of family room. The kitchen was on the right with a breakfast bar in the middle and one of those big

American refrigerators that for some reason are practically unobtainable in Britain. To the right of the main room was a master bedroom with its own pristine white en suite bathroom. To the left was the second bedroom that we came to use as a dining room. It was all airy and spotless.

As I pottered about, I inspected Henrik's CD collection and was stunned to see that he had nothing but AC/DC and a couple of Danish people I'd never heard of. I thought, 'This is never going to work!' I had a little chuckle to myself: 'A little bit of healthy competition won't hurt, girl. Nothing ventured, nothing gained, get your CDs out, my lass.' I arranged my favourites that I always travel with on the shelf next to AC/DC and put Barbra Streisand on the sound system.

Henrik's absence gave me a chance to unwind a little. I found my way to the supermarket and stocked up the fridge. Then I found that he hadn't got an ironing board and, wondering how the heck he ironed, I bought a board. It was nice to do my own washing in a place where I could do it properly. And a bath! That was a real luxury. After I finished unpacking the groceries and sorting everything out, I took my bikini and went down to the private pool. I remember swimming under water and as I surfaced, I found my depth and stood up, sparkling water rippling away and falling off my body in silver drops. At that moment, I thought: I cannot get any happier than I am right now.

I looked up and the sky was blue, the sun was dazzling, the air was scented with jasmine blossom and gardenias, I had a swimming pool with no one else in it, the palm trees were rustling gently in the breeze and I thought, 'This is heaven'.

'Oh, God,' I cried, my arms outstretched, 'this is it!'

FLIGHT TO DESTINY

Henrik was at work most of that week, but I was so grateful at being away from crowds of people that I appreciated having the space and freedom to just potter about, listening to music, reading and sunbathing. In the evening he would work on customising a powerful Harley-Davidson motorcycle. Afterwards, we would sometimes drive along the shore, swim in the sunset ocean and, afterwards, stop at a small fish restaurant in an out-of-the-way place to have dinner, where we'd watch the moon rise. It was one of the most idyllic, romantic periods of my life: I felt I could live like this for ever.

Drifting about the flat, even without a musical instrument, I started to write a song for Henrik, humming the tune in my head: 'Every time I hear a Harley, I think about the man in my dreams... riding on into the sunset sat astride a Harley machine...'

Feeling a bit like him Tarzan, me Jane – and with the ulterior motive of impressing Henrik – I decided I'd learn to cook. From nothing I suddenly had to jump in at the deep end. I wasn't a shrinking violet and had cooked for one or two boyfriends in the past but, where food was concerned, it had been fish and chips, eggs and bacon and Marks & Spencer's.

It became a joke with my family, 'If it didn't come out of M&S, it didn't get eaten in our Jane's house'.

I didn't envy anyone, but at that moment, I wished I could cook like my sister, Janet. A brilliant hostess, she had learned her skills entertaining her husband's business friends. Idly floating in the pool, I tried to remember some of the meals she had produced when I had been invited over to her house. I'd always wanted to be like our Janet, mainly because she was headstrong and did exactly what she wanted. I'd always felt like a wimp compared with her.

Thoughts of home reminded me that I hadn't been in Wakefield for over ten months. Waves of homesickness washed over me, a confusing emotion because I was so deeply in love with Henrik that I wanted to stay in Florida with him for the rest of my life. Over the coming months, this dual confusion was always with me until it resolved itself it in the most unexpected way – but again, I'm leaping ahead.

I already knew that Henrik's favourite dish was Indian curry. I decided to produce one that very night as a surprise. After years of cooking curries for the policemen who had lodged with us, my mother had become quite an expert, so I telephoned her for advice. 'You could try a chicken tikka salad with savoury rice and ready-made poppadoms,' she suggested. 'You can make it ahead of time – and if it goes wrong, you'll have time to get something else on the table.'

I wrote her instructions down carefully – my mother had always told me, 'Jane, if you can read, you can cook' – and then went to the organic Greek store just across the road to buy poppadoms, spices and chutneys. I followed Mum's instructions to the letter, experimenting with an added touch of my own, making raitha with cucumber, yogurt and finely chopped spring onions.

Unable to eat a bite, I watched anxiously as Henrik demolished the entire meal. Finally, he looked across the table and said, 'That was wonderful, Jane. I wish you could stay for another week.'

'If you're sure?' I said promptly. Well, they do say that the way to a man's heart is through his stomach – and here was instant proof! The very next day I went to Barnes and Noble, the big bookstore in Fort Lauderdale to buy a couple of cook books; like a witch, I'd brew up my own magic spells and love potion.

I cooked up a storm for the next week, buying so much food that most of it got thrown away, all the while on an emotional seesaw. I missed my Mum – and was heartbroken that I would have to leave Henrik. Did he love me? I didn't know. He was very much like my father in that he didn't show much affection. When I asked if he loved me, he'd always say, 'Of course'. It seemed just an automatic response, nothing more. I needed reassurance, needed him to plead, 'My darling, please stay! Please don't go!' I wanted the whole nine yards and then some. I'd always had that degree of adoration from previous boyfriends yet, perversely, it had always turned me off. When I left them, I never looked back over my shoulder. But this one kept me guessing. The more he kept me dangling, the more I wanted him. I wanted him more than I have ever wanted anything in my life. The words of the song I had written for Henrik kept pounding through my head: 'Be my rebel child… All this longing, wanting, is this the real thing?'

I knew that it *was* the real thing – but I insisted that I had to go back home, and Henrik didn't stop me. Even before I got on the plane, I was being tugged both ways though I didn't show it. Yes, I was that strong! I kissed him passionately, waved goodbye with a wide smile as I walked through departure gate – and sobbed my heart out all the way back to England. Each time I visualised how soon he would forget me, I sobbed anew.

When I reached Wakefield, as always, I went to see my Gran. 'You were right again!' I said, bending down to kiss her. 'Blue ship, white cross – and a real-life Henry!' She laughed, because she was always right. I had planned on asking her about Henrik, to see if there really was any hope for a future with him in America, but Gran wasn't very well at the time, and I didn't want to stress her by telling her how much I longed to return overseas. I suspect she already knew.

Instead I telephoned my friend Steve Holbrook, to see if he could fit me in for a reading that day. I always know that if Steve has a cancellation or can fit me in, that it's meant to happen. Steve was free and, after popping round to my house for a chat and a cup of tea, he spread out the cards and studied them: 'You don't live here, Jane. When I'm looking out the window of this house you live in, it's blue skies... I could probably say America... Florida'. I didn't say anything as he continued: 'You are going to marry this man... but you're a bit worried about some visitors – could I say that it's his mother?'

Henrik had mentioned that his parents were flying out to visit him shortly – and, although I had no expectation of being there, I said, 'Yes, his mother.'

Steve nodded. 'She's a redhead... very tall... that's where he gets his character. Now, I'll tell you how to treat her. Invite her into the kitchen, don't mollycoddle her – she's not the type. Treat her as a friend, not as your future husband's mother, and she will turn out to be your ally not your enemy, and you'll have a friend there for life.'

I hugged Steve's words to myself. Henrik and I had spoken

on the phone a few times but nothing had been said about my returning there. I had some money tucked away in the bank after ten months on the *Century*, but in my line of business you can never tell where your next cheque is coming from and I had many standing orders to maintain, including the mortgage on Silcoates Street, so I telephoned an agent and started working in the clubs again.

After the brilliant colours and sunshine of the Caribbean and Florida, I felt as if I had gone back in time to an old black-and-white photograph. Everything seemed tired and tawdry; I felt drained of energy, a hopeless case, my head and heart confused and muddled. Although I was glad to see my family, I wanted Henrik. Every moment of every day, I thought of him and dreamed about him every night, the words of my song haunting my sleep: 'Freedom in my soul, American dream I can't let go... All this longing, wanting, is this the real thing?'

At my lowest ebb, I said to Mum, 'Someone should have me put down to put me out of my misery.'

She replied, 'Well, you can't carry on like this, Jane. What are you going to do?'

'I'm going back,' I said, suddenly making up my mind. I thought, 'I don't want to be here in Wakefield.' I'd gone from a life of absolute luxury back to a small town in rural England and I realised for the first time in my life: 'I don't belong here any more!' That was quite a shock for me because I'd always belonged in Wakefield. Always. It was quite a lot to come to terms with. It upset me to think: 'I don't belong here, I've moved on from my childhood home.' At last I'd grown up.

I said, 'Mum, look, as much as I love you, I have to go back to Henrik.'

Mum nodded. 'I can see that. Has he asked you to go? Has he asked you to marry him?'

I shrugged with a feeling of helplessness. 'No, he hasn't asked – but I want to go anyway.'

Mum said, 'Well, do you know for a fact that he loves you, at least?'

I shook my head. 'No, but this is something I have to do.' I'd already made my mind up that I was going to leave the clubs. I'd tried returning and was miserable; I didn't fit in there any more either. The only way I could make that decision final was to sell the equipment – a full mixing desk, the best speakers – that I'd paid an arm and a leg for. I'd always had the best I could afford, now I let it go for peanuts. I sold the car, sold everything.

My bridges burned, I telephoned Henrik, telling him what I had done. 'So, do you want to come back and live with me?' he asked.

Weak at the knees, I could only nod.

'What are you saying, Jane? This is a bad line.'

'Yes,' I almost sobbed, 'oh, yes!'

My brother, Tony, was very upset by what looked like a rushed decision. He was my big brother, very close to me, who now felt that I'd be beyond his reach for help. He came round and we had a family conference, as we always did at such times. He said, 'What happens if it all goes pear-shaped? What happens if he beats you up? What happens if he throws you out?'

I said, 'I know he won't.'

'But I'm not there to come and get you,' Tony said protectively. 'I'm worried about you being on the other side of the world. I can't just drive up like I've done before and say, "Come on, lass, you're coming home".'

I said: 'Look, I've made up my mind. I'm going to America. If anything happens, I can just get on the plane.'

Then Mum started up, saying Henrik was foreign, he seemed cold, he didn't show his emotions, she could see my father in him. She reminded me of how strict Dad was and what a life she'd had with him. I could see her thinking, 'Oh, God, my daughter is going down the same path.'

I said, 'Mum, Henrik is good, kind, reliable, steady: he'll look after me.' Was I really speaking of the man on the Harley motorbike who I'd written that song for? I had a sudden flash of Henrik on his big bike and saw with perfect clarity that a great deal of his fascination for me was that he was the strong silent type. I didn't want a lapdog – I had always rejected 'yes men'. Henrik was a real challenge and I reacted well to challenges. He was so different from any other man I'd met that I was utterly captivated: I'd fallen for him hook, line and sinker – there was no going back.

Suddenly, Mum nodded, seemingly satisfied by the grilling she'd given me. She said, 'This is the right man for you.'

I said, 'How do you know?'

'Because you've told me you're going – not asked. You've actually said, "I'm going to this man",' she replied.

Despite having already burnt all my boats, I still wanted to consult one other person about my decision: Steve Holbrook. I knew I could always ring him for advice – mainly as a mate, not for psychic intervention, but if he got anything, it was great. We arranged to have lunch in a French restaurant in the centre of Leeds, not far from his salon. Over lunch I said, 'About this guy...'

Even before I had asked the question, Steve interrupted, 'Listen, you will marry him'.

I sat up. 'I don't know –' I said doubtfully, not because I had any doubts, but because Henrik hadn't asked me.

'You're going to be really happy with this one – you're meant for each other,' Steve replied.

I felt goose bumps as Steve described Henrik. I thought, 'God, you don't know him and you've got it so right'. Steve then said, 'You're filming. I've got TV cameras. There's seven people involved and you're going to be the star…'

'Give up, Steve!' I exclaimed flippantly.

'There's a film camera and seven characters in this thing – and you're going to come back and tell me all about it,' he said, sipping his coffee.

I laughed, 'Go on!' I'd never been on television. My mind ranged over the possibilities, thinking, America… I might get spotted in the States… it seemed so unlikely. Some time ago, there had been a time in the Torre Road Club in Leeds when Steve had been in the audience watching me sing. When the curtains had swished down behind me, he had seen instead the Stars and Stripes unfurling as a big backdrop, with me on another stage, a massive auditorium, with thousands and thousands of people in the audience. When I had come offstage, Steve, visibly shaken by the vision, had come up to me: 'Jane, you might think I'm crackers, but you're going to have a lot to do with America – you're going to sing in somewhere huge'.

I'd replied, 'Well, I wish it would bloody well hurry up!'

So far, nothing like that had happened – yet, here I was seriously thinking about moving to the States, having sold my car and equipment. I felt I had to take him seriously.

Now, back in the French restaurant, Steve continued, 'There's some kind of a chat show'.

'Oh, I can chat all right, talk the hind legs off a donkey,' I said. Then, getting back to my chief concern, I asked, 'You really think I'm making the right decision?'

He said. 'Yes – I really do.'

Budgeting carefully, I put aside enough money to pay the bills in Yorkshire for a few months with some to live on in America. With what was left, I bought the cheapest air ticket I could find. I left the house early one morning in August and almost screamed as Tony, who was driving me, was forced to crawl all the way through a heavy hill fog and low-lying clouds to Leeds-Bradford Airport from where I was to catch a flight down south to Gatwick to make my connection.

Tony hugged me tight after we had put my luggage on the conveyor belt. 'Call me if you need me. I'll come at once,' he said.

'I know, Tony. I love you,' I said, 'I'll call as soon as I get there.'

The Leeds plane took off late and by the time I arrived at Gatwick, I was a nervous wreck. Racing to the check-in desk, I found I had missed the flight by fifteen minutes.

Surrounded by people busy with their own affairs, I stood there and wailed, 'I can't afford another flight. I haven't got the money to pay for it!' I was so upset that I fell to my knees at the counter and in an Oscar-winning performance I begged, 'Please, you have got to get me out there. I am going to marry this man!'

I was so distraught, the staff must have thought I was flying out to my wedding day. The ticketing clerk (I think her name was Jill) was absolutely brilliant, and if she reads this, she'll know how much it meant to me. She could see the real distress I was in, sobbing because I didn't know what to do and convinced that my world was about to come to an end.

'I can get you on a flight,' she said, 'but it's via Canada – and it's not until tomorrow.'

'Anything,' I cried, falling on her neck.

I checked into the cheapest room I could find at an airport hotel and called my mother. 'I missed the flight,' I said. 'Henrik was meeting me at Fort Lauderdale – can you tell him I'll be flying in to Orlando instead?'

My mother was upset because I sounded so tearful. That's why, when she managed to track Henrik down on his mobile phone, she blurted out, 'Now listen, she's not on that flight. She's arriving at Orlando and you have to go and get her.'

Henrik was later to tell me that when he heard the very first words uttered by this formidable unknown woman, whom he had already decided was to be his future mother-in-law (though of course he hadn't shared this with me yet), he was petrified.

'I was in instant terror of her,' he told me in admiration. 'What a woman!'

It took me for ever to get to Florida. I set out from Wakefield on one day and, three days later, I ended up at my destination on a plane that was so old, I swear, it stopped for wood. Henrik had been working all day but he had to drive all the way to Orlando at three in the morning in order to pick up this distraught woman who looked like the wreck of the *Hesperus*. We reached the apartment and had about four hours together before he had to leave to fly to Alaska. But I didn't care; six weeks after I had flown out of his life, I was back: I had reached my man. I would be right there waiting for him.

☆　　☆　　☆

I discovered that even though Henrik didn't say a great deal, he showed his true feelings by deeds, often springing surprises on me. As soon as he got back from his trip, he said he had arranged a short holiday in Las Vegas. My heart jolted. To anyone else, Las Vegas might mean big shows and gambling; to me it meant just one thing – an instant wedding. MY instant wedding! Elvis Presley's version of 'Crying in the Chapel' is frequently one of the taped songs played at those drive-in places – but the Dixie Cups' version of 'Going to the Chapel (to get Married)' is more what I was thinking of, and I couldn't get the words out of my head when I phoned Mum to break the news of our trip. 'We're flying to Las Vegas. Don't be surprised if I come back married!' I said breathlessly.

Taking my birth certificate in my hand – just in case – we left from Miami Airport. I had never been across the States before and I wished that Henrik and I were bombing along on his big Harley, on the now mythical Route 66 as in *Easy Rider*. Some day, perhaps, we would make that trip – hopefully visiting Nashville and Memphis – two places I'd love to go to because of their strong music connections.

In Las Vegas, we followed the tourist trail. I remember standing outside Caesar's Palace, where Celine Dion was performing. Looking up at the blown-up image of her head outlined in neon stars, I said, 'I'll know I've made it if I ever sing here'.

'Some day you will,' Henrik said. He went and threw a coin in the fountain and made a wish that he's kept secret to this day. I'd love to know what he wished but you're not supposed to tell, or it won't come true. I threw my own coin in, closed my eyes and wished so fervently that Henrik laughed. 'That is some wish!' he said.

I can now reveal my wish: it was that we would get married.

I was so besotted, it remained all I wanted out of life for the two years until it *did* come true. Each time Henrik said, 'We're going out,' I quickly checked to make sure I had that birth certificate with me.

However, in Vegas, we didn't go anywhere near one of its famous wedding chapels. Instead, we did everything else, including taking a helicopter trip to the Grand Canyon that I'll always remember; not just because of the scenery, which was spectacular, but because as I was climbing up into the helicopter, in platform soles, skimpy shorts and a little denim top straining at the leash, (I must have looked a sight!) Henrik said, 'How much do you weigh?'

I'd been off the ship for a couple of months, but the weight was still there. Quickly, so it didn't sound very much, I said, 'Ten-and-a-half stone.'

Henrik said, 'If you lose about half a stone you will be just perfect.'

No one had ever said anything like that to me before. I replied, 'How dare you! No one ever speaks to me like that. I know I'm not perfect…'

Completely disarming me, Henrik said, 'But you're that close…' holding up two fingers a fraction apart. He was the only man who could have mentioned my weight and got away with it.

As soon as we returned to Florida, I got a personal trainer and worked hard to diet and tone up. I'm glad I did because I looked all right after that. Henrik's such a perfectionist, I'm sure he looked at me on the ship and thought, 'she's got potential,' and then proceeded to work out how I could achieve it!

Back in Florida, Henrik had more surprises up his sleeve. One morning he said mysteriously, 'I have something to show you.' We drove to the small town of Plantation some fifteen or twenty minutes outside Fort Lauderdale, turning off into the grounds of a former estate known as the Lakes of Newport. Henrik stopped the car and pointed to a large section of land staked out beside one of the several stretches of water on the huge property, and said, 'See this bit here?'

To me, it looked like a patch of barren land. I gave him a sideways glance, wondering what this was about, and said, 'Yes?'

He said, 'I've just bought it. We're going to have our house built here.'

I almost held my breath, as I realised that he'd said, 'our house'. So I *was* included in his plans for the future – and even though Henrik still hadn't said he loved me, it was enough for the moment. He took me to the builder's office and showed me the blueprints. At first, they were hard to visualise; but as the house went up and the ground was beautifully landscaped beside the lake between tall trees, I saw Henrik's vision and became excited.

Henrik was away such a lot that I was usually the one who drove out to watch our house being built. At first I used a hired car or a small second car of Henrik's, but some time later he was to surprise me yet again. I usually slept in late, after Henrik had left for work. One morning, he telephoned me to say that he had put something for me under the pillow. I looked and found the keys to a brand-new silver Mercedes. He had sold his prized Harley-Davidson so I would have a car of my own. Such a sacrifice finally convinced me that he really did love me. Brought up in Yorkshire, where men traditionally keep their feelings to themselves, I recognised at last what Henrik meant by this; but my artistic and creative side has always made me very emotionally expressive, and I still longed for just one special word from this caring but silent Dane.

I learned that Henrik showed how much he cared for me in other ways. I had begun to feel restless, not because I wanted to return to work, but because I felt that I should be contributing to my upkeep. More importantly, I had run out of money and was deeply concerned that soon there wouldn't be enough on deposit in England to pay the monthly outgoings there. Henrik was intuitive enough to sense my fears and asked what was troubling me. With a feeling of relief, I sat down with him and discussed what I wanted out of life. I told him that I didn't want to return to the northern clubs or be a production singer on the ships for ever, but I needed the money and didn't know how to move up another notch.

Henrik nodded. 'Why don't you take time off to consider your options, Jane, and not rush into the same job again?' Then he stunned me by offering to take over paying the bills in Yorkshire to give me the space I needed.

'You have so many expenses as it is,' I protested.

Without bragging, he said simply, 'I have money, Jane.'

For the first time, I learned everything about him as he filled in his background, how he, a Dane, had come to end up in Florida. After a career as a marine engineer, sailing around the world – even being attacked by pirates in the South China Seas – he had joined a big Danish marine boiler company that sent him and Ken Nilsen, a co-worker, to set up offices in Florida. Within days of their arrival, the company had closed down its US operations and Henrik and Ken had been left stranded without a job. When some of the existing customers asked Henrik if he and Ken could take over their contracts, they agreed. So many orders came in that Ken travelled all over the world for three months, from Australia to Russia. By the time he returned, Henrik had opened new offices, hired staff, everything was fully operational – all using their American Express cards to prop up their cashflow. This had all happened the previous year.

'We had some capital, but companies pay on sixty to ninety days – we had to bridge that gap,' Henrik explained. 'This year, we made a huge profit. It's going woosh – through the ceiling. Now we're opening new companies all over the world.'

My eyes widened. 'You've achieved all this in a year?'

'Well, maybe eighteen months,' Henrik allowed. 'My years on big tankers stood me in good stead – I know what I'm doing.'

The first time I had seen him he had been wearing a dinner jacket, but the second time, he had been in greasy overalls. To think that all this time I'd been under the impression that the love of my life was just another boilerman! I said, 'My God, Henrik, you're a dark horse.'

I was joking, but inwardly, I was beginning to feel very nervous. I was just an ordinary lass from Yorkshire, from a working-class background. A man whose own company had made a substantial amount in just their first year seemed beyond my reach. Did I deserve him, could I live up to him? It was easy when he was just a simple boilerman, but was I right for a businessman with rapidly expanding international connections? These doubts jolted my self-confidence although I tried not to show it.

As usual, my fears came out in my humour: 'Well, it's nice

to know you can afford me,' I said. 'Get your credit card out
– me brother's coming to dinner and I want to go shopping.'

That was how I broke the news to Henrik that Tony was
flying over in a few days to pay us a visit. I'd wondered how
long it would be before he'd decided to see for himself how I
was doing and to get to know this stranger I'd run off with. I'd
left Wakefield in August, it was only September before Tony
and Wendy, together with a couple of friends, just 'happened'
to book a vacation in Florida. Tony had tried to make it seem
more happenstance than intentional by renting a villa in
Naples, a small old holiday resort on the Gulf of Mexico, the
opposite side from Fort Lauderdale. I could even hear him
saying, 'Jane! What a coincidence, fancy you being here.'

When the group arrived, they rented a car at Miami
International Airport to drive across Florida, but with four
adults and several children, including my little niece, Katie,
there was no room for all their luggage and Wendy rented and
drove another car. The road to Naples cuts in a straight line
right across Florida, a large chunk of it through the swamps
known as the Everglades. What they didn't realise was that it
was locally known as 'Alligator Alley' and was enclosed both
sides in strong chainlink fences to keep the ravening beasts at
bay. Big signs at regular intervals warned people that if they
broke down, they were to stay in their cars and not get out
until help came. Somehow, our dozy Wendy didn't notice a
single sign – even though she drove past a dead alligator in the
middle of the road. When the boot of her car kept springing
open, she got out, walked unconcernedly to the back and
closed it. When she glanced up, she saw everyone in the other
car ahead waving vigorously out of the back window – so she
waved back. It wasn't until they reached Naples that Tony
said, 'Didn't you see signs, Wendy, about alligators?'

'Oh, I wondered why you didn't get out of the car,' she said.

When they were settled in, Tony telephoned. Without beating around the bush, he said, 'Jane, we're here, come to lunch. Bring Henrik.'

'I'll try,' I said, knowing that Henrik was not the type of man you told what to do. The moment I said I was going to spend the day with my family, I was sure he'd say, 'Well, you go,' and that would be it. To my surprise, he readily agreed to come with me.

I was delighted to see my family and their friends. Even though it had been just a month since Tony had driven me that foggy morning over the moors to catch my flight, I had missed him. After I introduced them, Tony and Henrik were skirting around each other, sizing the other up. It was only when someone mentioned that Tony was into bikes that the ice was broken, and they were instantly brothers in arms.

The villa, on the outskirts of Old Naples village, was very comfortable, with a swimming pool where the children were happily splashing about, and a Jacuzzi. They pointed out the lake at the back, inhabited by alligators and described Wendy's Alligator Alley adventure.

'I can't believe I drove all that way and didn't notice a single warning sign,' Wendy laughed.

'Well, that's typical of you – what would you have done if an alligator bit your bum?' I said.

'Climbed on car roof and yelled bloody blue murder,' Wendy said. We collapsed into our usual fits of giggles.

'He's nice,' Wendy said as we prepared the meal and laid the table, nodding towards the patio where Henrik looked completely relaxed, drinking beer. 'And you know Tony, we had to come, he couldn't settle until he'd seen that his little sister was okay.'

'He's always looked out for me,' I said.

Wendy continued, 'Not that he's come to check on Henrik – it was just that everyone at home kept saying, "have you met him, what's he like?" It looks as if you're here to stay, so we thought family should get to know him.'

While Henrik's English was good, Yorkshire, especially the slang, was hard for him to grasp. Over lunch, from time to time he'd say in his precise Danish way, 'What do you mean?' and either Tony would slow down and explain or, more often, I'd translate. I hadn't realised how much my own use of Yorkshire had been adapted on my travels so that people would understand me more easily – though I can lapse at once when amongst my own people.

When we had a moment alone, I said to Tony, 'What do you think?'

'He's a good lad. You're in safe hands,' Tony said.

'I'm like putty in his hands,' I joked. But I was very relieved, not only that Tony approved and could go home and reassure Mum, but also that Henrik had taken to him. I don't know what I'd have done if the two most important men in my life hadn't got on.

At the end of their holidays, although Henrik had to work, I invited the group for lunch at our apartment, which was on their way to the airport. Fort Lauderdale is a difficult place to find your way around and it's hard to get off the freeway. They rode around for ages getting hot and frustrated. Finally, they pulled into a diner to have something to eat and Tony went to the payphone to tell me that time was knocking on and they would have to go straight to the airport.

Worried, I had been looking out for them. Now I asked, 'Where are you?'

Tony told me the name of the diner and I said, 'I can see you from here!'

Still on the phone, Tony looked up and saw me, looking out of the window. I said, 'I'll be there in a minute'. There was only time for me to run across and chat, then they had to leave. I stood outside the diner, watching them pull away, sad that they were going but happy that Tony would be able to go home with a good report.

When Mum telephoned, she told me, 'Our Tony said, "she'll never get away with anything with that one. That one will keep her on her toes".'

'What do you think?' I asked.

Mum said, 'Well, perhaps that's a good thing. You've always needed a man you could respect.'

Later, it was my turn to meet Henrik's family. I was absolutely terrified. I cleaned and polished everything in sight, including my car, inside and out. I knew they didn't speak English, so I got Henrik to give me Danish lessons. I had my hair and nails done, I bought a new outfit, I went shopping and filled the big refrigerator so full of food I couldn't find anything – and still I thought there would be something they would find fault with.

When Henrik introduced me to his mother I nearly dropped dead. She was the tall, red-headed woman Steve had described. Quickly, I grasped the nettle and did exactly what Steve suggested.

'Come into the kitchen, Ruth, we can talk while I finish off fixing dinner,' I said.

Ruth sniffed the air appreciatively when she followed me into the kitchen, leaving Henrik to catch up with his father,

Ove. 'Something smells very good,' she said.

'I'm making lasagne, is that all right?' I asked.

'Of course! Let me do something,' Ruth offered at once.

I got her making the salad, leaving her to rummage through the fridge on her own. Her eyes widened, 'So much food is in here!'

'Henrik says I buy too much, but I love the stores here, and he likes to eat at home.'

'Oh, ja, he likes home cooking.' And despite the language barrier, we were soon chatting and laughing like long lost girlfriends.

I laid out a big family lasagne, a nice salad, garlic bread and a simple desert that Janet had shown me once: blancmange and mousse in wine glasses topped off with fresh cream – quick, easy and tempting.

The recipe for the lasagne came from one of my friends at the sunbed shop in Leeds where I had worked. I had written it down at the time and never forgotten it. My cheese sauce was spectacular, remembered from the kitchen at home from childhood, my mother saying, 'stir this sauce,' while she was busy doing other things.

'Well, Jane, that was wonderful,' Henrik said afterwards. I think he was telling me that I had passed the test with his family. The initial ice had been broken on both sides – with my family and now with his. Next he had to meet my mother. But before that happened, my life was turned upside down in a spectacular way that I would never have anticipated in a million years, with a telephone call from the BBC.

THE CRUISE

The winter solstice of 21 December 1996 was to be a red-letter day for us, the exciting day when we'd be given the keys to our house at the Lakes of Newport. For weeks, Henrik had been conferring with decorators, choosing all the colour schemes. We'd trawled the big stores in the malls for furniture, looking forward to enjoying our first Christmas together.

Henrik was away while I started to pack up the flat shortly before we were due to move. Most of the things were his, shipped around the world in his wake from the various places he'd been sent to by the Danish boiler company. Having left Wakefield with just a couple of cases, my own possessions were few – still, it's amazing how much a girl can accumulate when she's home all day with nothing else to do but go shopping!

I dropped in at my favourite Greek food store and asked for all the cardboard cartons they could spare, for packing smaller things like the lovely Danish dinner service Henrik's mother had given him, and for glasses, records and books. In the middle of carefully wrapping the items in newspaper before putting them into boxes, I was disturbed by the telephone. It was someone from the Celebrity office in Fort

Lauderdale, offering me a job. To say I was stunned, given that I'd said what I'd thought of them seven months earlier, was putting it mildly.

I could still see myself at the last-night party on the famed seventh of June, standing up in the bar, full of vodka and bravado, and saying to the officers: 'I will never set foot on another ship unless it's as a headliner – and I swear blind I will never ever set foot on the *Century* again'. Everybody had laughed, including me, but I'd really meant it.

But time can put a rosy light on almost everything. It seemed the Celebrity office was willing to ignore our heated relationship, while I was willing to consider an offer. Part of my willingness was the realisation that Christmas was looming and I had no money of my own to buy gifts. Henrik had been more than generous with his credit card – but somehow, buying someone a present with their own money didn't seem right. Of course I knew that even if I took a job – any job – at that late date, I still wouldn't have money in time for Christmas, it was just that not having money of my own made me eager to earn something.

'Jane, we've just launched the *Century*'s sister ship, the *Galaxy*. We want you to come aboard her maiden cruise as a headliner.'

'You've got to be joking!' I said.

They thought I meant I wasn't interested, when in fact, I was in shock. This was the offer I had always wanted – for it to come out of the blue, when I had least expected it, was startling.

'You'll have all passenger facilities and rights, and the pay will of course be in keeping with your status,' they said, trying to make an offer I would accept.

'If I agree, when would you want me to start?' I asked,

thinking that with such an important launch they would have got their entertainment line-up booked months ahead. Perhaps they wanted me for March or April, which would be fine, giving me plenty of time to move into the new house.

'Immediately – in time for Christmas and the New Year, for seven weeks.'

I sat down. Now I really did need a drink.

I talked it through with Henrik and decided to accept the offer. Four days later, the phone disturbed my sleep early one morning – and as all my friends and family know, I am not a morning person. Reaching one hand out from under the covers, I groped for the telephone. I said, 'This had better be good!'

A hesitant voice said, 'Hello, is that Jane McDonald? This is Christopher Terrill, of the BBC.'

'I don't do mornings,' I warned.

He laughed appreciatively. 'I was thinking of seven weeks – '

Now I sat up in bed. 'Where have I heard that before?'

'I got your name from the people at Celebrity. I understand that you're going to be one of the main entertainers on the *Galaxy* this Christmas.'

'Fame spreads,' I said.

He laughed again. 'We're making a documentary of life on a big cruise liner. Would you mind if we followed you around?'

I said, 'No, love, bring your camera and off we'll go.' I felt like giggling, it was so surreal, discussing all this while still in bed. If only he could see me now, I thought – not realising that was exactly how he'd like to see me – frowzy-haired and bleary-eyed, being normal.

When I established that this request was for real, that I wasn't still asleep and Chris wasn't some joker, we arranged to meet that evening in the lobby of one of the big hotels downtown in Fort Lauderdale, so he could assess my potential – and also to see if I got on with him. 'I'll be with you every moment over the next few weeks,' he'd said.

'What, like one of those fly-on-the-wall things?' I asked.

'I've never believed in fly-on-the-wall, as if the camera is not there,' Chris said. 'You have to be there, as the effects are dynamic, an interrelation. I don't use a crew, the camera is a big thing.'

'And you'll be holding the camera?' I said.

'Yes, I'll be right there, all the time.'

'Oh, in that case, I'll meet you in my lucky black trousers, love,' I said. 'Now go away and let me finish my beauty sleep.'

I'd had those trousers for years and every time I wore them something good happened (I still have them!). Sometimes, they didn't fit, with my weight see-sawing the way it tended to. I tried them on that day and they fitted because I'd really worked at trying to achieve Henrik's 'almost perfect' figure. With the trousers, I wore a leopardskin crew-necked top and a suede jacket with stars on it, a wide belt and high-heeled boots that added length to my legs. Tanned, with flowing long hair and scarlet lips, I knew I looked good as I waltzed into the hotel bar. Although we had never met before, we knew each other at once.

'You're Jane McDonald, aren't you?' Chris said, standing up and coming forward to meet me. He was a slight, dark-haired man, with an endearing smile and penetrating blue eyes. We sat and had a few drinks, getting on with each other from the word go. Chris told me that he'd known at once from my response when he'd woken me up that morning that

I would probably be the right person he was looking for as a 'character' in his film. 'It's this instinct thing,' he said. 'I know right away if it's going to work.' I nodded: I knew exactly what he meant because I've also always relied on a gut feeling – even if I am sometimes proved wrong.

Chris is an anthropologist as well as a film-maker, an interesting combination for a maker of documentaries that explore real lives in closed communities. He discussed what he was looking for in me as a person; humour, yes, but much more important was honesty. He said, 'If this project isn't right from the very beginning, the right mix of characters, with essentially one very strong lead who is prepared to show their frailties, trusting me enough not to exploit that, it can collapse from the outset. If we do this, you've got to be honest with me all the way through from start to finish. If you have any doubts at all, tell me. I will be with you from the time you wake up until you go to sleep. I'll be with you in and out of your cabin and in all of your conversations.'

I nodded and said, 'I'm just a northern club singer, is that enough?'

He said: 'Yes, it's great. People have to identify with you and your hopes and fears, your dreams – and they will. I'll be with you when you're worried, nervous, upset – and they'll see that too. Your vulnerability will be exposed in many ways and it takes courage to allow that.'

I said, 'What if there's something I don't want in the programme? Though I can't imagine what – my life's an open book.'

Chris said, 'If there's something you don't want and I think it is important to keep it in, we'll discuss it. If someone has something personal to hold back – and explains their reasons, I will respect that. When someone shows you their inner self you don't take advantage of that, you don't show it on camera in a way that is unfairly intrusive. At the end of the day it's only a film but that person has to live with it. These things are made on trust.'

He told me about other similar films he'd made – the most recent one, the award-winning *HMS Brilliant*, had followed the lives of sailors on a Royal Navy warship. He said, 'I do all my own research, or I don't get what I want, the thing that makes a film like this work. The secret is in the chemistry.'

'What made you decide on the *Galaxy*?' I asked.

'I wanted a ship that would agree to complete access and freedom. The *Galaxy* did. It's taken me a long time to find the right one.'

I nodded. 'I think we'll get on. I'm a straightforward Yorkshire lass, I call a spade a spade, and I can tell you won't take advantage of me.'

For the next three-and-a-half hours, we talked and entertained each other, getting on really well. I knew at the end of it that I could put my trust in this man, that he wouldn't let me down. Two days later we met again for dinner, joined by Henrik and several others who worked for the shipping line. I had worked on every single one of Celebrity's ships and knew everyone, including the company PR girl, who was an absolute scream. The two of us were the entertainment for the night, keeping everyone else in stitches.

'This is really going to work, you have so many facets to your personality, but most of all, you're sympathetic, the audience will warm to you,' Chris said when the party split up. He looked very pleased with the way things had gone. 'Can we start first thing in the morning?'

'You mean, when I come aboard the ship?' I asked.

'No, when you get out of bed,' he said. 'I'd like to show you packing your bags.'

'I don't think you appreciate just how much packing I'm doing!' I said, 'The apartment is a mess, we're in the middle of moving house.'

Florida was bathed in wintry sun and all the news was of plummeting temperatures when I prepared to sail, along with eighteen hundred passengers and eight hundred crew, from Port Everglades on the *Galaxy*'s inaugural voyage to the Western Caribbean on 20th December. I was leaving Henrik to move to our new house on his own the following day. I thought I'd done a wonderful job of packing all the cases – I even told him there was nothing left for him to do, but believe me, my bragging cost me dear. When Henrik came to lift the boxes up, the bottoms fell out, and his mother's china and our glasses shattered in a thousand pieces all over the floor. I was glad I wasn't there!

The morning of my departure, Chris came to the apartment with his camera and with Jonathan Mitchell, the sound man. Chris did what few have dared to do: he got me out of bed at the crack of dawn, to film me packing my suitcases and taking a cab to the Celebrity docks. Until then, I thought that cameramen shot film and then later on it would be chopped up and edited, being invariably put into a different sequence. What I didn't know was that this time, the very first moment Chris turned on the camera were the very first moments in the documentary. It was all absolutely as if it was live television, from the going on board to the sound of a string quartet playing '*Jingle Bells*', to greeting old friends and searching for my cabin on deck four. The cabin was the first where I'd had the luxury of so much space to myself.

'This is a bit of all right, isn't it?' I said as I looked around. 'I'm going up in the world.'

I could see Chris out of the corner of my eye as the day progressed, getting a little buzz off him. He was there all the time, up close. Sometimes he'd shoot from different angles, or he'd go off at a tangent and shoot background footage and other people who would later be cut in on the edit. He never, however, made me repeat or 'fake' anything – not once did he say, 'Can you do that again, Jane, and this time, would you do it this way?'

When we had a break for dinner that evening, Chris turned to me and said, 'Jane, this is going absolutely brilliantly. You're a natural – it's all far more spontaneous than I'd ever hoped.'

'Oh, I'm a natural all right,' I said. 'Very earthy, love.'

He told me that he was shooting the film like a drama, with hardly any commentary. 'I want people to see it as if they are right there with you. I want them to feel, as I do, that it's a privilege being allowed so close to you – not a right.'

'Is there anything different you want me to do?' I asked, not able to believe how straightforward it all seemed. I'd always thought you had to rehearse things over and over again – this was very relaxed.

'No, I don't want to "tell" you to do anything,' Chris said. 'You're in control. You lead, I'll follow.'

As we talked things through that first night, I saw that there was a certain degree of insecurity, maybe a tussle in my own mind as to whether I should present myself in the right light – the kind of façade that we all show to the world – instead of exposing the real me. I think that everybody has that desire to hold back, to act out a role that they think others want from them. As I got to know Chris, it became easier when I didn't think of the potential audience who would be watching this film. Chris had told me that he worked for the BBC in London – but for some reason I believed it would be shown only in America, simply because that was where we were shooting. In a way, that element of distancing myself from the people who really knew me – my family and friends at home in Wakefield – was what lowered that wall and allowed me to truly be myself.

Chris was no longer 'the camera', but increasingly became the mate I could confide in. When I was talking about personal things, it didn't seem that I was doing it on camera, but directly to Chris himself as he followed me everywhere sharing my tears, my triumphs and my innermost thoughts – like the night when everybody walked out of my performance. I was shocked and mortified and turned to Chris almost in tears. 'They're all leaving! What's wrong? Is it me?' I was extra nerve-wracked because, not only was the event being filmed, but that was my very first time as a headliner. I'd been announced as having performed at the London Palladium, which wasn't true, and I was ridden with guilt over that – had the audience cottoned on? Did they think I was a fake? All these things were whirling around in my mind – and were painfully revealed on camera.

I discovered that it wasn't my singing; the audience was rushing out to a newly scheduled midnight buffet – as if they didn't have enough to eat all day! It was the timing that needed rearranging, and once this was done, my audience stayed, applauded, then rushed to feed at the trough.

Chris was there when I went ashore on Christmas Eve at Cozumel in Mexico, in order to meet Henrik who was flying in to join the ship for a few days. I telephoned my mother from the quay, standing under swaying palm trees filled with squawking red and yellow macaws, watching pink flamingos flying across the lagoon. Despite the exotic location, as soon as I heard Mum's voice, I missed her so much, especially when I heard that they were having a white Christmas back home in Yorkshire.

'How are you, Jane?' Mum said.

'I'm stranded here in Paradise, but I'd rather be there with you,' I said, wiping tears from my eyes.

Mum said, 'Where's Henrik?'

'He's joining me. I'm waiting for his plane to land.'

Henrik had agreed to be filmed – but not that first moment when we greeted each other. I was a bit concerned that Henrik would do his nut having a camera follow him – after all, I was used to all this attention, having performed for years, but he is a quiet and very modest man who had specifically said, 'Jane, I want to greet you first when I come on board before we go on camera'.

I discussed it with Chris beforehand. 'Don't freak him out with a camera. This is my boyfriend, I haven't spent all that much time with him. Men hate all that sloppy stuff that we women like – all that sloppy hug-hug, kiss-kiss, darling I've missed you kind of stuff – and I don't know how he is going to react with the cameras there, watching every move, recording every sentimental word.'

'Of course I'll do what Henrik wants,' Chris said. 'But it will be a very powerful moment. Can you take some time to reconsider? Do you think that Henrik will really hate it, or is he reacting to the idea of it being potentially embarrassing?'

I sat and thought about it for a while, coming to the conclusion that Henrik was a good sport and trusted me. By shifting the responsibility of trust away from Chris to me, I felt that Henrik really wouldn't object – and there was always the final edit. Chris would never let editorial control out of his hands, but he had promised a debate and, if Henrik did freak out, we could reconsider; at least, the actual moment would be captured instead of being lost.

So Chris secretly wired me and was filming from a distance. We were chatting – and that was all in the film. I didn't know how Henrik was going to react towards the cameras being there but surprisingly, he took to it like a duck to water. In fact, he was more relaxed than I was!

That evening, as I dressed for my Christmas Eve performance in a silver and black sequinned jacket and matching black pants, Henrik said, 'Do you realise that this will be the first time I've seen you perform on stage, Jane?'

My hand stayed, putting on mascara. 'Are you sure?'

'Yes, when you were on the *Century*, I would snatch some sleep in your cabin while you were on stage – don't you remember? It was the only time I got any sleep when we first met. I did sometimes drop into that cabaret room where you performed some nights, but I don't count that.'

I laughed. 'I remember. I can't believe you've never heard me sing on a theatre stage after we've been together for nearly a year. So you only know me as Plain Jane, which is nice.'

Henrik looked at Chris, who was recording all this, and said, 'I hope she's good'.

'Cheeky bugger!' I said as I headed down the long corridors to the back of the stage. In my past, boyfriends had got crushes on me as a singer, and not as a person. Because he had never seen me perform, Henrik had shown that he cared for me for what I was, not for the unreal figure up there in the spotlight. Waiting in the wings, I was assaulted by my usual panic, then the music started to play a fast arrangement of the song 'How Do You Keep The Music Playing?' written by one of my favourite composers, Michel Legrand – and I was on. I felt like calling out to Henrik sitting somewhere in the audience, 'Well, lovey, what do you think – are you going to keep me now you've heard me?'

I had my opportunity to say something towards the end of the show when I told the audience that my man was there for Christmas and the next song was for him. As far as I was concerned, the song 'The Power of Love' said it all, as I sang to Henrik that I was his lady and he was my man.

The spotlight hit Henrik, and if he wilted under the glare, he didn't show it. He always seemed so cool and in control. He even agreed to be filmed practically still in bed the next morning when he handed me my Christmas present, an intriguing little box wrapped in gold paper.

I was so excited, thinking at last, an engagement ring! I could see from Chris's wide smile that he was sharing my excitement – probably he was also visualising what the viewers would be thinking. (A year later half of England was going 'Aah!' at that moment when they watched it.) In real time, I was also going, 'Aah!' as I opened the box and I saw the flash of lovely diamond-cut gold earrings.

I was thinking, 'Jane, you're still not engaged!' and hoping the camera wouldn't reveal too much disappointment. I'd been praying to get married to this man. At that moment a degree of panic hit me over what I was doing. We could have fallen out over the cameras being there; Henrik could have walked off the ship. And that would have been the end of that!

Instead, I took a deep breath and focussed on the earrings, which were gorgeous. For Henrik to have bought them when he'd had so many expenses with the house, was surely another example of how much he really did love me. Feeling that I was nearly home and dry, I thanked him most graciously. Still, I couldn't help saying to Chris, 'I had thought it might be an engagement ring, but we've decided we're not bothered by all that.' Then to Henrik I said, 'Isn't that right, darling?'

'What?' Henrik said.

'We're not bothered about getting married.'

'Oh, sure,' Henrik replied.

Later, when I eventually saw the film, the raw disappointment in my face at his words, which I thought I'd kept concealed, was there plain for half the world to see. There was no commentary, but there didn't need to be. I understood then what Chris had meant by saying I'd be exposing my vulnerability, that the film was like a drama – it was; and what was left unsaid said more than any commentary could ever have added.

If Christmas wasn't all I wanted it to be that year, Henrik and I did share a sublime, spiritual moment. Wherever the ship went, there were always dolphins leaping ahead through the sparkling waves. I longed to know these mystical creatures better and whenever the *Century* had anchored off Cozumel, along with Nicky, Charlotte and a few of the dancers, I had taken the tender across the bay to the Sacred Paradise Wildlife Gardens and the Cancun Dolphin Nature reserve, where we learned to scuba dive. Long days were spent in the warm waters of the Gulf as we learned how to be mermaids. I was entranced by the sensual grace of the dancers as they slid and glided underwater with the dolphins. While I didn't have the agility of the others on land, the sea evened us out, making me as graceful as they were until I felt as much a part of that undersea world as the fishes. As I said to Nicky, 'If I ever stopped singing, I could always dive for treasure.'

The Caribbean is stuffed with gold and silver, the treasure of the Incas. In one hurricane alone a few centuries back, over a hundred overladen Spanish galleons sank somewhere off Cuba where the Silver Shoals lie.

With Henrik now with me, I seized the moment, assumed the mantle of a siren and lured him into the magical underwater world where I felt so at peace. They say the oceans are alive with music, with the sound of whales and porpoises singing to each other across thousands of miles. The truth, however, is that when you get underwater, you can't hear anything except the sound of your own breathing.

Chris was able to follow us underwater because he could dive and had underwater housing for his camera with him. Just to load the dice and ensure we got plenty of visitors, buckets of bait were tossed over the sides of the boat. It looked dangerous, but I felt quite safe, even though I did camp it up a little, telling Chris, 'You have to be joking. I'm not going to be a shark's dinner for your film!'

That day, as Henrik and I sunk down to the bottom, about twenty stingrays drifted up. It could have been frightening but I sensed that they were as curious about us as we were about them. I nodded to Henrik – 'Oh, look, they've come to see you.' He smiled, giving me the thumbs up sign. Stingrays – and make no mistake, they do have razor-sharp tails that can inflict deep wounds – swim quite flat and close to the bottom, so I got flat down with them. One very big one swam up to me, undulating its fins slowly. I held my breath as, for a sublime moment, we looked into each other's eyes. I put up my hands, and it made contact. It was like velvet running over my hands. Gently, exactly as if it knew what it was doing, it floated the length of its body over my finger tips. It passed,

Me on the *Galaxy* – headlining a show at last.

Together with Captain
Korres during filming
for *The Cruise*.

Me with boyfriend
Henrik in the early
days of our romance.

On the set of the *Cruising into Christmas* video.

With Chris Terrill, the man who I owe so much to.

Singing in theatre concerts was a big change for me after the clubs and cruise ships.

Signing autographs for my fans, who I value so much.

Mum and Gran backstage at Blackpool – it was a great day for all of us.

My wedding day was
a dream come true.

Me and Henrik with
Jack and Granville,
two friends who also
starred in *The Cruise*.

Together with Henrik:
my husband,
my manager,
my love, my life.

Filming in New York for *OK!TV* with
Nigel Havers (top). I loved New York and
went on the biggest shopping spree ever!
Nick Fiveash (below), a good friend who
has helped my career enormously.

Meeting Prince Charles at a Prince's Trust event.

On the set of my TV show, *Star for a Night*.

then turned around and repeated the performance. There had been an undeniable bond between us.

Henrik left the ship when we arrived back in Fort Lauderdale, leaving me on my own again for the New Year cruise. I went ashore on New Year's Day at Cozumel to do a little shopping from the tacky Main Street stalls. I knew that Henrik, who had been born in the cool blues and green of a northern landscape, was painting our new kitchen in the strong, burnt earth colours he loved. I decided that I would buy some of the vibrant scarlet and orange plastic shellfish wall hangings I'd seen on my numerous visits there, to spice the colour scheme up further. 'He'll probably hate them,' I told Chris, 'but the colours are fabulous.'

Shopping done, I found a payphone to call Henrik. 'Happy New Year, darling.' I said. 'What are you doing?'

'We've run out of paint for the kitchen, I have to go to the store,' he said. 'What are you doing?'

'I'm in Mexico. I've just bought a few bits and pieces for the kitchen.'

He sounded cautious, 'What kind of bits and pieces?'

I looked at Chris and winked. 'Oh, bright things, a few plastic lobsters and so on.'

As anticipated, I could tell by his reaction that Henrik wasn't convinced about my good taste. I don't think plastic was what he had in mind for our house. After a little more chatting, I said, 'I love you lots.' When Henrik said, 'I love you lots, too,' I almost dropped the phone. I said to Chris when I hung up, 'This is big! This is really serious.'

It was one of the most important moments of my life – and it was being filmed! Not realising that his voice was being recorded, he'd finally said he loved me. It was such a big thing to hear and so unexpected, I couldn't conceal my excitement. When moments like that were ultimately broadcast, everybody was watching, everyone wanted to know what was going to happen next, the viewing figures got bigger and bigger – everyone asking, 'Did you see Jane last night?'

Chris had foreseen the potential drama of life on a ship and had told me that he wanted to extend his intended one-hour documentary into a far longer series.

'Jane, we've got something very special going here. Are you up for it?'

Without missing a beat, I said, 'I'm totally at your disposable.'

Chris telephoned his bosses at the BBC back in London outlining his excitement. 'I've got something really special and out of the ordinary,' he said, asking permission to stay on longer. He managed to convince them, probably because of his already proven track record in making unusual and powerful films that pulled in the ratings. He was given carte blanche to stay on and film as much as he wanted.

We had discussed the background to life in a luxurious cruise liner in order for Chris to get an understanding of what made us all tick and react the way we did to situations that might seem different ashore. As an anthropologist, Chris of course would see things that perhaps I wouldn't. It was obvious why everyone perceives a cruise as being one of the most romantic of holidays. It is a romantic thing, there's Champagne, beautiful scenery, sunsets, the rocking of the boat. Below decks, life is rather different for the crew. The *Galaxy* was a world of its own, with every human drama going on, from illnesses to stress to fights. Everyone's there for a reason, using the ship as a retreat or to save money.

Whatever the reason, it's not easy being on a ship with a thousand other characters who you have to live with.

I told Chris, 'The *Galaxy* has a big heart and a personality of its own. That's what I like about it. But there's also a lot of scandal below stairs, a lot of feuding and fighting.'

Chris had filmed me while having a massage, talking to one of the pretty young beauticians about this. Over the years, I had seen far more of this aspect of ship life than she had, although she wasn't naive by any means. She said, 'Everything's very glamorous but behind the scenes, it isn't. Everyone goes off with other people's boyfriends and girlfriends.'

I said, 'I know, all morals go out of the window on a ship. You do things here you'd never do on land – and you end up with people that you would never look at twice on land.'

Chris's film wasn't looking for scandal. It was about dealing with difficult things, about human endeavour. He said, 'It's about striving. I want to show people's fears, triumphs and tears, their loneliness. It's not just about filming you singing and having the audience in the palm of your hand – though we're glad for you – but it's also about showing your fears when you're off to find out how you've done in the ratings. Will you be fired, or will you win? Your story is a parable of vulnerability as well as success – and look at people like Dale and Mary and Granville.'

Chris was talking about some of the others he had also filmed. There were Dale and Mary Nathan who had lost their home in England during the recession of the Eighties and were looking to save hard by working in the casino and starting over; Granville Bailey was the ever-cheerful Jamaican cocktail waiter who didn't see his family from one month to the next. His son had had a bad accident but

Granville couldn't get off the ship to see him; despite that, every night, we saw him pray with moving sincerity for his family's well-being, for the safety of the ship and for everyone aboard.

There was also the elegant Amanda Reid, who I had known first as a dancer, now the ship's social hostess. The camera captured her sadness about her mother's health and Amanda's growing acceptance that she was on her own. The hyperactive DJ from Tampa, Scotty O'Brien, was another engaging character. He thought he had finally found his dream job – only to be told that his super-energy wore everyone out and his ratings were not up to scratch. On camera, we saw his anguish when he was 'let go'. Then there was my friend Jack Failla, the gentle American dance captain, far from his home in California, who always looked for the good in everyone; there was even the Captain, Iakovos Korres, who was gloomy at first because he said things weren't as perfect as he'd like them to be. 'Passengers notice everything on the hotel side,' he told Chris. The nautical side, no – but if things aren't just right with their cabins or the cruise, they complain.'

And complain they did. Chris filmed a very vocal woman from the Home Counties who had come aboard to find she was sailing in the wrong direction and wanted a full refund. What intrigued me was the fact that she travelled everywhere with her teddy bear, Edwina (named after her heroine, Edwina Currie) who was seated at table and given full meals. And if Edwina's food wasn't up to scratch, heaven help the bemused waiters.

We also saw the larger than life professional American gambler – known as 'Stormin' Norman' – who swore at Mary Nathan because she couldn't allow him to smoke cigars at her blackjack table and because she turned down his offer of his $30,000 watch as security against a $100 bet. We did, however, also see the uncomplicated, flip-side of the coin, in a delightful middle-aged couple who had been on sixty-eight cruises and still had energy for more; and a shy young bride in a sweet short, white frock who was married on Grand Cayman.

Ashore one day on Key West, with its wide streets and Spanish-style adobe buildings, Chris filmed me having a psychic reading by a well-known clairvoyant at a place named 'Heaven'. Where my career was concerned, she told me that I would be successful if I could get over my self-limiting belief that I didn't think I deserved it. This was so spot-on that I asked my next questions: would I be happy with Henrik and would we have children and if so, would I be able to combine a career with a family?

She said, 'I see within the next three to five years there will be children. I see you're very gifted in loving – you will give those children wings. Everything is coming your way. You will have a career and a family – all you have to do is take the first step. You know the old saying, a trip of a thousand miles begins with just a single step. So, you have to take the step into your destiny.'

Chris wasn't a believer in spiritualism, although he was curious to learn more. When he heard that I had some psychic ability and read the tarot, he asked if he could sit in on a session. 'I stopped doing it,' I said. 'Something I saw on the *Century* was too upsetting.' But in the end, I decided to give Mary Nathan a reading, mostly because I didn't see anything alarming in her future. Everything was going on a fairly light-hearted note until I asked her if she suffered from some kind of sleep disorder. She looked astonished.

'How did you know!' she replied. 'For ages I had an undiagnosed sleep disorder. Once or twice a year or so, I fall asleep for two weeks and then I wake up and I'm fine until the next time.'

Mary hadn't mentioned this to anyone because obviously it wouldn't help her job prospects. Then I asked her if she suffered from some kind of rash or itchiness. She looked puzzled. 'No, not at all.'

A few days later, after Mary and Dale had spent the previous day swimming in Montego Bay, Chris walked into their cabin early one morning, to see Mary sitting dejectedly on the edge of her bunk, smothered in red spots. Dale, somewhat sensationally garbed in a mask and rubber gloves, looked concerned.

'What's up, Mary?' Chris asked.

'I have rubella,' Mary said, unable to believe it.

Chris was quite taken aback and admitted later that was when he started to wonder if perhaps there was something in clairvoyance because of the timing he'd seen for himself. There'd been several days' delay between my forecast and Mary actually waking up with the measles. With Chris shooting it exactly in the sequence it happened, when it was eventually aired, I ended up getting sackloads of letters. Chris got himself in terrible trouble with the ship's doctor because he had inadvertently crossed quarantine barriers by going into Mary's cabin and could have spread the highly infectious virus around the ship.

The paragliding episode gave Chris another slight start. He told me he thought it would be a wonderful thing if we could pull off an interview up there in that setting, talking about Yorkshire and things poignant to me.

'Have you ever paraglided before?' Chris asked.

I said, 'No, but the older I get, the more risks I enjoy taking. Let's do it.'

We hadn't been up for long when I felt waves of nausea wash over me – only, odd as this sounds, it wasn't me feeling sick, it was a transference. I said, 'Oh, my God, we've got to go down.' Although I couldn't see or hear him, I'd picked up that Jonathan was throwing up over the side of the boat pulling us far below. When he felt better and could do the sound recording, we carried on. Now I really did know what it felt like to be one of those birds floating high over dad's allotments.

A full year had now passed since I'd met Henrik. Valentine's Day came round again and I'd just finished my stint on another ship. It seemed unbelievable that only a year ago I had been sobbing my heart out, so depressed that I'd written a letter of resignation. Chris and I hugged each other when we parted, in order for him to fly back to England with all his tapes and a long edit ahead of him.

'When do you think it will be ready?' I said.

` 'Not for some months. In any case, I was hoping that you and Henrik would come to England to do some taping in Yorkshire. I'd like to film your mum if she's agreeable.'

We left it that Chris would contact us and I rushed off to the car where Henrik was waiting for me as he used to do the previous year.

'I can't believe I'm going home at last!' I said.

Henrik smiled, 'I hope you like it, Jane, everything's done, the house is painted, the furniture's been delivered.'

As we walked in, Henrik said, 'I have a surprise for you.'

Well, I'd heard that before and always been blown away. I

couldn't think what it could possibly be. I'd seen the house, a large, ranch-style bungalow, go up – but I hadn't seen it decorated and furnished. From the time I walked in through the front door, I was saying, 'Oh, my God!' almost every moment as something new revealed itself. Never in a million years did I think I'd have a house like this.

The whole place was so full of colour and vitality it was like being inside a painting by Van Gogh. Perhaps because of his cold northern roots, Henrik can't stand white, it reminds him of hospitals. He'd gone the other way, choosing rich burnt earth colours, mustard yellows and burnt siennas, bright oranges and oxblood reds and Mexican tiled floors throughout. Our bedroom was old colonial-style, with burnt orange walls and rustic tiles. There was a massive four-poster bed and heavy furniture with solid brass fittings. The kitchen was pumpkin yellow with blond waxed wood surfaces and cupboards.

'Wow!' I said, looking around. An imp made me continue, 'I can see just the spot for my red lobsters to hang.'

Henrik smiled. He knew me well enough not to be drawn by this. I walked across and looked out of the window and drew my breath. The kitchen looked out on a lake surrounded by palm trees, the skies were bright blue; it was unbelievable that this Yorkshire lass who'd spent most of her life looking out on a scrappy backyard with a brick khazi and a lean-to made of junk, should be looking out on a view like this.

'Come and see,' Henrik said.

We walked through into the lounge which had a classy Italian look, with magnolia walls and pale peachy drapes and furnishings. But I only had eyes for a seven-foot concert grand, over by the huge picture windows.

'Oh, my *God*!' I said, letting out my breath in a rush.

'Do you like it?' Henrik said.

But I couldn't speak. I sat on the piano stool and sobbed.

A few days later, we flew to England so that Chris could round off the series by showing us going home to meet the mother I had talked of so constantly on the cruise.

'People will feel they know her, Jane, so they'll want to see her at the end,' Chris told me.

I didn't need an excuse to go home, but if one dropped into my lap, I was ready to grab it. Mostly, I was really looking forward to showing Henrik off to my family. Chris met us at Manchester Airport and we drove up the M62 in the rain, Henrik feeling the cold in a brown leather bomber jacket and a Hawaiian shirt, and me looking distinctly Florida in a white linen jacket and the new hairdo I'd had done on the ship. The house looked smaller than I remembered, the rainy streets duller and shabbier – but nothing mattered when I saw Mum's warm, smiling face and outstretched arms. Then we were in the house and Tony was there with Wendy and Katie and Janet with her husband, Gary.

Ten minutes later, Henrik was eating one of Mum's large bacon butties washed down with cups of tea. (Mum had even bought some Danish blue cheese for Henrik, although she doesn't like it.) In the cramped little kitchen while everyone laughed and chatted in the living room, I whispered to Mum – 'Well, what do you think?'

'Perfect,' she said, 'he's just right.'

A CORPORATE WIFE

A short week later, Henrik and I returned to Florida, where I was to spend the next six months practising the art of being a corporate wife to Henrik. I use the term 'wife' loosely because we weren't married. However, he needed someone to act as his hostess, particularly for business dinners, which I was delighted to do – anything that kept me in the frame. And even though marriage hadn't been mentioned, we had discussed having a family. 'I know I'd make a wonderful mum,' I had said, my face softening.

'Yes, you would,' Henrik agreed. 'But I think we should get to know each other properly first. Children are a big commitment.'

Word had spread that our interior decoration was like something from *Homes and Gardens* magazine, and we had the neighbours from all over coming round to see what 'the Europeans', as they called us, had done. Everything was Henrik's taste, but not backward in wallowing in his reflected glory, I invited Ken, Henrik's business partner, to dinner. I made chicken fricassee with a white onion and mustard sauce, served with Henrik's favourite savoury rice. Our dining room was very elegant, with a real Italian white marble table and the most beautiful contemporary chandelier. I set the table, lit the candles and stepped back to admire it.

During the meal, they were talking business when Ken stopped and said, 'This is really good...' and carried on talking.

I smiled to myself. Then he stopped again and said, 'No, this is really, really good. In fact, you should stay. Everyone has noticed how much Henrik has mellowed under your influence, Jane.'

If it seemed that Ken didn't seem to realise that I had been around a while, it was because Henrik hadn't got around to telling the people at the office about me until I casually dropped by one day to see him. Shelley, the secretary, didn't know what I was talking about when I said I was Henrik's girlfriend. It emerged that after he had first met me on the *Century* and had called in to say he needed to stay on board longer, Shelley had joked, 'Have you got a girlfriend out there or what?' There was a long silence and she'd thought, 'Oh God, I've just put my foot in it with my boss!'

When I tackled Henrik about why he hadn't mentioned me, he said, 'Of course I mentioned you. I just kept it very low-profile; I didn't brag, "I've met this singer". Think how embarrassing if it didn't last.'

'My love, you'd better believe it – this is going to last,' I said.

After that first meal with Ken, I had more confidence and invited some of Henrik's friends round to a small house-warming. I made one of Henrik's favourite dishes, pork steaks in parsley sauce, and I marinated a selection of meats ready for the barbecue and put out big bowls of salad with my special mayonnaise, made with lashings of fresh garlic, and warm French bread. One of the women said, 'How did you do this? I can never invite you back, this is all so good.' To me, it seemed so simple; but then, I remembered how I used to look at Janet and think, 'How does she do that?' When you start doing it yourself, it becomes easy. Also, I think it helps that I'm organised and quite artistic, I will plan a meal like a military campaign and, with everything under control, I can relax and enjoy it.

Word spread that I always cooked fresh food, not frozen or from a packet, and there was always plenty of everything. People started dropping by unannounced; some nights we had six or seven for dinner. I'd say, 'No problem, I'll put another chop on,' and it was done. It was all worth it when Henrik told me that I was a good homemaker.

'I know, lovey,' I said, 'it runs in the family, like Mum's bacon butties.'

He roared with laughter. The entire week we had been in Wakefield, Mum had plied him with so much food – particularly her famous butties, which had grown bigger, higher and fatter in ratio with his appreciation of them. If we hadn't left when we did, I think Henrik would have been trying to sink his teeth into the buttie equivalent of one of Desperate Dan's cow pies! Mum's eased off a little now, bless her heart, and gives him daintier morsels.

When I first met Henrik, we both had salty tales to relate to each other, of storms and freak waves and basking whales. When he had first gone to sea as first engineer on an oil tanker, he had sailed regularly over the top of the world, from Singapore or Hong Kong to Anchorage in Alaska, experiencing all that extreme Arctic conditions could throw at them, from icebergs and ice sheets to gales that were so severe they couldn't be recorded. But it was his stories of pirates in the South China Seas that fascinated me the most. I'd not even been aware that pirates still existed and here was a man whose ship had actually been boarded by them on several occasions.

'Did they make you walk the plank?' I teased.

'It's no joke,' Henrik said seriously, 'people have been murdered.'

One hot night at the end of July 1997, as we sat out on the patio of our house, watching the fireflies flashing their entrancing little signals to each other, Henrik said, 'I have to go to Singapore for a couple of months, Jane. Would you like to come?'

'Oh yes, I'd love to!' I said at once, fantasising about the images I had from old films of this tropical island at the tip of Malaysia; a rough-and-ready port of rickshaws, opium dens, pirates and pearl luggers. A place where you could drink gin slings under languorous ceiling fans at Raffles Hotel and walk along quays where three-masted merchant ships had once berthed. Henrik filled me in with some history. According to legend, he said, a Sumatran prince had encountered a lion when he came ashore for water, and so founded Singapura, or 'Lion City'. Lions have never roamed there, so he must have seen a tiger, some of which are still found in the jungly heart of the island. By the time Sir Stamford Raffles sailed by in 1819 and decided it was a place of military importance between China and India, there was nothing left of the mythical Lion City – and Raffles founded his own rakish port on the swampy river.

Rudyard Kipling once said, 'When in Singapore, feed at Raffles'. One of the last grand hotels of the East, it was a place I had always wanted to stay in. As well as Kipling, people like Somerset Maugham, Noël Coward and Ava Gardner had all stayed there and had suites named in their honour. But, at a thousand dollars a night, we decided that booking a double room would do.

A week later, we were there. With wide, breezy verandas, lush tropical gardens and, of course, gin slings in tall, misted glasses tinkling with ice cubes, it was like stepping into a world where time has stood still.

'I could live like this for ever,' I said, slowly sipping my drink after a refreshing shower. I spoke before I realised that Singapore is on the Equator, and while it is not always baking hot, there are frequent violent thunderstorms, after which the humidity hits you like a soggy wet towel. But for that first evening at least I was lulled into a sense of bliss by a combination of air conditioning, gin slings and a view of sampans illuminated by lanterns poling across the darkened river.

Henrik had arranged that for the next two months we would rent a spacious apartment from a colleague, at a place called Spanish Village, off Holland Road. As its name suggested, it looked very Spanish, with stuccoed walls and cool tiled floors. Property prices are sky-high in Singapore, and even though the complex had a massive swimming pool and beautiful tennis courts, when I was told how much the apartment was worth, I couldn't believe it. Life in the apartment was like a camping expedition. I had my little washer (each morning I'd hang the clothes out of the window to dry). I had a little microwave combination oven that I had no idea how to use properly – I'd switch it on and hope for the best when cooking meals. As I slaved away over the wash tub and the hot stove, I thought, 'I bet he's really glad he's taken me – a bit of domesticity, his clothes washed and ironed!'

I'd go shopping at the market across the road and instantly

be overwhelmed by the potent, rotting stink of overripe jackfruit, a small greeny fruit that looks like a pineapple. It is a smell that still haunts me, bringing back instant memories of Singapore. Long days passed in humid heat. My chores over early, I went swimming, read all my books, listened to my CDs. I was bored silly.

Henrik was away for long hours, driving to Malaysia; in fact, he went so often, his passport was stamped full and he had to get a new one. When I went with him, I was fascinated by the wild hilly interior of Singapore, the exotic tropical trees and plants and the quick flashes of colourful birds I saw skimming through the branches. The Causeway, which is half an hour across the island from the city, has quite a history. It was blown up by the Japanese during World War Two when they invaded, crossing quickly and unexpectedly from the rear – when all the defences were facing out to sea on the opposite side of the island where the city and docks were. J. G. Ballard's wonderful novel, *Empire of the Sun*, relates his adventures as a small boy during and after the fall of Singapore. Once over the Causeway and on to the long peninsula of Malaysia, the road to Kuala Lumpur sweeps through lush, tropical forests with, here and there, stalls by the side of the road that sell local fruit and produce.

Gradually, I started to explore my wider surroundings. Much of Singapore is like the City of London's modernistic Lloyds' building, where the old has been razed to make way for the new. There's very little of the old districts left, but I hunted them down, wanting to experience the authentic flavour of the East. In this incredible multicultural city, everywhere seems to be named after somewhere else in the world. The crowded streets of Chinatown, where fortune-tellers, calligraphers, incense-sellers, chop- (a type of stamp) makers and temple worshippers jostled for space, gave way to Little India, with its curry stalls and glittery Temple of One Thousand Lights, which gave way in turn to Arab Street, a traditional textile centre where I bought batiks from Indonesia, silks from China, sarongs from Malaya and rattan goods from Burma.

Henrik raised his eyebrows when he saw the amount of shopping I'd achieved in a few days. 'I'll need to hire a freighter to take that lot home,' he said. 'Jane, we're going to be here for two months, you should slow down a little.'

'But it's so cheap, and I can have this silk made into some wonderful outfits for work, so it's an investment,' I said.

'Yes, you're right,' was all he said.

He could have said, with accuracy,' But darling, you don't work any more. You haven't worked for months, and have no plans for returning,' – but he didn't. It was his good humour and what he didn't say that made me realise that I was a kept woman – and loving it, or so I thought.

I was delighted when one day I found Oxo cubes in a shop in Tangling Mall and bought loads for my shepherds pies and beef stews. Moving on through the warren of shops, I was browsing for opera and classical music, when I heard two English girls talking beside me. I turned around and said, 'By heck, that's not from around here, is it?'

They gave little shrieks and even though we had never met before, we all clutched each other in delight. They introduced themselves as Wendy and Victoria, expats, whose husbands worked in Singapore. I said, 'I'm so excited, I've found Oxo cubes!'

They said, 'Oh yes, it's quite English out here. And Chinese – and Indian – and Malaysian!' We all laughed. Vicky said, 'Come on, let's go and have coffee and a good gossip.'

Over coffee, we compared notes and learned that we were all ladies of leisure. I told them about coming from the States, that my partner had a marine business based in Florida and he was opening a subsidiary company in Singapore. I didn't realise how grand that must have sounded to them, because, when I said I was a singer, they took it with a pinch of salt.

I returned to the apartment with a spring in my step, feeling that I now had some friends to meet up with. I'd already bought some Andrea Bocelli CDs; now I listened to them again and, even though I didn't have an instrument to work out the chords, I felt inspired enough by the anthem-feel of his music to write my own songs. A little later, after Vicky and Wendy discovered that I really could sing (I'll get to that), I told them that I was also writing some songs and invited them to the apartment for lunch. I was halfway through writing a song at the time that I'd called 'Winner' and I read them the lyrics aloud, which told of love and survival, perhaps describing how I felt about emotional rather than financial success.

Vicky said, 'That's fantastic, Jane. We're really honoured that you've shared that with us early in the creative process.'

I was very pleased with the way these new songs worked, not having the faintest idea that one day in the future I would actually be recording them on major labels – or that I would be singing them at the Albert Hall and the London Palladium. But all that was to come.

Vicky and I bonded really well and agreed to meet again, even though she lived on the other side of town. She called me and we went out the next day. I was surprised to find how familiar she was with MRT, the subway system; hopping on and off so casually, she made it look easy. A midwife, she seemed to know everything, lending me books on subjects I would never have thought of reading about.

Having lunch in McDonalds, I was shocked to see a very old Chinese woman who said she was eighty-five, doing hard, menial tasks. 'She's so old!' I said. Vicky told me that there were no pensions in the East. If their families didn't look after the old and incapacitated, they had to work. When I told Henrik later about the old woman, he said, 'That's why you've got to have fifteen kids out here – it's the Third World pension scheme. It's why so many of them go to sea on ships – to escape poverty and to send home the bacon.'

One day, Vicky suggested we meet another friend of hers over coffee. She said, 'You'll get on really well with each other.'

As predicted, Bea, a psychologist, and I bonded at once, in no time chatting and giggling at ninety miles an hour like a couple of teenagers. Vicky and Bea showed me the best places to shop, and we'd meet up almost every day. One afternoon, Bea and I went to a cinema where *Paradise Road* was showing, a film that showed how bad the Japanese army was to the English during the occupation. The only two English faces in a sea of Singaporeans, we slowly slid down our seats and then crept out. Outside, we leaned against a wall, killing ourselves with laughter. Small things, but it shows what fun we had, how frivolous we always were when together.

Drinking tea in an English café, Bea introduced us to two men, one from Huddersfield, had a boyfriend from Singapore, and offered to show us the bits of Singapore that no Westerner ever really got to see. I felt almost exuberant, shoes off, sitting cross-legged in an authentic Chinese tea shop, drinking green tea from little eggshell cups. To me it was marvellous that an English girl from Yorkshire should be halfway around the world, making friends and absorbing local culture and traditions. This included going to see the stone lions on the island of Sentosa, which Henrik had told me about, as well as visiting Haw Par Villa, an incredibly tacky Chinese mythological theme park, and the beautiful Jurong Bird Park.

As I confessed to my new friends, without their companionship I'd have been in danger of spending my time ironing Henrik's shirts and reading my books! And I did have a wonderful time during our weeks of exploration – apart from the food poisoning I got three times from eating shellfish from the harbour: a small price to pay for tasting an incredible range of dishes I would never otherwise have got the chance to do.

With Henrik usually away until very late, Vicky, Bea and I arranged one night to meet up at a nightclub where the girls knew the manager. I hadn't been dancing or clubbing since the cruise days, so was looking forward to letting my hair down. I'd bought four beautiful silk evening frocks, which in any other part of the world would have been wildly expensive, but here were very reasonably priced. Even so, I did feel a little flicker of guilt because my own money had run out long ago and it was Henrik's I was spending, though he never complained. Putting my guilt to one side, I slipped into one of the new dresses, admiring the way I looked in the mirror before leaving for the club.

I was a little late and the girls were already there having fun. We drank a lot of Bacardi and coke (something I don't even like!) The band was good, and we were on the floor for every dance when, growing ever louder, Bea shouted out, 'My mate's a singer!'

The lead singer called from the stage, 'Come up here then and give us a song.'

I was thinking, 'Bloody hell! What do I do?' when everyone pushed me up with the band and started clapping. I asked, 'Do you know, "I Will Survive"?' A microphone was stuck in my hand and off we went. Automatically, my years of training put me into professional mode. I do remember that there was a brilliant PA system and the club was filled with rowdy revellers all having a good time. In fact it was only because I had really missed singing that I continued. I was singing for me, I was singing for all my dreams and all my hopes, lost in my own world. That little stage and the noisy club receded as I sang my heart out, my voice filling the room.

Everyone got up and started dancing as I sang on. When I stopped and stood in the spotlight, my arms embracing the audience, the place went ballistic, and everyone started screaming, 'Do you know this song – do you know that one?' I was so tipsy that I couldn't think of any of my usual numbers, so I did Chaka Khan's 'Aint Nobody'. When I returned to our table, Bea and Vicky were stunned. 'We didn't think you meant it,' Vicky said, 'but you weren't bullshitting – you can really sing, can't you?'

We had the best night I can remember in ages. We didn't pay for a drink after that – as if we needed any more! They even offered me a job, which I declined. I was still on such a high when I returned to the apartment towards dawn, where Henrik was asleep in our big bed, that I insisted on waking him up to recount every detail, telling him how much fun I'd had, and how I missed singing. I don't think I realised just how exhilarated I sounded because he didn't say very much. He'd not seen me like that before. The next day, he was very introspective. I had absolutely no idea at all, because he disguised it so well, that he thought he was holding me back from doing what I loved best: singing. Henrik had spent the night thinking of a way to let me return to work.

'What is it, love?' I asked him.

'I've had a shock, Jane,' he told me. 'We're skint. You have to go back to work – we need the money.'

I slumped into a rattan chair, feeling the draught from the ceiling fan overhead and stared at him. 'Of course I'll help!' I cried, shame flooding me. 'Oh, sweetheart, I've been going on and on talking about myself, when you must have been feeling terrible.' Growing guiltier by the minute, I said, 'I bought four really expensive frocks yesterday – I've worn one, but I can take the others back. We'll go back home and...' Another thought struck me. 'I don't know if I can make enough money to pay for the house – will you have to sell it?'

'I don't know,' Henrik said, sounding quite depressed. 'Right now, anything will help.'

'I'll go back to work at once,' I vowed. 'You've been keeping me for a year, paying all the bills, now it's my turn. I never thought – I've been so selfish, but I will make it up to you,' I promised.

'Are you sure you don't mind?'

Like Henrik, I disguised it well. 'Oh, no! I love singing and I've really missed it,' I said, making myself sound as enthusiastic and convincing as possible.

We were still so unsure of each other in those early days that we kept our true feelings hidden. I thought that Henrik wanted me to be his 'housewife' and didn't want me to work, while he thought I was pretending I didn't want to work to please him. Between the two of us, we set off on a path of mutual pretence, thinking each was pleasing the other. It was just like something from a Shakespeare play!

As soon as we returned to Florida, I packed a few things and flew home to Wakefield. I didn't want to go back to the clubs, but all the way on the plane, all I could hear was Henrik's voice in my head, saying, 'I can't afford to pay for everything with the business so stretched'. He'd been paying all my bills in England while I was out buying frocks and spending money like it was going out of fashion.

When I arrived, Mum said, 'What on earth is wrong, Jane?'

I said, 'I can't even begin to explain how badly I feel. I have abused Henrik's money for a whole year and not even questioned it. How selfish can I be?'

Mum looked puzzled. 'I don't think it's that bad,' she said. 'Are you sure Henrik meant that?'

I said, 'Of course I'm sure. His words are engraved on my conscience.'

What I didn't know was that Henrik's story, made up on the spur of the moment, in fact was a big white lie. He'd previously had one or two conversations in Florida on the phone with my mother, in which she'd expressed her sense of regret that I appeared to be abandoning my career, something I'd worked so hard for so long to achieve. 'She was a headliner on that last cruise,' Mum told Henrik, 'I know something exciting is about to happen. She has to get back to work for her own self-esteem.'

When Henrik had seen my delirious reaction after that night in the club in Singapore, he thought that my career was more important to me than I was letting on – that I had dumped it to be with him. In fact his business was booming but, heroically, he denied it, putting himself in a bad light, seeing this as the only way to get me back to doing what I loved best – singing.

Although I concealed it from Henrik when I flew out of

Miami, I felt my heart was breaking. I didn't want to leave our lovely home in Florida, the sunshine and a way of life I enjoyed. I didn't want to be back in Silcoates Street, back in the clubs where I'd started. I'd made a conscious decision to leave it all behind, to sell up my life and move on. I'd told everybody in Wakefield that I was leaving to go to America to be with my love – and here I was back where I'd left. Some people sneered, 'Oh, so she's failed, has she? She can't have been much good.'

I had to eat my words. I rang an agent in Manchester who I'd worked through before, who welcomed me back with open arms. I didn't need my own PA system because the clubs in Manchester – which are always packed out with people – have the best house equipment and I have often wondered why other clubs don't follow their lead; it is quite pointless lugging heavy equipment around. Henrik bought me a car, and I still had a closet full of my trademark posh frocks and my high-heels. I was ready to work, doing something I did not want to do – and hating it.

Now I had to run the gamut of a new lot of people in Manchester, saying, 'We thought you'd given up?' – and I was saying, 'Well I'm over here because I've got a TV show coming up.' – 'What are you back in Manchester for then on a hundred and fifty quid a night?' they said, obviously thinking the TV thing was just a cover-up story. But of course I thought I still had to pay my mortgage, I still had to earn the money I thought Henrik hadn't got. I was out there saving like mad, trying to get some money together.

Night after night, I got in my car and drove to Manchester. I was filled with such despair that one evening, for the second time in my life, I lost my voice. I apologised to everybody in the club, saying to the audience, 'I'm so sorry ladies and gentlemen, but my voice has gone. I promise you I'll come back and do a free night for you – I'm so sorry.' The people in that club were so nice, saying that they understood. I was in tears as I drove back home.

The next day, I saw a throat specialist. She said, 'I think you should see a psychiatrist, Jane. There's nothing physically wrong with your throat – it's all in your head.'

I was angry with life and absolutely disgusted by her words. I thought she had to be hiding the truth from me – that there was something drastically wrong with my throat that she wasn't telling me about. I was in such a turmoil that I went home and sobbed and ranted to my mother, 'Half of me wants to sing, the other half wants to be a wife and a mum!'

Mum said, 'If you really want to have a family that badly, Jane, then that's what you must do.'

I was in such a state that at once I went the other way. 'I don't know anything about children!' I wailed. 'I've never had anything to do with them, how can I handle all that? At least I know how to sing.'

Mum lost her patience and shouted at me, really letting me have it. 'For God's sake, Jane, you make me sick! Make up your mind! You want this, you want that – you don't want this, you don't want that. It's all me, me, me!'

Shocked, I stared at her. Her voice softened. 'I know you're miserable, pet, but you've got to stop all this nonsense. You're like a butterfly dithering around and, frankly, driving me crazy. Life isn't a bunch of flowers that you can choose. Life is bloody hard and even the richest amongst us have hard decisions to make.'

Mum and I sat down and talked it through. Some years ago she had put the fear of God into me because she'd said, 'You've got a God-given gift – if you don't use it, you'll lose it.'

I reminded her of that and said, 'When I came back and I couldn't sing I thought it was retribution. I thought: God's taken it away because I'm not using it, it's my own fault because I've turned my back on my career.'

Mum shook her head, 'Lovey, I never meant to scare you! All your life you have had this insecurity. You've needed a little push – and I've seen how, once you are out there singing, you love it. Afterwards, you're on a real high. I believe in you and know you were born to sing – but you also have so much love in you, you'd make a wonderful mum. There's no reason why you can't do both when the time is right. But you must decide what you want – can't you sing in America and have a family? Plenty of women do.'

Suddenly, my head cleared. Mum was right! The dilemma was that I couldn't sing in the States because I didn't have a Green Card. *That* was why I was back here in Yorkshire.

I rushed to the phone and called Henrik. 'I'm coming back!' I said. 'We have to talk. I need a Green Card – can you start the ball rolling?'

Miraculously, my singing voice returned. I completed the bookings I had for that month and, late in September, I returned to Florida for two weeks to have a long-overdue heart-to-heart talk with Henrik about the future.

The first thing I had on my mind was the bizarre story Henrik had told me about his business problems when I had seen no sign of trouble at all. When I tackled him about it, he admitted that it wasn't true.

'Then why did you tell me such a cock-and-bull story?' I exploded.

'It was what I saw that night in Singapore,' Henrik said.

'You normally get excited when you sing – but that night you were radiant. I said to myself: "Bloody hell! This must be good!" You were really on a high, and I thought we must do something drastic to sustain this.'

'Yes, it was drastic,' I said. 'Very drastic. I became ill – I lost my voice. You have no idea what it was like.'

'I didn't know that would happen – I thought you would be happy going back to the work you loved. I thought I was the one making the sacrifice. God, Jane, I'm so sorry.'

We continued to discuss it long into the night. We'd been told by Chris Terrill that *The Cruise* was going to come out in the autumn, quite imminently, we thought. If it came out and people saw it, perhaps I would get bigger bookings. If it was shown in America, as we believed, then perhaps it would lead to the offer of work there.

'One of the points you have to consider,' Henrik said, 'is that if *The Cruise* does well, by going back to the clubs and getting into singing again, you'll be ready. Your voice won't be rusty.'

'I almost had no voice at all!' I said.

But I realised what he was getting at. After a year away, I could never just pick up and continue where I'd left off. All those months while I'd been running our house in Plantation, I'd only tinkled on the piano, writing a little music, but not putting any effort into it. Mostly, I had lounged around the pool, gone shopping or watched the telly.

Some time ago, Gran had told me that Broadway was the key to the door of a dazzling future that would be mine if I grasped the nettle. Henrik had already approached a lawyer to put my Green Card application in motion. While it was being processed, I would return to England to continue with my bookings in the Manchester clubs – and, hopefully, by then *The Cruise* would be out and we'd consider any options at that stage.

On my last day in Florida, before Henrik left for work in the morning, Valerie, my American lawyer, telephoned to ask if I was planning on getting married in the near future. When I asked why, she said that my application process would be harder to get in that case because I'd have no status as Henrik's wife. Immigration would almost certainly think that I was marrying him just to get a Card, and my application would be rejected. 'You're not even thinking about it, are you?' she asked.

I looked at Henrik and repeated, 'We're not thinking of getting married, are we?'

Very firmly, he said, 'No!'

I couldn't help myself: I was so hurt, I burst into tears after he had left for work. I thought, 'He really doesn't want to get married after all. This is the perfect excuse.' Dismally, I wondered if I didn't get a Green Card, was this to be my life in the future: working in England and snatching brief interludes with the man I loved? I didn't want to spend my last evening miserable, so I tried to pull myself together by having a cooling swim.

As I lay on my back and gazed up at the sky, dotted with those huge puffy clouds that often come in from the sea in the afternoon, I planned the menu for dinner that evening. Because of the late summer heat, we'd been eating a lot of salads, but this was my last day, tomorrow I was to fly home and I wanted everything to be special. I know that shepherd's pie isn't very exotic but, if well made, it can be sensational. It was one of the very first dishes I had ever cooked for Henrik and he'd said it was the best thing he'd ever tasted, so I decided I'd make it for that evening.

It might sound an odd choice for a special meal but on the cruise liners, where there were at least a hundred and forty different items on the menu each day, from lobster to Beluga caviar, the British crew members couldn't wait to go ashore at Bermuda where there was an English pub that served sausages and mash or baked beans on toast! I can even remember waking up in the middle of the night, moored off some palm-fringed beach with the moon making a silver path across the water, dreaming of Mum's meat pie with cabbage and gravy. It's true that too much luxury can pall and you crave the simple things in life. Although I'm speaking as someone who grew up working class, I don't know if my taste would have been any different if I'd been born rich.

As I climbed out of the pool and picked up my towel, I knew such trivial thoughts were concealing the unbearable sadness I carried like a heavy stone inside. Was I mad to be returning to a bleak English winter when I could stay here in the sun with Henrik? I felt as if I was being torn in two because my instinct told me to go and my heart was telling me to stay. Unhappy and confused, I walked into the house and slipped on a shift dress. In the kitchen, as I assembled the ingredients for supper, I caught sight of my plastic marine tableau and smiled.

I remembered how Henrik had wanted the kitchen kept plain and simple and how he had sounded quite alarmed when I'd told him I'd bought a large assortment of plastic shellfish in Mexico. I loved my three-foot red lobster with that gleam in his eye and the little spotted crab draped with fake seaweed and coral. Along with a lot of interesting bits of driftwood from the beach, I'd hung everything up and thought it looked rather good, lending a nice touch of humour to the room. 'What do you think?' I'd asked Henrik at the time, stepping back to admire my work.

'Well, you live here too, it's your home as well,' he'd said enigmatically.

I had known he was being polite about the decoration but, on a different level, his words had thrilled me, though I wasn't entirely sure then what he'd meant. Perhaps I worried too much. We were very happy and Henrik never asked anything of me – in fact, so far, our relationship was very one-sided, with him giving me everything and me content to grab with both hands. But I didn't want to be a mistress – I wanted to be a wife.

I stood stock still. 'My God,' I thought, 'you're just insecure, that's what the problem is – that's always been the problem, and until it's resolved, it will never go away.'

I cranked up the air conditioner to keep the kitchen extra-cool while I cooked. I had made the shepherd's pie and put it in the oven when, at lunchtime, Henrik came in from the patio at the back of the house. I hadn't heard his car because the music I was playing on the CD really was very loud.

'Something smells good,' he said.

'I'm cooking shepherd's pie for dinner,' I replied, turning down the music system. As usual, whenever I saw him, my heart did a somersault. I'd seen a documentary about love and it said that in many cases it hurts so much because it's a compulsive addiction fuelled by hormones – well that was me, addicted!

It was unusual for Henrik to come back in the middle of the day and I wondered what was up. 'Is everything all right?' I asked.

'Sure, I just forgot something,' he said.

He stood at the counter watching me finish my preparations for the meal. I thought there was something odd about his expression. He was looking at me very intently. Our gaze locked. I felt breathless, like I do before I go on stage – excited but sick. It was like that moment in time when I walked down the stairs on the ship when I first saw Henrik at the bar.

'I really do love this man,' I thought, in a great wave of tenderness.

'So, will you marry me?' he said, just like that.

I drew in my breath sharply. 'Yes,' I said in a rush, feeling faint.

In the other room the CD switched to Bryan Adams singing the theme song from *Robin Hood, Prince of Thieves*, '(Everything I Do I Do It) For You', a song that always gave me goose bumps. It described exactly the way I felt for Henrik, a love so intense that it actually hurt.

'What brought this on so suddenly?' I asked, as always making a joke at my most emotional moments.

'It's not been sudden,' Henrik said seriously. 'It's been on my mind for some time. Marriage is a big commitment, Jane, I wanted to be sure that it was what we both wanted – that we could live together for the rest of our lives. These past two years have shown me that we can.'

GOING BALLISTIC

Chris Terrill was very good about keeping us informed over what was happening with the series. We already knew that it had been extended to twelve half-hour episodes, and were expecting it to be broadcast some time in October, late at night. I hoped that someone might see it and something might come of it. When your career has been spent in northern clubs and adrift at sea, any opportunity, however remote, is worth waiting for. But time had passed; October, November and we were into December and still we'd heard nothing.

But now I had other far more exciting things on my mind – my wedding. We planned an early Spring ceremony after I'd finished my last bookings in the clubs, which ran through to the end of January. Henrik flew in on December 24th to spend his first Christmas in Yorkshire. It was very cold, with sleet lashing over the moors, the car rocking in the high wind as we drove home to Silcoates Street from Manchester Airport. He peered through the windscreen and said, 'The moors would be spectacular if I could see them – but I think I would rather be in Florida with you.'

'So would I, love,' I said, 'but we'll be back there soon, planning our wedding.'

We'd discussed the matter of the Green Card and, as is so

often the case when you're madly in love, it no longer seemed as important as getting married. I knew which certificate I would rather have and I was sure that, somehow, things would work out. That night, Henrik came to one of my shows in Manchester. It was the first time he'd seen me singing in my native environment, a club, and the first time with a 'real' audience, not a captive one on a ship where I happened to be the entertainment for that night. The place was packed and he managed to squeeze in at the bar. Afterwards, he said, 'You were sensational, Jane. You need a larger stage.'

That struck me as funny because the stage was about as small as it could be. 'Oh, I know, ducks, we could all do with a larger stage,' I said flippantly – but I did know what he meant.

We got in after one o'clock in the morning. I gave Henrik his Christmas presents – probably because I couldn't wait to see what he'd got for me! It was all a bit of a culture shock for him. In Denmark, presents are handed out on the night of Christmas Eve, after a big family dinner, not on Christmas Day. Henrik was jet-lagged and ready for bed. The last thing he wanted was to rip open a gaily-wrapped package and dance around the Christmas tree. 'Can't we do this tomorrow, Jane? It doesn't feel like Christmas yet,' he said yawning.

I said, 'This is the life of a singer, always working when other people have fun. You'd better get used to it, my love.'

I watched as Henrik unwrapped my gifts: a pair of socks, a shirt and some aftershave. He kissed me, then started to laugh, holding up the socks. 'You kept me up for these?' he said.

'It's the thought that counts,' I said, 'Don't you like them?'

'Yes, of course, they're wonderful socks!' Henrick replied.

I was still giggling as I unwrapped the slim package he

handed to me. Inside was a red leather box. My eyes widened as I opened it and saw an exquisite diamond necklace. 'Oh, my God!' I gasped.

'Do you like it?' Henrik asked.

'I don't think I'll be taking it off this Christmas,' I said, getting Henrik to help fasten it around my neck. I went to the mirror and stared at my reflection. The diamonds sparkled brilliantly, reflecting the pointed lights from the Christmas tree. 'Bah gum, lad,' I said. 'This beats a pair of socks any day'.

Apart from the fun we had exchanging gifts, the thing Henrik remembered most about that Christmas were the brace of ducks. Usually the whole family, some dozen of us, had always crowded into Silcoates Street for a feast that started at noon and segued to tea time, when we removed the turkey and the ham and brought out the Christmas cake, mince pies and sherry trifle. That year, however, we went over to Janet's for dinner – a break with tradition because her house was posher than ours.

Beforehand, Janet and I had discussed what we could do to make Henrik's Christmas as nice as possible. I told Janet that in Denmark they ate duck, not turkey. Unfortunately, I didn't know that traditionally they cooked them whole, on the bone, golden-skinned and crispy. Janet had achieved wonders in decorating her house, the table looked festive with candles, and Christmassy centre-pieces all on white linen. The ducks were beautifully prepared; but boned! I could see Henrik's face as these two peculiarly shaped objects were triumphantly brought out and sliced straight through in thick slices, stuffing and all; but he ate his portion manfully. On the way home, he said, 'However nice something is, it's not the same if it's not what you expect.'

'Never mind,' I said, 'I'm sure you'll get a proper Danish duck at your Mum's next week.'

Now that we were officially engaged, Henrik was taking me to Denmark for New Year 1998 to meet the rest of his family. I'd been preparing for the moment since October, as soon as I had returned from Florida, by taking a course in Danish at Leeds University, really eager to make an impression. I knew none of the Brixens spoke English and as my family are always telling me, I can chat the wind up.

Shortly before we left, Chris telephoned me to say that the BBC publicity machine wanted me to do some interviews. Could I cut short my trip to Denmark?

'What's it all about, Chris?' I asked him.

He said, 'The powers that be have seen the programmes now and have got excited. They say it's pure escapist television. They've made big plans to bring the series out early in January, because people are sick of winter by then and dreaming of holidays in the sun.'

'That's great!' I said, relieved that at last things seemed to be happening. I asked Henrik and he agreed at once that we would return early.

I loved it in Denmark, absolutely loved it. The village of Simmelkaer was very small, set in the middle of Jutland, west of Copenhagen, in flat countryside with fields all around. When Henrik mentioned that the population was about three hundred, I said, 'What do you do round here for entertainment – watch the traffic lights change?' He said, 'We haven't got any traffic lights.' I couldn't stop laughing, he started laughing and since laughter is so infectious, even though they couldn't understand the joke, the family started laughing too.

The ice was broken, even if they did think I was a bit touched in the head.

Henrik's father worked in a local carpet factory. His mother, he said, was the hairdresser. I repeated, 'Oh, a hairdresser.' – He said, 'No – *the* hairdresser – the only one. There used to be three,' he mused, 'I don't know what happened to the others.'

'Don't tell me – she undercut them,' I said. It took half a second before Henrik got it; we were so close that our humour needed just a match to the blue paper and it was flaring

Naturally, everybody wanted to know about me. Casually, Henrik mentioned, 'She sings,' and that was it. I could have sung in a church choir as far as they were concerned, but whatever I did, they were impressed that I'd taken the trouble to learn their language. Although I wasn't that proficient yet, at least we could communicate. I was already good friends with Henrik's mother and father, Ruth and Ove. Now I met Ruth's mother, Mor-mor (which means 'mother's mother') who had been very close to Henrik in his childhood, and also met his brothers, Palle and Flemming, their wives and also the aunties. I had thought that, at over six-foot, Henrik was tall – but he was the smallest out of the three sons. The parents, too, were giants. My eyes would meet their stomachs and just rise on and on up.

I said to the brothers, 'What happened to you then – did you fall asleep in a greenhouse?' But they didn't get it. To Henrik I said, 'Ee, lad, you'll have to sleep in a growbag.' Henrik tried to translate for their benefit, but my sense of humour doesn't always translate well.

Henrik's other grandmother, Far-mor (which means 'father's mother') asked him to bring me round for coffee (in

England we have afternoon tea; but coffee is the Danish national drink) so we could talk. Panicking a little, I said, 'I can't hold a conversation, not on my own!'

'You'll like her and I know you'll understand each other well. Besides, I'll translate if you need it,' Henrik reassured me.

Grandmother's house was immaculate, beautifully decorated and filled with fine polished furniture and exquisite crystal, but I had eyes only for her. It was impossible to believe that she was eighty-seven. She was just stunning, like a beautiful doll with dark-hair and vibrant eyes, very elegantly dressed in tailor-made clothes, reminding me of my own grandmother at the same age. When we were introduced, she grabbed my hands and said. 'Oh, flot! Flot!' which means 'beautiful' in Danish. For the rest of my visit she held my hands all the way through, releasing me only so I could drink my coffee and eat a little cake. As Henrik had predicted, ours was a meeting of kindred spirits. I was very moved when she said to him, 'I'm so glad you've waited for the best.'

I felt she wanted to chat freely, girlie talk; I certainly did, but we were restricted. Henrik translated, but, being a mere man, it wasn't the same – another reason why I wanted to learn Danish well. Communication with those close to you is so important.

Henrik's home was also lovely, everything beautifully decorated for a traditional Christmas; it was so immaculate that I was terrified of tramping in dirt and took my shoes off each time I came in. Every room was so nice and warm, filled with even heat from large traditional stoves, that I could walk around in bare feet. The highlight of the visit was the Christmas dinner prepared on New Year's Eve for Henrik's benefit since he'd missed out.

The thing I remember most was the duck, served on the bone, succulent, crisp golden skin: 'A proper bird!' I said to Henrik, watching his eyes light up when the big platters were carried in. It was cut up at the table and we were served a quarter each, with caramelised boiled baby potatoes, tossed in brown sugar like toffee, lots of sweet and sour boiled red cabbage, and a rich sauce. To follow was riz almande, the Danish equivalent of our plum pudding. It is a basic rice pudding in which is hidden an almond, instead of a silver sixpence, served with a delicious hot cherry sauce. Whoever gets that almond, gets a mystery prize.

In Denmark it was the custom to eat between six and eight in the evening, finishing with coffee. At about nine o'clock, when the meal was cleared away, we sat around the Christmas tree, singing songs. To get a little exercise after so much food, everyone grabbed hold of everyone in a chain, like a conga, and we danced around the entire house through every room, upstairs and down. Finally, the presents, which had been waiting under the tree all day, were handed out as a grand finale.

I said to Henrik at the end of the festivities, 'No wonder you flipped when I gave you your present the night before in front of a half-dead fire. This is so much more fun!'

No one could have predicted the frenzy when *The Cruise* was broadcast a week later, at peak time, right after *East Enders*, winning a regular audience of twelve million viewers. I was shocked when I first heard myself described as a celebrity. One minute I was Jane McDonald, club singer, and the next, the series went out and I was Jane McDonald, on the telly, in the papers, plastered everywhere. Far from wanting to be out there, wallowing in my new fame, I wanted to run away and hide: 'This isn't me, it can't be real,' I kept thinking when I woke each day. It's true that I was well-known in Yorkshire and had sung before large audiences for many years, but that was within a closed kind of world, a world I was used to. Suddenly, I was projected into national prominence. No one can prepare you for sudden fame and when it happens, it is very daunting.

Wherever I went, in Yorkshire at least, I was stopped in the street or in supermarkets shopping with Mum – even when I dashed around to the local fish and chip shop (thank God my hair wasn't in curlers!) People would say, 'We saw you on telly, Jane.' They all wanted to stop for a good gossip because they felt they knew me personally – and I suppose in a way they did. I was the girl next door.

When the hosts on all the TV morning shows asked me what it was like being the new docu-soap queen, I'd reply: 'At the time, it didn't seem like I was being filmed for a television series. It was like going out with my mates.'

Henrik had returned to Florida by the time *The Cruise* aired. Sitting down and watching some of the episodes with Mum brought it all back to me as if I was still there on the *Galaxy*: talking to Cruise Director, Doug 'you can be humbled in a heartbeat' Jones; backstage in that now infamous sleeveless gold lamé frock with a roll collar ('Look at all those chins!' I exclaimed to Mum, wincing as I watched. 'That's the first thing that's going – we'll turn the dress into a lampshade for the lounge!') Behind scenes, walking up and down, drinking a glass of water to calm my nerves; telling Chris Terrill that he was a little dreamboat with gorgeous legs ('My God, did I really say that!'); splashing about in the cascades on Dunns River Falls in Jamaica with larger-than-life Scottie O'Brien (after eight hours with him, I ended up saying, 'Beam me up, Scottie – *please*!'); a grey day, with rain pelting on the decks, the lounge chairs and empty swimming pools looking abandoned and sulky.

I turned to Mum as we watched, 'And people say it never rains on a Caribbean cruise.'

'You'd think they'd enjoy a little rain,' Mum said, 'a change from all that sun.'

As I watched the programme, I suffered with the cast when they suddenly had a new show, 'The Goldwyn Years', thrust upon them with two days notice before opening. I winced as I saw how one dancer broke his toe, another twisted his back and the lead singer lost her voice due to bronchitis, all in the space of twenty-four hours. 'This is what I did for seven years: struggle bloody hard,' I said to Mum with feeling.

I was there once again in the candle-lit glow of Jack Failla's cabin, as he talked me through some ideas for improving my act. I lived again the hilarious moment when Anna, one of the best stylists on the *Galaxy*, put highlights in my hair. When she pulled a rubber cap down over my head, I said, 'Oh my giddy aunt, it looks like a giant condom'. Then as she pulled strands of my hair through the little holes, I exclaimed, 'Oh, my God! I look like me dad's allotment!'

And was that really me, trawling through Marks and Spencer in the Galleria on Grand Cayman, brazenly shopping for knickers? 'I can't believe that twelve million people now know the colour of your drawers,' Mum said, her jaw dropping.

Watching some of the programmes was for me a very cathartic experience. It was as if my entire life was unfolding before my eyes, preparing me for the big changes that were about to happen. From the time the series went out, the telephone in our little terraced house didn't stop ringing with requests for interviews and appearances. When he discovered that I was being swamped beneath an avalanche of demands, Chris telephoned me, 'Jane, please ask me if you need any help with all this. I'm here at any time to advise you. I'll try to protect you if I can'.

I said, 'I've been asked to sing on the Midweek Lottery with Carol Smillie and press the button for the draw, what do you think?'

Chris said, 'That's great! It's prime time TV, you'll be seen by a lot of people, which will definitely help your career.'

A few days later, I caught the train down to London and did the show, wearing a heavily sequinned, short black halterneck frock with bare shoulders and full-length sleeves, with a large silver dragon design at my waist. The song I chose was the upbeat 'Dancing in the Street' – and before I was very far into it, half the audience had left their seats and started dancing in the space between me and the cameras, instantly making what had been a terrifying experience for me into a great deal of fun.

At that time, I still carried on with bookings at the clubs in Manchester because I didn't know what was going to happen. Despite the furore, I still had two more bookings to fulfil. *The Cruise* went out Tuesday and Wednesday and I was at two clubs in Manchester on the Saturday and Sunday. When I arrived, people were queuing up around the block to see this Jane McDonald who was on *The Cruise*. The clubs had to turn people away, there was even an all-out fight because the club members couldn't get in, and I was struggling in this melée trying to get through the door.

The club managers thought they had a little golden goose there, and were milking it for all it was worth, with huge posters plastered everywhere, and big advertisements in all the papers. I rang up the agent and said, 'You've got to cancel the next show.'

All I could hear down the phone was a loud squawk. He got his breath, and howled, 'I can't do that! They're over the moon because they've got Jane McDonald coming.'

I said, 'Whoever this Jane McDonald is, she's not doing it.' I tried to explain that I wasn't ready for a bunfight; I needed time to catch my breath. The agent wasn't happy, but he had no choice.

When things settled down a little and I felt I could poke my nose out from my hiding hole, I tried to thank Chris for what he had done for me, for seeing something in me that I didn't know I had. He said, 'I'm delighted to have set you on the way, Jane, but you've taken your luck and run with it. You've created your opportunities.'

I'd already broken the news to Chris that Henrik and I were – *finally*! – engaged. Ever the professional, at once he said, 'Can we film the wedding? It would be wonderful to have something later in the year to follow up *The Cruise* with.'

We talked it through, with Chris already visualising the entire programme in his head. He asked if there was anything special I was going to do in the near future. 'Yes,' I said, 'I'm going to give a concert at my local Working Men's Club as a kind of thank you to my roots. With everything exploding the way it is, I might never do another WMC again, and this is one of the places where I used to go dancing with my dad as a kid, one of the first places I ever sang professionally. I feel it's like looking back before I can look forward.'

The concert at Crigglestone WMC was arranged for

February 14 – St Valentine's day – a day on which something nice always seemed to happen. I think the entire town of Wakefield turned up that night. When I arrived with my family, the place was packed out and people were being turned away. A doorman put his arm out when I approached. 'I'm sorry, love, you can't come in, we've been full since half-past six.'

I said, 'You daft bugger, I'm the turn!'

Once I got going, it was a great evening with a wonderful spirit of goodwill. My backing was Trevor and Colin from my favourite club in the old days – and they were fabulous. Everyone danced with each other: lovers, mums and dads, dads and daughters, young girls. It was like it had always been throughout my teenage years, and I was loving every moment. I felt Dad's presence, right behind me all the time. This was his world and I knew if he missed anything at all it would be this.

'By heck, why wasn't it always like this, Dad?' I asked him in my head. 'Everyone nice and friendly, enjoying themselves.' There was no answering that – such is the nature of showbiz. Some you win, some you lose, eh Dad? It seemed the natural moment to sing the song I'd written for him, which likened life to a gamble because you never really knew what was going to happen. You threw the dice, played whatever game was going, and took your chances. Whatever life threw at you, you fought on – that was how it was with Dad and me – we were both fighters and grafters.

As if to tell me what was what, some little imp put a spanner in the works in Leeds, at the club where it all started; from where I'd run away to sea after Dad's death. I'd agreed to do one final show there as my big farewell to the clubland that had nurtured me. It should have been fun, but I was very badly let down. Upfront, I said I would do it for £150 expenses, adding that as I no longer had my own PA system, I'd need to borrow one. The agents who had booked me in said, 'Don't worry, we'll sort out PA out for you.'

True to their word, they did get a PA in; but there was some sort of a misunderstanding and the guy who owned it took his gear down and left. I said to the agent, 'What am I going to sing through now?'

He shrugged casually and said. 'Oh, use the comedian's,' seemingly oblivious of the fact that the place was huge, packed out to the rafters with coachloads of people coming in, thanks to the management heavily advertising that I was top of the bill. The comedian's mike was all right for someone to talk through, but he understood when I said I needed more amperage.

Luckily for me, there was a Scottish singer I knew in the audience, who said, 'Hang on, Jane, I've got me PA in the car'.

During the bingo, he went down the fire escape and brought all his equipment up. Thanks to him, I could do the show, such as it was. The doors were opened at half past six, to get everyone in so they could start drinking. There were two support acts on first. By the time I was on, from 10 p.m., a lot of people were drunk. I didn't have a compère, it was get on and get off, sort yourself out, we don't really care. The radio and the press were there in force. I knew if I'd walked out it would have been a nightmare, with destructive head-lines the very next day. I just knew in my heart of hearts that after that night I would never do a club again.

☆   ☆   ☆

People who wanted to contact me did so via the BBC and I'd started to follow up on some of the calls, including one from a top agent who I had talked to on the telephone in order to set up an appointment. A friend had fixed up an interview with another big London agency that I'd been to see, taking with me some of my own material, which they seemed very enthusiastic over. They said they had contacts with all the major record companies and would set up appointments as soon as I gave the word. I mentioned them to someone at the BBC who told me, 'No, these are not the right people for you'. It was very confusing.

The next time I was in London doing an interview, the PR person at the BBC handed me yet another stack of phone messages and faxes from major record labels who were interested in talking to me about a deal. 'What should I do?' I asked Chris. 'My head's spinning. Everyone says do this, don't do that. Even if I go to see them, I wouldn't even begin to know how to talk to them.'

Chris glanced through the names and whistled. 'There are some big players here,' he said. 'A deal with any one of them would be fantastic. You need a good entertainment lawyer to represent you.'

Chris had already helped me so much that I felt I couldn't ask him to come up with a lawyer as well. Vaguely, I thought I'd ask one of my old friends on the club circuit if they knew anybody I could approach. Returning to Wakefield on the Intercity express, I sat across the table from someone who looked like a lawyer from his clothes and the bulging briefcase. I said to myself, 'Well, Jane, here's your chance, go on, ask him if he knows anyone.'

I said, 'Excuse me, are you a solicitor?' We started talking. I said that I was in a dilemma, I needed some good advice, someone to look after me.

He said, 'Why, what do you do?'

I said, 'I'm a singer. I've just become quite famous on a documentary and I'm getting phone calls I need to make decisions about. I need a manager, or a lawyer to help me sort out a record deal.'

Handing me his card, he said, 'It so happens, I am a solicitor. I must admit that I've never heard of you, but I might be able to help you. I'll put you in touch with a friend of mine. Give me a call.'

By the time I got out at Wakefield, I was walking on air. I told Mum, 'I've met a solicitor on the train, he's going to help me sort out my life, thank God.'

'You met a man on a train?' Mum repeated. 'Shouldn't you find out a little bit about him?'

'It's all right – he gave me his card,' I said.

The next day, I telephoned the solicitor and he told me about another lawyer he had gone to school with, and who he had also studied law with. 'He's gone into entertainment law. Why don't you give him a call?' he suggested.

I did so, and set up an appointment with the new lawyer. A few days later, I went down to London to a meeting in his smart West-End offices. We seemed to get on well, apart from the fact that he was a bit show-bizzy, seated behind a massive, circular desk in a large, throne-like chair, while I was given a little, low chair to perch on like a schoolgirl in the headmaster's office.

He said, 'I've never seen you on television, but I'll watch *The Cruise* and let you know what I think.'

I felt a little deflated when I returned to Wakefield – it had seemed a long way to go to London for a 'maybe'. However, true to his word, the lawyer did watch the show, made a few enquiries and found that it appeared I *was* all the rage; people who'd had time to watch television knew exactly who I was. He told me he had found an agent who was interested in taking me on, so I returned to London for another meeting. To my astonishment, within an hour of arriving, I at once met the agent for a late brunch in a hotel. He was peculiarly dressed in a green plaid suit with red socks – very Toad of Toad Hall I thought – but otherwise he seemed to be on the ball and expanded at length on what he could do for me. Over croissants and coffee, he agreed to represent me; he was to later introduce me to a record company who signed me up. I felt dazed, it seemed so fast. I wished I had someone to talk to and was so glad that I would be with Henrik very soon.

After I got over the joy of being back in Florida, Henrik and I discussed my astonishing news: I had a record deal!

He was perceptive: 'What's the matter, Jane?' he asked. 'You don't seem to be over the moon.'

I shook my head. 'It's silly, isn't it? It's what I always wanted and yet it all seemed to happen so quickly. I just felt I needed more time to think.'

Henrik said, 'It's probably just an initial reaction.'

I agreed, 'Yes, you're probably right. The walls of the record company were plastered with gold and platinum discs and big pictures of all their top stars – so why do I feel uneasy?'

Henrik said, 'Jane, you're a professional singer. This is the next step up the ladder for you. You've been around, you've won awards, you deserve this – and you'll see, it will be sensational. You'll take the world by storm.'

All my doubts, like the cold weather in England, seemed far away and started to fade. The sunshine and being with Henrik restored my natural exuberance and I was so happy to be home that I walked around with a spring in my step. I started to make lists of songs for my album and spent hours working out arrangements and practising some of my favourites, such as 'Wind Beneath My Wings', 'You're My World', and 'I'll Never Love This Way Again', thinking of the words in relation to my ever-deepening love for Henrik, coming to see that I had never really sung these songs with the depth of emotion they deserved.

Often, I would talk to Henrik about the different degrees of love. There was the love I had for my father, who I felt was still very much with me, since I sincerely believe that death is a change of state, not an end. My love for my mother was a constant, as was my love for Tony, Gran, my sister and all the others closest to me. Then there was Henrik.

'I feel as if we have met before,' I said. 'We were intended to meet again.'

'I want to understand your beliefs,' Henrik said, 'but I'm very much a pragmatist – can you see it, can you hear it, can you feel it, does it exist?'

'That's the engineer in you,' I said. 'But what about television waves? The air is full of pictures zapping around and through everything and we can't see any of it. I'm sure you will tell me that there's a scientific explanation, but without a TV receiver, those waves are invisible. Maybe some people are receivers for another kind of signal.'

I wasn't preaching. It was a normal part of my life. 'One day it will happen to you. You are around me and it will happen, you'll realise what I mean,' I told him.

It happened sooner than I thought. For a few days following our conversation, Henrik seemed to be bombarded with information about the psychic world at every turn: on television, in the news, in magazines. Finally he said, 'OK, I will check this out for myself, no preconceptions. If I'm going to be married to a psychic, I should at least know what it's all about.'

He went to a place I'd mentioned, to ask for a reading. The psychic wasn't there, only the owner of the property. They got into a debate, the proprietor saying he'd heard people say the psychic was good. 'He's Mossad,' he said, 'an Israeli.' He said that the man had moved to the States where he now worked with the FBI, aiding them locate missing people and solving murders. 'When he started with the FBI they didn't believe him – but he got it right time after time. Now they call him in for every unsolved crime.'

Henrik was taken aback. Mossad is the name of the Israeli intelligence service – utterly incompatible in his mind to all this irrational spiritualism I believed in. 'Well, one spook is very much like another,' I'd joked. 'Come on, Henrik, there's no such thing as "types" in spiritualism any more than there are in Catholicism, Buddhism or any other belief.'

Henrik made an appointment and, still very sceptical, checked the psychic's credentials before returning a week later, fully expecting to see some cuckoo with gold earrings and a crystal ball. As soon as he walked in through the door, he could feel the whole atmosphere change. He didn't say anything, but the Israeli seemed to know what he was thinking. He smiled. 'Now you're in the spooky world!' he said, gently mocking.

Henrik wasn't amused. Before they proceeded, he wanted to talk to the man, to see if he was normal (insane was what he actually meant, but he was too polite to say that!) After half an hour, Henrik had run out of questions. Deciding that the man seemed rational, he indicated that they should continue in earnest.

The psychic said, 'You're going to travel.'

Henrik said, 'I travel two hundred days a year, don't tell me that one.'

He said, 'You're going to make a trip very soon that's going to change your whole life. There are some very strange happenings here. Have you just formed a new company?'

Henrik said, 'Yes, we're expanding rapidly. Every half year I open up a new company somewhere in the world.'

The psychic said, 'No, this one is completely different. Within ninety days you're going to be learning a new business – something completely different from anything you have ever done before.'

Henrik shook his head. 'No, impossible. I am the director of companies that are starting up and need my full attention, no way am I going to change direction.'

The psychic repeated, 'Within ninety days you're going to change profession. You're either going back on the school bench or you're going to change abilities.'

Henrik laughed. 'No way,' he said. 'That is so far off, it's ridiculous.'

The psychic ignored him and continued, 'You have a girlfriend, but I don't see her. She's not here.'

Henrik said, 'Yes she is.'

The psychic said, 'No, she's not, I can't see her here. You might get married but you won't live here, not in Florida. I see some mountains and a lot of water. Everything's going to change. Where your girlfriend is concerned, there will be large problems. If you can sort them out, you'll be all right. You have to do your homework, be prepared.'

Henrik told me all this when he returned to the house. 'So, what do you think?' I said.

He said, 'If it happens as he said, then I might believe it – until then, well, I'll keep an open mind.'

☆   ☆   ☆

On my return to England, I was due to sing at the legendary Opera House in Blackpool's Winter Gardens. Chris Terrill would be filming it as lead-in footage, together with the Crigglestone evening, and some clips from the final *The Cruise* episode for his proposed *Cruise Special*, the story of my wedding which was to be broadcast later in the year. I flew back to rehearsals, both for the concerts and for recording the album.

I started work in London at Abbey Road Studios, instantly bowled over and seduced by the wonder of being in a place so filled with music history that it practically bounced off the walls. From my first moments in my pram at Eastmoor Road I had listened on the radio to songs recorded there by the Beatles and Cilla Black. In Mum's big kitchen as I'd rolled out my little bits of pastry, I'd sung along to 'She Loves You'.

That week in Abbey Road, I went beyond the, 'Is this really happening to me?' stage to the, 'Oh, my God, I'm numb!' stage. Most of my fears vanished. This was pure profession-alism. There was a massive real-life orchestra, as opposed to a bank of synthesisers; there were experienced session singers to do the harmonies; there were classical arrangers and producers; I liked the people I was working with.

'It's great!' I told Henrik during my regular goodnight telephone call from the tranquillity of the Richmond Hill Hotel overlooking the River Thames. Every morning a car would take me through Richmond Park, past herds of deer grazing beneath spreading oaks to the recording studios – either Abbey Road where the orchestral work was done, or to R.G. Jones where I did the bulk of my singing in more intimate surroundings. Riding through the ancient park where Henry VIII had hunted, I felt like a queen.

Henrik flew over to be with me for my debut in Blackpool

on April 11th and 12th. The Opera House was the Mecca of the North. Never, in all my wildest dreams when I had driven over the Pennines with Dad in some rusty old van to a backstreet club in Blackpool, did I think I would be performing there. It was the first time in my life that I had walked through a bona fide stage door, as opposed to a door with peeling paint halfway up a fire escape. Eventually, I would get used to it, but at that moment I had to keep reminding myself that I was allowed to do this; no one would stop me and say, 'Hey! Where the hell do you think you're going?'

It helped that once again, I had Chris a few feet away, a camera on his shoulder. 'Ee, lad, feels like old times,' I said, in broadest Yorkshire.

When I walked on the stage and saw the serried ranks of seats stretching almost to infinity, I said, 'Oh, my God, look at this stage! It's just a little bit different from Crigglestone Working Men's Club, isn't it?'

After rehearsing, Henrik and I climbed to the top of Blackpool Tower and looked down on the Winter Gardens, which even from that height looked very big. 'Now I'm on top of the world,' I said and really meant it. The time for the show came almost too quickly. Henrik was there to help zip me up in a form-fitting silver lamé gown and slip on my silver high-heeled shoes like Prince Charming with Cinderella, then he vanished into the auditorium to mingle with the crowd and get a sense of what they were saying about the show.

I looked into the mirror and said, 'Oh heck, I feel like Cinders, I just hope my frock doesn't turn to rags on stage and I'm left sitting in a pile of ashes.'

Chris said, 'You look lovely, Jane. Nervous?'

'Very!' I said.

Chris asked, 'What would you say to someone who says it's

unfair. You happened to be there. It's luck you happened to be on the telly, you happened to get the breaks – why you and nobody else?'

'I'd say, damn right! I have been very lucky, Chris. There's so much talent out there – but I was in the right place at the right time.' I checked myself one last time in the mirror and said, 'Come on, let's get out there. I'm going to see if I can do Henrik proud and do a good show for him. I'm really going to enjoy myself tonight.'

No words can describe what it was like to actually be there on that big stage: the audience warm and receptive; the laughter building; the sheer welcome that I got. Many of these people were fans I had known for years in the clubs. They were there for me that night, old friends, wishing me luck and willing me to do my best. For Mum and Gran and the rest of my family to be there, too, for my first ever theatre concert, made me feel very special. After the show, we gathered in the dressing room to drink Champagne, and when Gran said: 'I just lived for this day. All I wanted was to see you be a star,' I didn't think I could hold in my emotions for much longer.

I was brought down to earth when Mum said, 'You were good, Jane'.

I said, 'For my mum to say that, it must have been good. She usually says, "Oh, but – ".'

Mum smiled. She said, 'I've got to keep your feet on the floor. You were great.'

After Blackpool, my manager and I parted company, Henrik returned to the States, while I returned to London to finish recording the album. As soon as I'd sung the last note and everyone was satisfied, I flew to America, very relieved to get away from a storm brewing on the management side, to start preparing for my wedding which was to take place on

St Thomas, in the American Virgin Islands. With the promise of a very large cheque from *OK!* magazine in exchange for an exclusive story on the wedding and a first look at my dress, I'd decided to blow the lot on inviting fifty friends and family to join me on a cruise where, for the very first time in my life, I wasn't working. It was going to be romance and fun all the way.

THE WEDDING

When I arrived in Florida, Henrik was in the throes of running his company's stand at a cruise ship trade fair in Miami. As he got dressed early on the first morning, he said, 'Do you fancy coming down on the SBS stand?'

I said, 'Yes, when I've had a chance to wake up. It'll be fun.' Later that day, I put on a saucy little miniskirt and jacket, stuck Henrik's SBS company logo prominently on my front and off I went. I hadn't been on the stand for more than ten minutes, when the word went round the fair – 'Jane McDonald's here!' Representatives from the other stands started dropping by. I'd been around for some years and knew all the UK ones: Cruise Scotland, Cruise Ireland, you name it, they were all there. They'd all seen *The Cruise*, but none of them knew I was Henrik Brixen's fiancée. The question on everyone's lips was: 'Why is Jane McDonald on the SBS stand?'

We got free gifts from everywhere, whisky from Scotland and Ireland, gin from England, Champagne, perfume, fruit cakes. Run off my feet, greeting people, signing autographs, receiving gifts, having my photograph taken, it was amusing watching the reaction of everyone from the big stands, wondering what the connection was. Henrik hadn't breathed a word about the television series, so Ken was completely baffled. He came over to me and asked, 'What's going on, Jane? They're saying, "Golly, SBS must be doing well".'

'Well, you *are* doing well – aren't you?' I said enigmatically, as I posed for yet another photograph and accepted another case of single grain malt.

'Whatever it is about you – we'd like some more of it. Can you come back tomorrow?' Ken asked.

'No, tomorrow I'm going shopping,' I replied.

The BBC had asked if Mum and I would like to be their guests on a morning show that did total make-overs. 'We'll choose a wedding gown for you, and your Mum's wedding outfit if you agree,' they said. I jumped at the chance of getting the help of experts to do everything, including a tiara and veil, my hair and make-up. Unfortunately, Henrik was to see a photograph of my wedding dress, leaked by the *Daily Mirror*. As superstitious as any bride-to-be, I knew I couldn't tempt fate. And there were financial considerations: even though I hadn't yet got the money from *OK!* magazine, its promised fee was crucial – I could hardly cancel all my guests at this late stage; I needed a new dress. With no time left to buy one in England, I decided to go shopping in Florida – and I knew just the place.

Two years earlier I had admired Suite Suzanne's on Lasolas Boulevard, wistfully dreaming that some day, if I became a bride, I would buy my trousseau there. Now, thanks to the leak, that dream was about to come true. I grabbed hold of Josie, our next door neighbour in Plantation and, waving Henrik's American Express card, I said, 'Come on, lovey, we're going shopping'.

Well, the phrase 'shop till you drop' was just coined for me. I tried on everything in sight and bought enough glamorous undies for the honeymoons of a dozen brides – all of this filmed by Chris. I didn't buy absolutely indiscriminately; when shown a flimsy bit of black lace to wear on my wedding night, I said, 'Oh heck, I'd look like a bag of spanners in that'. As for the see-through bit of white nonsense we found, I couldn't help remarking, 'It's kind of virginal – virginal on the ridiculous!' I was so used to Chris there that I had forgotten what I was doing until he laughed loudly – I don't think he'd ever heard the kind of irreverent chat that goes on in women's dressing rooms.

'You little tinker! What are doing here? Go on, lad, out you go, this is no place for a man,' I said firmly, closing the door on him and his camera.

Shopping for my basic essentials completed, Suzanne produced the perfect dress that fitted me exactly, right off the peg. It was a traditional gown made of heavy, raw silk, thickly encrusted with bugle beads and modestly cut with a scooped neck, front and back, a hint of a bustle and a very long train. I decided on a delicately pretty tiara of flowers made of pearls and crystal and a veil. This bride was going to be one hundred per cent traditional all the way to the altar, even if that altar turned out to be a strip of golden sand along a palm-fringed shore.

It was a strange stroke of irony that the ship cruising to the eastern Caribbean and the Virgin Isles was the *Century* – the ship I swore blind I'd never set foot on again. But, at the end of the day, it was the sister ship to the *Galaxy*, where, not only had I had a great time, but astonishing doors had been opened for me. I was happy to make my peace with the *Century*, the cruise liner I'd dubbed 'the ship from hell,' since I'd met my beloved on it.

Amongst our fifty guests were Henrik's parents and three

of his longtime friends from Denmark – all of them called Henrik, including Henrik Ovesen, the best man. Not only did they look alike, but whenever I called out my fiancé's name, four heads swivelled as one!

It was bitter-sweet to be back on the ship, particularly since many of my friends from the previous trip, including Granville Bailey, the cocktail waiter from Montego Bay, and Jack, the dancer who had helped me so much, were there as the ship set sail from Fort Lauderdale on 23rd May. The night before our wedding, which would be on the 26th, we drank to the success of the next day with our guests. I felt a surge of pride as Henrik said, 'Jane's a very honest person, a caring person – and she loves me'.

I told everyone how excited I was to be there. 'It's going to be a long day but I'm looking forward to it.'

Before turning in, I stood at the railing on my own and thought of my father. The day before I had left Yorkshire, I had paid a visit to the old allotments where we had scattered Dad's ashes. The once-neat beds were a riot of dandelions, sparkling in the sun and I remembered all the childhood years when he and Mum had looked after me and kept me safe.

'Thanks, Dad,' I said, looking up at the sky. 'I know you're up there somewhere, and I know you've got a lot to do with all this.' I almost turned around, expecting to see him there as he always had been, with his packet of sandwiches and flask of tea, giving me the thumbs up.

For the first time, I was back on a cruise ship, not as a singer, not as a worker, but as a guest and – call it fanciful – I knew Dad was still there behind me, lending his support every inch of the way.

I was in my cabin getting ready for bed and completing a few finishing touches for the next day, painting my nails a soft pearl colour, when panic hit me. I wasn't having second thoughts – I was just scared witless. I crawled into bed, willing sleep to come, but instead I lay awake all night long, experiencing one of the biggest attacks of stage fright I have ever had.

'Ee, lass, you're going to have black rings around your eyes come morning. You'll look like a panda, not a bride,' I told myself as I tossed and turned. It was no good counting sheep or sea shells or going through the words of every song I knew – nothing worked. By dawn, I was wrecked.

Henrik and I took a stroll around the deck, watching the sun come up and the dark colour of the sea lighten to pearl and then to aquamarine. The green hump of St Thomas lay ahead, red roofs showing through the foliage here and there. Overhead, sea birds floated on the off-shore thermals and gradually, I felt all tension easing away.

Sensing my mood, Henrik took my hand. 'Sure, darling?' he asked.

'Very sure,' I said. 'I'm more sure of this than I've ever been of anything in my life. I really love you.'

'And I love you very much,' he said.

In a day that was going to be very public, that was our own private commitment to each other, our own very personal moment.

While Trevor Sorbie, the hairdresser who had flown 4000 miles to do my hair, back-combed and piled it up so it would hold the tiara and veil in place, I telephoned Gran at home, ship to shore. 'Hello, Gran, I'm just about to get married,' I said.

Gran had bought a new outfit and was sitting in her chair,

ready to drink a toast to us. Her voice sounded faint and far away. It seemed so sad that she wasn't strong enough to travel, the only one in the family who wasn't there. 'Are you shaking?' she asked.

Starting to cry, I said, 'I am, yes. I just miss you so much.'

'I'll be thinking of you all day,' she said.

I put the phone down, snivelling and wiping the tears away. 'I'm so pathetic. I can't cry, my mascara will run,' I said to Trevor. Rallying, I joked, 'Well, time to get into my scaffolding.' I struggled into a white satin corselet and then slipped my gown on, helped by my sister, who was looking very smart in a navy and white outfit with pearls and a navy straw hat. My veil was put in place, a few tendrils of hair were artistically arranged, my lips were given one last coating of gloss and I was as ready as I would ever be. I stared in the mirror and gasped. Could that really be me, that ravishing bride? (I felt I could think that because it looked nothing like me.)

Granville came in with Champagne on a tray. Raising a glass he said, 'My very good luck and prosperity.' We all took a sip, and he added, quoting from one of the songs he'd heard me sing during the years we had been friends, 'This really is the moment you have been waiting and longing for'.

'Thank you. It took me a few years to get this one!' I said, breaking the emotional bubble – for the moment. The whole day was filled with emotional moments.

Mum was by the gangway exit, along with the rest of the party who were waiting for me. I started to sob in earnest now. Mum looked so pretty in a café au lait and peach dress and jacket in heavy crêpe with a scattering of bugle beads. Her big hat was so smothered in cream and peachy silk roses, it looked like a giant cabbage rose in its own right. 'Love your hat,' I said, 'Mum, you look fab!'

'So do you, darling,' she said, her eyes going moist behind her glasses.

'At this rate, we'll never get off the ship,' I said, taking my bouquet of large lilies, pink and cream roses and sweet-scented white stocks from Janet. I'd gone for an old-fashioned cottage garden look, and got it; the bouquet smelled delicious. Telling everyone I hoped I wouldn't be pursued by bees and wasps, I grabbed Tony's hand, to be escorted down the gangway to the white stretch limo waiting on the quay. As we drove off with my immediate family in the car, Tony said, 'Henrik said, don't go shopping on the way'.

I said, 'He's a cheeky devil. I can't believe that the next time I return to the ship I'll be Mrs Brixen. It took me two-and-a-half years to get him to ask me to marry him – and you know what? It was shepherd's pie that did the trick, so thanks, Mum.'

Mum said, 'It was ironing did it for me.'

Janet nodded. 'Cooking for me,' she said.

We all waited for Tony; but he looked coy. 'Come on, Tony,' Janet pressed. 'How did you catch our Wendy?'

'I can't talk about it in company,' he said, making us laugh, thank goodness. It was either that or cry all the way. As we drove through lush, tropical foliage, passing the exotic flower gardens of the little red-roofed houses I'd seen from the ship early that morning, we exchanged family memories. The one about the shepherd's pie had reminded us of the very hard time during a long drawn-out miners' strike when Mum had cooked proper teas – often shepherd's pie with all the trimmings – for Tony and Wendy each evening, and I had taken it around to their house. Things like that had drawn us very close together as a family.

Twenty minutes later, we arrived at Bluebeard's Castle,

where the ceremony was to be held on a grassy lawn beside the sea. I could see a collection of white chairs beneath the shady palms, and the guests in their gaily coloured outfits, including Henrik's parents and my dancer friend, Jack, in a fabulous red check suit.

This was to be the exotic and very romantic wedding I'd dreamed about for so long. I proudly took my handsome brother's arm as we walked down a short flight of blue-painted wooden steps leading from the road and crossed the lawn past bushes of scarlet hibiscus to the tune of 'Here Comes the Bride' played on steel drums.

Henrik was there, waiting for me. He gave me a heart-stopping smile and I almost swooned on the spot. 'Now, Jane, hold yourself together,' I lectured myself. 'Not long now – he's not going to run away.'

The pastor had obviously had some prior experience of nervous brides. He said, 'We have come together this afternoon to celebrate the marriage of Henrik and Jane. In honour of the pledge you are about to make, please join right hands.' In a small aside he told Henrik, 'Keep a grip on her – this is where they slip away!'

I felt Henrik grip just a little bit tighter.

'Henrik, do you take Jane to be your lawfully wedded wife, to have and to hold from this day forward in sickness and in health to love and to cherish, so long as you both may live?'

I held my breath as Henrik said firmly, 'Yes, I do.'

'Jane, do you take Henrik to be your lawfully wedded husband, to have and to hold in sickness, in prosperity or adversity, to love and to cherish, as long as you both may live?'

'Yes I do,' I said with absolute conviction.

'Take both rings and put them on,' the pastor said. We were

married with a ring on the left hand, as is usual in England, but because Henrik wanted to show how much he loved me, he had bought two huge engagement rings – so I had a wedding ring for my right hand as well! As I told everyone, I was doubly lucky – and I wasn't talking about diamonds, however much I made a light-hearted joke of it – I was talking of the man standing beside me at two o'clock that afternoon in the tropical sun.

We completed the vows, promising to love, honour and respect each other and not to forsake the other. Henrik put a very reassuring emphasis on the word '*not*'.

'According to the laws of the United States Virgin Islands, and more importantly, by the highest power that rules the land and the seas, I pronounce may you henceforth and hereafter be known to all as husband and wife.'

I couldn't help myself. I declared a triumphant, 'YES!' I'd finally made it! Henrik threw his head back and laughed: I think he'd enjoyed the chase – though I wondered who was really doing the chasing. I'd been so transparent, he'd played it so close to his chest; but at the end of the day, we both had exactly what we wanted.

The pastor said, 'Ladies and gentlemen, may I be the first to present the new Mr and Mrs Brixen.'

Everybody clapped as we kissed and said a simultaneous 'I love you'. Out of the corner of my eye when I surfaced from the kiss, I saw little boats offshore on the blue-green sea where gentle waves lapped against the golden sand. A small group of beach belles in bikinis waved. It was just perfect. I know Dad would have approved. After all those hard years lugging my stuff around in the cold and the rain, he should have had some of this sunshine – I just wished that he'd been there in person rather than in spirit.

Everybody threw rice, then it was Champagne on a lace tablecloth and cutting the first slice out of the apricot and buttercream tiered sponge cake that was decorated with a single red camellia on a large green leaf. Henrik said, 'Be careful Jane, don't let the slice flip over,' as I carefully tried to balance it on a plate. It was a tradition in Denmark that if the first slice tipped over to lie on its side – rather than remaining upright – the mother-in-law is going to be a right witch. Luckily, the slice stayed upright and Henrik breathed a sigh of relief. 'So my new mother is going to be all right,' he said.

We toasted each other, Henrik said, 'To us'.

I said, 'Cheers, darling, may we always be as happy as we are today.'

We were still dancing as evening drew in. Henrik and I slipped away and walked on our own along the beach in the gently lulling waves. It was almost the perfect end to a perfect day; all that remained was the party on board the ship that evening. I will never forget Henrik's short and moving speech.

'Jane, you look absolutely gorgeous and I am extremely proud to be your husband. I want to thank you for being so brave and having the courage to give up all your ties in England, for having such a belief in our relationship that you left everything you hold dear: your home, your family, to come to Florida to be with me – for that I'll be thankful for the rest of my life. This is the biggest day of my life...' (at that moment he looked directly at me standing by his side and softly underlined, '*it is*') '... I really, really look forward to sharing the rest of our lives together.'

I broke in and whispered, 'me too...'

'I hope our marriage will also be blessed with kids because you will be a wonderful mother. I have tried to find a good way to end the speech, so I am just going to let everyone know

– *and you* – that I love you very, very much.'

All I could say was 'Oh God…' before I started to weep, unable to hold myself together for a moment longer, not caring that my mascara was running and my nose was red. It was all, and more, that I had ever hoped for in a speech on my wedding day.

Maybe it was the high level of emotion, but there is always a coming down from being at a great height. A couple of days later, heading back to Florida, Henrik and I were sitting on our own in a sheltered corner of the deck. He sensed something was wrong.

'What's up Jane? You're very quiet.'

I wasn't going to bother him with my problems, but I had to. I said, 'I can't face going back.'

Henrik said, 'What are you telling me?'

I said, 'I can't handle the pressure. It's like Russian dolls. I'm looking at people and they're not who they seemed to be, there's somebody else inside and it's scary. I want you to come back with me to sort a few things out.'

'Well, maybe for a few days,' Henrik said slowly. 'But you know, Jane, I have a lot to do over here. Things are going well. We're expanding so fast that Ken is away most of the time. I have to be on hand to run things.'

I stood up and walked to the rail, gazing sombrely out to sea. Heavy green rollers marched on to the horizon. I felt totally adrift and rudderless. Almost at breaking point, I turned and faced him and took a deep breath having come to a decision. 'If you can't take over the reins of my career and manage me, I'll give it up and stay here with you. I need your protection.'

Henrik said, 'Are you telling me that you're in danger?'

I said, 'No, not physically. All my reason and instincts are screaming that my life is spiralling out of control. Henrik, I'm almost at breaking point. There are so many people who want a piece of me. I need a manager but I don't want a stranger – I want you.'

Henrik said, 'But I've never managed an artist's career before. I wouldn't know where to start.'

'Of course you can do it,' I said with real fervour, believing implicitly in him. 'You've got a great brain and you're a good businessman. You can do anything.'

Henrik put his arms around me and held me close. I relaxed, leaning into his strength, feeling secure. 'I can see that you're in pain,' he said. 'I'll come back for a couple of weeks to try to sort things out.' He sounded very positive, but I could tell that he was deeply perturbed and I wondered what I was doing to him and his business.

BREAKING RECORDS

We didn't have much time for a honeymoon, as I had a previously confirmed booking in England which, as I don't like to let people down, I had to keep. Henrik remained behind in Florida for two weeks in order to look after our guests, but he joined me as soon as he could, armed with a book I'd bought for us on the music industry. The first thing I did was take Henrik round to Tony and Wendy's home, where I'd set up temporary offices in their conservatory so he could go through the avalanche of mail that had poured in – fan mail, offers of work, requests for appearances, begging letters, demo cassettes from people asking if I could advance their careers. Wendy had suggested that since she was at home all day with their little daughter, Katie, she could act as my unpaid secretary and PA. At first Henrik's face was a picture when he walked in and saw the filing cabinets standing next to Katie's outdoor toys and the computer set up on the potting table, but he was soon impressed when he saw how organised the files and the diary were.

'No wonder your head is spinning,' he said, as he scanned nearly fifty offers from television production companies alone for me to front an incredible variety of shows.

I said, 'How do I decide what's for the best?'

Chris Terrill was so busy filming his new series, *Jail Birds*, that I didn't want to keep bothering him to ask, 'what do you think I should do?' each time another offer came in. In the end, I'd told Wendy just to send them a polite 'I'm thinking about it' letter, hoping that in the meantime I could sort out the wood from the trees.

Henrik seemed to have a very quick grasp of things. He said, 'Daytime TV is great to go on and promote your record and concerts, but I don't think you should do a day-time series, it's not suitable for a singer.' This, at a stroke, got rid of eighty per cent of the offers. 'These are the companies you should talk to,' Henrik said, showing me a shortlist.

'How did you do that?' I asked. 'You don't know anything about the entertainment business.'

He said, 'Businesses are much the same. It is a matter of applying logic and common sense. You are very creative, Jane, so it is hard to mix the two.'

One of the things confirmed was a summer season of Sunday shows at Blackpool's Opera House, which would fit in well with promoting my forthcoming album, and we snapped it up at once. This was to be followed by a major thirty-date tour of the UK in October, including a sell-out night at the London Palladium in November. There was some urgency in getting everything set up properly because there was just a month before we opened in Blackpool and Henrik had to return to the States to complete some work. Everything was new to both of us, particularly to Henrik and he had to learn fast – very fast.

Things didn't go well when I introduced Henrik to my record company. For a number of reasons, the meeting broke up with a great deal of bad feeling on all sides. Henrik was quiet as we left the building. On the way back to Wakefield, he said, 'This is not going to be easy.' I knew he had been hoping that at the meeting some things could have been ironed out, leaving him free to commute between his business in the States and mine in the UK. Now he saw that I really did need his full-time help. For instance the first concert in Blackpool was looming and I was starting to panic. We had the orchestra, the dancers and some backing singers but no help at all in organising it. I asked Sue Ravey, a brilliant singer in her own right, who had opened for Marti Caine and other big acts, to sing backup for me.

'Do you mind, Sue?' I asked. 'I know you're a star performer with your own act.'

'It's an honour,' Sue said. 'I would never get to sing in places like Blackpool Opera House normally.'

When I had first met Sue, some fifteen years earlier, she had been working as a duo with her sister, June. Ours was the kind of friendship that took up where it had left off. When I had gone to see Sue perform in Leeds shortly before my wedding, jokingly she had said, 'Would you like another bridesmaid?' 'Absolutely!' I had replied, and had been very pleased that she could come.

At Blackpool, even during rehearsals, I knew things weren't right. My backing singers worked hard, the orchestra worked hard and I sang my heart out but something was badly wrong – there was no stardust. I felt empty, unable to put my finger on the problem. I'd find my hand straying to clutch my throat. Mum always recognised the signs from the times when I had lost my voice before and she'd get out the sherry, measure out a few stiff tots and I'd relax enough to continue. The first night, I was a trembling mess. I had to force myself to walk to the wings and wait for my cue. A deep breath, shoulders back – and on I'd go, a wide smile pinned to my face, full of terror inside. I knew that I'd failed to come up to my own high standards because, although the audience clapped and there were some cheers, there were few curtain calls and no standing ovation.

The album was being released on July 13, to coincide with the broadcast of the *The Cruise Special* and there were numerous media interviews set up to publicise it. I had met Nick Fiveash, the PR man appointed to look after me, before my wedding, when I'd come down to do an interview with the *Sunday Times* in Soho House, a media club in Soho. We'd taken to each other like a long-lost brother and sister – I simply adored him from the word go.

'I wanted to meet you the moment I saw *The Cruise* on telly in January,' Nick told me. 'I'm a TV addict and saw all the trailers of the programme. As soon as I sat down to watch it, I fell in love with you and when you sang, I was hooked! After the first episode went out, I said to the friend I was with: "I want to work with her, I really want to work with her".'

Nick had gone on a mission to find me. He had called the BBC which told him that I was no longer in the country but that if he wrote a letter, they would pass it on.

'Oh, you did write to me!' I said, remembering.

'I was very keen! I did you a little intro letter saying who I was, the other artists I represent: Barbra Streisand, Neil Diamond, Harry Connick Jr, Elaine Paige and so on. A couple of weeks went by and I didn't hear anything. Suddenly I thought, maybe she's received this letter from this person she doesn't know, listing all these top people I represent in PR and she's gone, "Bloody hell, I can't afford him!"'

I laughed. 'You're right! I was scared to death when I got your letter. I thought you must have made a mistake, I'm not in that league.'

Nick continued, 'That's why I wrote an amusing little follow-up note saying: I've had second thoughts, you probably have read my letter and gone, "Ooh, I haven't got a chance with him". But it's not about money, I wrote, if you need any help, I'd love to have a cup of tea and a chat.'

A couple of days after Nick had sent his second letter, the project manager on my album had telephoned him to say she was really excited as she'd just got her first independent commission. When Nick had heard it was to promote me, he had gasped, 'Jane McDonald! I've been writing to her! I don't believe it!'

When we met, I'd grabbed hold of both his hands and said, 'I feel like I've known you all my life.' I knew that whatever else happened, I had found a kindred spirit, one I could totally trust. Later, as the media campaign to promote me hotted up and I got to know him better I telephoned to ask if he would like to come to Blackpool on the following Sunday to see the show. I was very anxious for his opinion.

He did come, and disappeared to sit somewhere at the back. At the end of the evening, there was no sign of Nick. We were getting ready to leave, when he came into the dressing room. Henrik said, 'Well what do you think?'

Nick said, 'Jane was fantastic.'

Henrik said, 'Full stop?'

'Yes, full stop.'

'OK – we need to talk.'

We had to be in London the next day to attend to some business. Afterwards, the three of us met in the St George's Hotel, where we sat and talked. When I had met Nick he had only seen *The Cruise*, he had never heard me sing live. His reaction after the show was not good. But I knew I had to sit and listen to what he had to say if we were to have an honest relationship with each other. He'd already told me that he couldn't promote anyone if he didn't one hundred per cent believe they were brilliant – so his verdict was doubly nerve-wracking. Would he want to dump me before we'd even begun?

'So, where is it going wrong?' Henrik asked in his forthright way.

Nick looked at me. 'I thought you were absolutely fantastic, Jane – but the show! It was just appalling. You had dancers, a band – it was a whole show, but it was just not *you*. I sat there in the audience watching, and then wondered, what was I going to do? I was supposed to go around to the dressing room afterwards. I said to myself, *I can't*. I walked around the Winter Gardens, and it's quite a big block, thinking what am I going to say? I still wanted to work with you, would you listen to me? Then I thought, if this is the way I want to go on, I have to be honest and if honesty is not what they want to hear, so be it. I took a deep breath and went back and into the dressing room: it wasn't easy.'

I nodded. 'I knew at once, as soon as I saw your face.'

Henrik said, 'So, what's the problem?'

Nick said, 'I think you were trying to do a cabaret show in a venue that holds three thousand people. You've been used to playing in clubs, and the cruise ships are still a bit cabaret-style on a certain level. A friend of mine went to Blackpool last week. She sat upstairs and she said, "I saw the top of Jane's head the whole time. Did she forget there were people up there?" You can't just play to the first ten rows.'

I stared at him aghast, knowing he was right.

Nick continued to detail all that he thought had been

wrong, such as the running order and the lighting. Part of the problem was that during the rest of the week, Monday to Saturday, *Summer Holiday* was on, and we weren't allowed to change their lighting, which left very little leeway for me. 'Well, maybe we can do something,' Nick said. Henrik said his piece as well while I listened quietly. When they'd thrashed it out, I just looked at Nick and said, 'Do it.'

He said, 'What do you mean?'

I said, 'You're telling me what's wrong with it – so get it right. Come up early on Sunday and we'll go through it.'

He said, 'I've never done this before. Yes, I've watched and worked with loads of people, but you're taking a big chance.'

I said, 'Let's give it a go.' Nick had been around, he had some top clients, very well established stars. If he didn't know what it took, then no one did. We sat and did a new running order of all the songs, By the time we split up, my confidence was beginning to build again.

The following Sunday, Nick joined us in Blackpool, where he sat with the lighting guy, who proved to be very helpful, showing Nick what lights were available. As I moved about the stage, they worked out a first-rate lighting plan. The whole afternoon while I was rehearsing the new running order, Nick walked all round the inside of the Opera House and was waving to me to make sure I was looking up and projecting to the people up in the gods. While actors learn to do this when they are students, I had very little experience of singing to three tiers of seats and needed to take a crash course in this. By the end of the afternoon, we were all excited and re-energised.

That night, I went on and got a standing ovation during the show – which I hadn't heard the week before. When Nick joined us backstage, I was bubbling over. I ran across the back of the stage, grabbed hold of his hand and said, 'You did it! I trust you with my life, thank you so much'.

Nick said, 'No, you did it. You're the one who takes the audience on that journey. You lead them by the hand through that roller-coaster of emotion, roaring with laugher one minute, in tears the next.'

'Oh yes, that's me,' I said.

The show continued to get better. I ended up by becoming the second biggest grossing artist in the theatre's history. Things really started to explode when *The Cruise Special* was aired. The television viewing figures were sensational. There's no doubt it helped the sale of my album, which shot into the charts at number one from nowhere, something which apparently has never been achieved before. The next thing I knew, it had gone platinum, I had achieved superstar status and was in the *Guinness Book of Hit Records*, getting even more headlines. It felt like it was all happening to someone else.

On the Sunday when the charts become official, I was up in Blackpool enjoying a little celebration which the press put on. They were all coming up to me saying, 'Well done Jane, this is fantastic!' But I was numb – worn out by all the problems and all the work I'd done to promote the record. I felt that I had stood on the street corner and personally sold that album one piece at a time, I had gone to every radio station and every TV show.

I travelled the length and breadth of the country, sometimes with just a bored driver. I can remember sitting in the back seat, specs on, peering at a map directing him to some obscure radio station, getting hopelessly lost – usually in a summer thunderstorm, unable to see a thing while rain cascaded down and while the driver muttered about women navigators. Exhausted, I would totter in to do my interview, pretending that I was on top of the world, and just thrilled to be there.

Thank God for the times when Nick escorted me, which he did more frequently when he realised how depressed I felt. He was always being mistaken for Henrik, not because he looks like him but because people got used to seeing him with me. They'd say, 'Oh, you've got your lovely husband with you.'

Once, on a plane going to Aberdeen to do a charity concert, I was instantly recognised by the staff, which is nice because you get the extra glass of Champagne. Nick and I got very giggly, as we always do when we're together. For some reason the plane was circling for a while before landing, during which time the cabin staff continued to be extra nice to us, plying us with several more glasses of Champagne. An announcement came over the tannoy: 'Ladies and gentlemen, we will soon be arriving at Aberdeen airport but we are just delighted to welcome aboard this morning's flight Miss Jane McDonald and her husband.' The whole aeroplane applauded. Nick sank down into his seat, trying to hide, while I smiled glassily. Unfortunately, we both got a fit of the giggles. I'm sure everyone thought we were drunk and deranged – but I put it down to the altitude playing havoc with the bubbles.

On another occasion, we were put up in a really beautiful hotel in Dublin by the people at the top talk show there. The night we arrived, we went up to our rooms to unpack and had a walk around the town, enjoying looking at the Liffey and other historic places while looking for a restaurant. But, as usually happened, we decided that we were both too tired to eat out and would have dinner in the hotel restaurant. Nick and I were animatedly chatting, the waiter hovered attentively. Presently, I yawned and said loudly, 'Oh, God, Nick, I can't wait to get to bed!'

Discreetly, the waiter took a step back and, hastily, I said, 'He's not my husband,' which made it worse.

The waiter coughed and said, 'Madam, your secret is safe with me.'

I said, 'I don't care if my secret's locked up in the hotel safe – he's still not my husband.'

At the show the next day, we had already sent the track for 'Some You Win, Some You Lose', the song I had written for my father, which I was going to perform in the studio before a live audience. When the TV producers listened to it, they decided it would be lovely to have a gospel choir standing behind me on the set. When we got there for rehearsals in the afternoon, the place was full of schoolkids in jeans and sweatshirts and trainers. We rehearsed the song, it went well and I went to the hotel for a rest. In the evening at the studio, I got dressed and made-up, ready to go on stage. I walked out of the dressing room into the corridor, to find all these kids now in their white choir robes and little blue collars filing by. I was telling them how nice they looked when a tall bearded man followed behind in a hessian robe with a bit of rope around his middle.

I said, 'Blimey, you could have dressed up, couldn't you?'

A deathly hush descended, a few of the teenagers tittered. One of the productions assistants hurrying by said, 'Oh, hello Father Peter.'

Nick and I completely lost it: I was crying so hard with laughter, tears ran down my cheeks. In a few minutes I was more composed, standing in the wings waiting to go on. I started to relay this story to another production assistant when I realised that Nick was elbowing me. Looking up, I saw the monk was standing within two feet of us, sombrely watching me. Instantly, I was convulsed again, my eyeliner and mascara, running down my cheeks.

The theme music started, they'd gone live on air, and I was on first. Nick said, 'Your face!' He grabbed handfuls of tissues to rub smudged mascara off my cheeks. He rubbed hard, spat on the tissue and rubbed some more, but there was still a little bit that wouldn't shift. 'It won't come off!' he said. 'You can't go on with a dirty face. Imagine the close ups.'

A production assistant quickly produced a mirror. 'That's my mole!' I said. That set me off yet again, laughing like a maniac. They had to physically push me through the curtains, the audience started to clap and I tottered across to the mike. Instantly, I was in professional mode, straight into the song; then went on to chat for twenty minutes on the couch – with the monk standing to one side, watching, arms crossed, with a strange smile on his face.

In mid-July, Nick and I flew to Spain where the ITV morning show was broadcast from a villa for the duration of the holiday season. The moment we arrived at Heathrow, the lady behind the counter said, 'Jane McDonald! You're my first celebrity of the day'.

Delighted we'd been recognised, Nick said, 'Any chance of an upgrade from the steerage we've been booked on?'

She said, 'We are absolutely full up front – but I will put you at the back of the plane and give you four seats so you'll be nice and private.'

They plied us with vodka and tonics the whole journey across and by the time we got to Marbella, we could have been sitting on the tail fin for all we cared. I already knew that my call was at the ungodly hour of six o'clock the next morning, to go live on air at ten past seven. I always try to sing live, but even if I hadn't been so dehydrated, I knew my voice wouldn't be warmed up, so I'd asked for the record company to send a backing tape for me to mime to. By some mix-up, the tape that arrived was a DAT, which was the size of a matchbox. The engineers there didn't have a DAT machine to play it on. By the time they'd rounded one up, I didn't have time for a run-through.

I was filmed in a kind of chapel at the top of a tower – singing to the wrong mix, as I discovered halfway through, when the chorus cut in at the wrong place. Quickly, while I was trying to figure out where on earth in the song I was and what my lips were supposed to sing next, I put the mike up to cover my mouth and kept on miming. For the viewers, it looked as if I sang the entire song eating the mike: it was a close call.

My first album came out in July and, by October, I was in the middle of a thirty-date, sell-out tour. But while everything was very glamorous up front, things weren't running smoothly behind the scenes due to issues that I don't want to go into too deeply here. I was upset when I was told that the budget wouldn't stretch to paying for my backing singers; so I paid for them myself. Then I couldn't understand why the roadies, the guys behind the scenes who set things up for the show, always seemed exhausted – until I discovered that they weren't getting enough sleep and precious little food. It appeared to be usual practice with some tour companies not to provide suitable accommodation for road crews, and since the lads had not yet been paid, some of them were too broke to eat properly. While I had separate accomodation arranged, the roadies were expected to stay in cheap hotels that were often miles from where the show was. This meant that they would crawl into bed at 4 a.m. and then have to get up at 6 a.m. in order to build the set in a new venue for that evening's concert. As soon as we found out what was going on, we insisted on getting the roadies a proper bus with bunks, so that they could sleep overnight while being driven to the next venue.

At times, I dreaded going to Blackpool between the tour dates. This was partly because the tour show was different from the Blackpool show and I'd had to be familiar with both; but it was also because of having to travel nine or ten hours from wherever I was in order to get there for the Sunday night. People thought my life on the road was sex, drugs and rock and roll but the reality was quite ordinary. After a show I would always do signings, which could take as long as the show itself, but I would never ever stint on that because the fans were, and are, so important. I would recognise faces from places like the Maid Marion Club and be cheered that they had bothered to come – although seeing myself on a Jane McDonald T-shirt and even on the pen I was signing with freaked me out! Then afterwards, like Cinderella, it was bath, bed and a cup of tea by midnight. I really loved that quiet coming-down time on my own, while Henrik went out and talked to the MD or sorted out whatever needed to be done for the next day.

During those weeks, both Henrik and I were on a learning curve and the tensions were telling on my relationship with him. He was already feeling the strain of trying to sort through the treacly morass of my business affairs and deal with constant crises, while at the same time running his own business at a distance. He was constantly getting phone calls in Florida and, at a moment's notice, he would catch the redeye and be back in England within twenty-four hours. He was trapped in a growing dilemma: would my career get to the stage where I would make money, or should he concentrate on his own business for our living?

'Jane, I'm torn apart by all this,' he said one night.

Scared, I asked, 'What do you want to do?'

He said that he'd been weighing it all up. While some people, who shall remain nameless, said that my career was flash-in-the-pan and wouldn't last, Henrik had seen the reality of the sold-out theatres, the standing ovations and the wonderful crowds at the stage doors. Most of all, no one could argue with an album that had gone straight in at number one and stayed in the charts for twenty-six weeks.

But I was worn out and dispirited and felt out on a limb on my own. I said, 'Things are very hard here, every day there's a new battle: I hate it. Why don't I give in and return to Florida? Now that I have my Green Card application approved, I could find work in the States.'

I'd given up on getting my Green Card after being warned by the American lawyer not to marry Henrik. But as soon as I went to number one in the album charts, they took me seriously and pushed my application through.

Henrik said, 'No, we should stay. There is no doubt at all in my mind that you will achieve even greater success. Your career is worth fighting for, so let's fight.'

At the end of our discussion, Henrik contacted a Swedish guy, the best sales person in his previous company, whose dream it was to retire to Florida. They agreed that they would split Henrik's share of SBS, leaving Henrik with some interest but a lot less responsibility. Shortly after our long talk, everything was put back into perspective when my old stamping ground, the Maid Marion Club, rang Henrik and asked, 'Will Jane come back and do a night?'

Henrik said, 'Well, she travels with a fourteen-piece orchestra.'

'Oh, the lass knows our backing, she'll get on fine with house band,' they said.

The Maid Marion has the best punters in the world and I'd always enjoyed working there, but now there was a wide gulf between the club singer I used to be and the polished performer I had grown into. I felt sad, but you can't go back.

By the time I got halfway through my tour, I no longer felt that I didn't deserve to be there. I was glowing and confident and in love with my vast army of fans. *They* had put me where I was – and I adored them for it. My first album had deliberately been produced to be quite low-key and soft, so people had no idea that I was any other kind of singer. Many of them came up to me afterwards, saying what a surprise they'd got when I belted out some of the really big songs. They admitted they'd come out of curiosity over *The Cruise* – and left as fans.

The mid-point of the tour was to be marked by a grand night at the London Palladium on November 8th, to be filmed by the BBC for broadcast on New Year's Eve. Nick and I went in the afternoon for a run-through and a sound check. While I went in through the stage door, he went round to the front. Three minutes later, he came running backstage. 'It's fabulous! The sold out sign is up.' We clutched each other and did a little jig of glee.

When we walked out on to the stage, Nick said, 'It's so tiny!' I looked about and gasped, It seemed impossible that it would hold two-and-a-half thousand people. All the tiers are stacked up almost vertically, so the back row and the circle seemed almost in your face, whereas somewhere like

Blackpool is so vast, the circle seems a long way off.

Henrik's family were coming that night. During my first visit to Denmark they had treated me with affection and kindness as the girl their son had chosen, without knowing anything more about me. When *The Cruise* went out in Denmark, they were startled. Now, here I was at the Palladium and they, as well as Ken, Henrik's partner from the States, were flying in to see me perform live for the first time. Despite my new confidence, I couldn't help feeling slightly jittery. Everybody wants to play the Palladium; all my idols like Judy Garland had been there, and the thought that I'd be following in their footsteps was daunting. Also, I'd heard that London audiences can tear you limb from limb, and leave you bleeding in the gutter, your career in shreds.

Nick told me that when a leading American artist came over to tour, his promoter said to him, 'You've had a great tour, you're now playing the Dominion. Don't expect them to get up out of their seats. They'll applaud, they'll cheer, but London audiences don't react the same way as the rest of the UK'. The American actually got them on their feet, a feather in his cap.

'But the promoter was right,' Nick said to me, 'London audiences are a bit like, "OK, impress us". So don't be too downhearted if they just clap politely.'

Chris Terrill came with his camera, ready to film the entire show in his special, intimate way. The very first thing he did was to ask me to stand outside on the pavement, looking up at the Palladium lights and the posters and the sell-out signs. He said almost nostalgically, 'Do you remember how you were during *The Cruise*, when the Cruise Director said you'd been on at the Palladium?'

'Don't I just,' I said with feeling. 'I was that scared I'd be caught out. Now look at me! Scared silly in case I bomb.'

When the show eventually started, I sang a cappella offstage to begin with and, almost from the very first note, everyone went wild, the roof seemed to lift. The noise went on and on as I walked into the limelight and stood there on my own. And then they hushed while I continued singing Whitney Houston's 'One Moment in Time'.

Chris had problems because he was told he couldn't go on stage, he had to stand behind an invisible line in the wings and not step beyond it – and no one tells Chris Terrill what to do. He told me that he wanted to capture the evening from my point of view; the nerves, the microphone, the audience out there beyond the footlights, the whole mood and feeling and intensity of it all. To start with, he filmed the whole thing from the wings, but he needed more.

He said, 'I just knew that you wouldn't mind. So I waited till the last song and then I had to go on. You didn't miss a beat, so I knew I'd done the right thing, even though I got into a lot of trouble with the management afterwards. I got my film.'

'I was so used to you,' I said, laughing. 'After you'd shot my nostrils on *The Cruise*, nothing you did could phase me.'

It was such a special night. Everyone crowded into the dressing room afterwards – my family, Henrik's parents and grandmother – everyone amazed at the profusion of flowers, bouquets from everywhere, including a huge basket of roses from Chris with a card that read: 'For my cabin mate'. We drank Champagne and continued with the party back at the hotel. Nick said, 'To be standing at the back of the Palladium when the house lights went down and all I heard was your voice – well, it was goosebumps time.'

☆　☆　☆

After I'd got over the excitement of that unforgettable night at the Palladium, I had the great honour of an invitation to sing on the Royal Variety Show. I had met Prince Charles before, at a Prince's Trust event, and we'd got on quite well, I thought. He was taller than I had expected and I could see that he had a great presence. I'm sure, however, that he's got a healthy dose of Yorkshire blood in him because he has a wicked sense of humour: the droll, deadpan kind that's really quite down to earth. It's almost as if his humour flies by you and suddenly you think, 'Hey, that was funny!' The trouble is that most people are in awe of him and I imagine that very few respond to Charles's subtle wit. It's a pity, since I'm sure he would like to be treated more normally at these starchy events – at least they would be less boring for him.

Charles told me that he had watched *The Cruise* and enjoyed it. I was amazed. Before I could stop myself, I blurted, 'Where on earth do you find the time? You don't think of royalty with your busy lives and all your dinner parties having the time to watch TV!'

Charles laughed. 'Well, we do get some time off, you know.'

The Royal Variety Show was to be on a Sunday. We rehearsed the day before at 11 a.m. I'm definitely not a morning person; apart from the sheer pain of getting up early when the night before perhaps hasn't ended until one or two o'clock, the voice, which is a muscle, needs time to warm up. I was in such terror of even rehearsing in front of some of the big established stars who were on the bill that Nick, who lives just outside London, very kindly agreed to come up from the country to help Henrik hold my hand that morning.

Henrik had chosen my song for the show. Now that his American commitments are so much fewer, he stays with me every day throughout my tours and sits far back in the audience each night so he can be a part of them, getting a sense of what they like best. When we were discussing what I should sing, he said, 'Jane, "Somewhere" is the song that they really like. It stops the show every night.'

'Well, love, I could do with a show-stopper with all that competition,' I'd said. I'd been joking a little – that was before the reality hit home that I'd come from nowhere and was going to be performing with some pretty big players. 'Somewhere', from the musical *West Side Story*, has meant so much to me over the years, even though I could never sing it in the club or cruise days because I didn't have the confidence. Well, nothing boosts confidence like a little success, but even so, it was a big song to handle on such an important occasion – and I had decided to sing live. About four others also sang live but most of the acts, especially the groups, mimed to a tape, which surprised me. Personally, I wouldn't do it on stage because I have a horror of the tape sticking. On the other hand, when you sing live, you have to hit the high notes – you get no second chance.

Nick picked us up from our hotel early that Saturday morning, we got to the Lyceum and waited in the wings for my call. There are some very big notes in 'Somewhere', especially in the middle and end. Nick had already said, 'Don't belt it out now – no one else is putting out their best, it's just for cameras and lighting.' But I always give my best and didn't want to look as if I couldn't cut it. I belted the song out. My voice didn't sound right, I missed a couple of notes. I stood shaking in the wings, until Nick, who'd been seated in the auditorium, joined us. I grabbed hold of him and said, 'Get me off the show, I'm out of my depth.'

He said, 'Jane, don't be so silly. It's too early to sing. Keep

271

it down, talk your way through it. They're only checking the cameras.' Gradually I calmed down and realised that Nick and Henrik were right – nobody was batting an eyelid, the producers didn't come up to me and say, 'Hell, you can't sing, who do you think you're trying to fool?'

For the show I wore the beautiful gown we'd borrowed from Isabel Kristensen. It was a pale *eau de nil*, cut across the breast, very tight in the waist then skintight all the way down to the ankles. 'Very lovely, darling,' Nick said when he saw me in my dressing room, 'You look like a Grecian urn.'

'I can't walk in it!' I said. 'I'm going to fall flat on my face.'

I was terrified that if I took too deep a breath, I'd split it. I'll draw a veil over the size I'd been for years, thanks to all that lavish food on board the ships – let's just say that my borrowed plumage was a size ten but I'd lost so much weight through nervous energy and hard work during the previous months that I could just about wriggle into it, with Henrik on hand to zip me up. Actually walking across that huge stage, however, was another matter, as I was shortly to find out. To make matters worse, I was wearing four-and-a-half inch stilettos and was weighed down with half a million pounds worth of borrowed diamonds from Hennells the jewellers.

'Guard them with your life,' I'd been told, 'Sleep in them if you have to – just don't take them off.'

'I could superglue them on,' I joked weakly, as I stared down at the brilliant chunks of ice mounted on gold lying in the satin-lined boxes. 'Up north, you could buy twenty good houses for this lot – an entire village complete with church, golf course and mansion if you're good at haggling.'

Nick had asked for the piano to be set on stage when it was my turn to sing. I was to wait behind the curtains so that, after they'd introduced me, the curtain would go up and I'd be discovered in front of the grand piano with one arm raised, looking like the trademark Venus on Colombia Films.

The stage manager indicated that I had to move forward onto the stage to wait behind the curtain. 'Oh, my God,' I said, 'This is it!'

People were wishing me luck and Henrik kissed me as he always did, and said, 'You look lovely, Jane. You'll be fine.'

'Why do you do these things to yourself, Jane?' I asked myself for the tenth time as I got into position. I'll say one thing – wearing a dress that's too tight does wonders for your deportment.

'OK?' my pianist asked as I got into the Grecian urn pose next to the piano.

'Oh sure,' I said. 'My dress is going to split, I'm going to trip over my stilettos and land flat on my face on the stage before the future King of England and all those people who've paid a great deal of money to watch me make a fool of myself.'

I didn't know how much the tickets had cost, though I did know that all the proceeds for the night went to a kids' charity. Suddenly I wasn't going to be singing for Prince Charles and all those celebrities in the audience – I was singing for kids who had nothing. My nerves left – and then, from the other side of the curtain, I heard Ulrika Johnsson say: 'It's Jane McDonald!'

Everyone applauded. Back swished the curtain and beyond the bright lights I saw the good-natured crowd packed into the auditorium of the Lyceum, and felt their warmth reaching out to me. I had played the Palladium a few weeks before at the end of my first British tour and that had been sensational – everyone wants to play the Palladium, don't they? But the Royal Variety Performance had a special ring to it that seemed to say, 'You've arrived'. The first ever show had been for King Edward VII and, since then, some of the greatest actors and artists of all time have been invited to perform. I can still remember being struck dumb when I got the call saying they wanted me.

My instinct as a performer took over. If my dress was going to split, then let me use it I thought. 'Fab frock – pity I can't walk,' I said as I bent down, hiked the skirt up and, camping it up, walked like a duck to the front of the stage, hearing the first ripples of laughter from the audience.

I thought, 'Keep the humour going, girl.' It was what I enjoyed, building a rapport with the audience. Thanks to all those years in the working men's clubs up north, where you gave back as good you got, I was never short of a word or two. I looked down into the pit where the orchestra was and said, 'Nice to see a working pit'.

I couldn't get my mike right, so a boy came and set it up but, even as I joked about that, I felt my right leg starting to judder. All I could think was, 'Oh, my God, they're going to see this on camera.'

'Who watched *The Cruise* then?' I asked.

A faint cheer came from the crowd. 'Oh, seven of you,' I said. The laughter continued to build. Remembering my conversation with the Prince, I looked up at the royal box and said, 'Sorry, eight...'

That got a good response and, apart from the vibrating leg, I started to relax. I had the stage for five minutes and the producers had been very strict about timing – but I wanted to pay a special tribute to Dad. I started to feel the tears welling up as it hit me that he wasn't there to watch from the wings as he'd watched so many of my shows over the years. I started to tell the audience how much I was missing him and how he had helped to get me to where I was now.

I could feel my voice cracking and on those high heels, both my legs were now wobbling. 'Just get me through this, Dad,' I prayed silently as the music started, and I launched into 'Somewhere', a song that is almost a hymn – and perhaps reflects both what I feel about life here on earth and in the next world. Like the words, I fervently hoped that Dad had found peace and quiet – somewhere.

I could hardly hear myself through the monitors because they are kept so low for TV and 'Somewhere' is slow and emotional, not a fast song you can get into. Things seemed to be going well judging by the rapt faces I could see beyond the spotlights – but it wasn't over. I thought, 'Sink or swim, girl, you've got that top D to hit yet.'

I hit that top note at the end perfectly and when the last notes of the piano died away, the audience went wild. It was unbelievable, the applause I got from that one song – but like most televised royal events, the show had to run like clockwork and we were told not to hang around milking our moment of glory but to get off quickly. I bowed to the royal box and headed for the wings. Now that I had finished, I felt exhilarated – how I wished that I could have felt like that while waiting to go on stage!

As soon as I was safely in the wings, I got the full luvvie treatment with everyone clustering around, hugging me and telling me I had done well.

'Was it all right?' I asked, still not believing that I had lived through the ordeal – only now it wasn't an ordeal any longer, but fun, a moment to remember and treasure. 'I could hardly breathe!' I said, rolling my eyes and camping it up a little. 'I felt like a Christmas cracker – that's the last time I shoe-horn myself into a dress.'

'Where have you been?' a voice said.

It was Bryan Adams. I gawped at him and almost swooned into his arms. This was the man who had sung, '(Everything I Do, I Do It) For You' to me at the moment Henrik had asked me to marry him. Why did he want to know where I'd been? Confused, I replied, 'On stage.'

That set everyone off laughing because Bryan had meant, 'Who are you – why haven't we seen you before?'

'Oh, I've been all at sea for years, darling!' I said.

Everyone laughed again but, ruefully, I thought it was all too true. To coin a phrase, I'd been a big fish in a small pond for a long time, because the world of shipboard entertainment is a small one. Out of sight, sailing the ocean blue, really is out of mind as far as mainstream show business is concerned.

At the end of the show, all the performers crowded on to the stage for a grand finale. After the curtain calls and a standing ovation, the heavy drapes swished down for the final time and we were all lined up for the official presentation. I was next to the Spice Girls, who were as bright and chirpy as usual. When Prince Charles came along the line, he stopped at me and smiled, 'Delighted to see you here, Jane'.

As I bobbed a curtsey, I heard another voice saying, 'Why, Jane, how lovely to see you again!'

Charles said, 'Oh, do you know each other?'

It was King Constantine of Greece, who of course has a beautiful Danish Queen. They had been special guests of the owners of the Celebrity line when I had been asked to sing at some of the stateroom parties, and they recognised me at once, which made me feel very special.

Instead of going straight to the cast party as everyone else was, I'd agreed to do a couple of interviews – then, feeling like Cinderella, I had to rush back to my hotel to take off the borrowed diamonds. Our hotel was a few hundred yards away so we walked, the Isabel Kristensen gown hoiked up and hidden beneath a long overcoat. With Henrik holding my arm to guide me through the crowds, I was unlikely to get mugged.

My feet were killing me in their spiky stilettos, and I was grateful to get into our suite, kicking off the shoes as we entered the door, my stockinged feet sinking into deep-pile luxury carpet. Henrik patted the jewel-cases, 'Some day you'll have your own diamonds and won't have to borrow them,' he said.

'I do have my own,' I reminded him. 'You gave me my exquisite necklace as a Christmas present, remember? I'll always treasure it.'

Worn out by all the excitement, I was still in bed early the next morning while Henrik went for his shower. The phone rang beside the bed and I answered it. It was a messenger at the front desk, asking if he could come up and collect the jewels. Within a few moments, he was knocking on the door and I handed them over. 'I was scared to death with that lot around my neck,' I said with a smile. 'I'm glad they're in your hands now.'

As I closed the door, Henrik came in from the bathroom in a towelling robe, rubbing his hair dry. 'Who was that?' he asked.

'Oh, just a messenger to collect the jewels,' I said casually, brushing my hair at the dressing table.

'Give me the receipt and I'll file it,' said my husband, the ever-efficient businessman.

I swivelled on the stool. 'Receipt? I didn't ask for a receipt.'

'You mean, you just handed half a million pounds worth of diamonds to a total stranger?' Henrik said.

'He said he was from the jewellers,' I protested, never having seen such a thunderous expression on Henrik's face before.

'I can't believe you were so stupid,' Henrik yelled, pulling on his jeans and grabbing a shirt before racing out of the suite with wet hair. Not waiting for the lift, still buttoning up his shirt, he went two steps at a time down the staircase, through the foyer, ignoring the startled glances, and out on to the pavement.

How he recognised the messenger, I'll never know. The man was about to step into a taxi when this berserk, half-dressed Dane charged at him from twenty yards away.

Henrik got his receipt and I learned something: that my normally docile husband can be a tiger when aroused. His anger had scared me because I had never had it directed at me before. No relationship can be sweetness and light all the time. Moods and circumstances vary. You find things out about each other, you express your feelings and these forge a bond between a couple over the years. In that instance, Henrik had shown me his business face, it had not been personal: he was saying, 'Jane, please be more cautious, don't be so trusting'. I realised he was right, that he was seeking to protect me and I found that very reassuring. I had made the right decision in asking him to manage me.

That spectacular year of 1998 ended with my Christmas single going into the charts at number ten and with me appearing on my childhood favourite programme, *Top of the Pops*. The real highlight came when I was voted Yorkshire Woman of the Year. Michael Parkinson won the Yorkshire Man of the Year at the same time. As we clutched our awards, he said, 'If you knew how many years it's taken me to win this award – and look at you!'

I told him, 'My opening line at the clubs used to be, you can take the girl out of Yorkshire but you can't take Yorkshire out of the girl, and bah gum lad, it's true.'

The people of the north are warm; you don't get that sense of loyalty and pride in your location further south because the south is full of people from all over the country. True, Londoners might have that sense of unity amongst themselves but, sadly, I feel that there's no real sense of southern identity, whereas my roots are very strong. For me now, 'home' is more a sense of self than of location. Wherever I hang my hat is home, everything else is bricks and mortar. There's great warmth in Silcoates Street, but if my mother's out, the warmth isn't there, so it's all due to her.

As I reflected on an astonishing year in my life, everything looked rosy. I had married the man of my dreams, I had found success. I should have been deliriously happy. There was only one problem: success had not reached my bank account yet.

FOLLOWING MY DREAMS

One of the first things that Henrik had done when he had taken over as my manager, was to move us out of Wendy's conservatory and into new offices in a handsome old Georgian town house in the centre of Wakefield, conveniently situated near the railway station. Oddly enough, from the windows, you could see Piccadilly, the district where my family had first lived when they'd come down from Scotland before I was born. Those old back-to-back terraces had been long demolished; there was nothing there now but a large carpark and some cash-and-carry businesses. But it had been a fresh beginning for the family then – maybe, I'd thought, it would be a fresh beginning for me. It had resembled the three stooges, watching Wendy's brother, Tony and Henrik putting the office furniture together from flat packs, with me sitting killing myself laughing at their antics.

I had been on a high that day; everything had been looking good. By then Caroline Eccles, who had been at school with Wendy and me, had given up her long-term job in an architect's office to work for our new company – Jane McDonald Limited – and we made a good little team. There had been Blackpool and the tours coming up with a massive support team behind me – and I can remember wondering how one woman could create so much work.

Six months later, reality hit home. Henrik said we needed to discuss the future. We were like the generals in the field having a meeting in the tent before the big battle the next day. I felt as if we had been through hell. I was upset and angry because it seemed incredible that I could have sold millions of pounds worth of records and still be so hard up because in the music industry it takes so long for money to come through. We'd gone to number one in the charts and Henrik had spent a fortune subsidising my business but now, once more, I was wondering if it had been worth it.

The various business difficulties almost led to the break-up of our marriage. We were still in love; but you can't rant and rave about things week after week without some of it rubbing off. Constant anger against people who seemed to be untouchable or, the other side of the coin, constant tears and moans, can be very wearing on the person you live with, however close you are.

During those months when we were at our lowest ebb, we got an incredible amount of support from Sue and John Pickles, two friends who had been very well established in the music business for some fifteen years. I certainly came to see that if you don't have true friends, you can't survive many of the storms and pressures in the entertainment business. Henrik and I would often go and stay in Sue and John's peaceful home in the Dales, taking trips into the glorious scenery of the Lake District. We would stay in restful hotels, eating well and sleeping deeply. Often, as I walked through the ancient castles and abbeys that dotted the landscape, the deep spirituality of the places soothed my soul and I could feel the tension fade away. It was my time to come down, to prepare myself for whatever fresh hell from others might be waiting my return.

Sometimes, when Henrik and I felt very low, we'd escape the office and walk around one of our favourite places, the Newmillerdam, a lovely spot just outside Wakefield. One cold and frosty day just after our crisis meeting in the office, we crunched fallen leaves underfoot, watching swans glide on the serene, reflective waters of the lake, also reflecting on our future together. Sometimes you can confuse one fight with another. Were Henrik and I fighting a nebulous *them* or were we fighting each other?

With me being who I am, I wanted to walk away. I said to Henrik, 'Let's leave it, why are we even putting ourselves through this?' I could see my house going, I could see my life going. All I wanted to do was go back to the safe existence I had in Florida. I decided that I was going to be a wife and a mum, and I was happy with that. I wasn't bothered about fame; I really wasn't. I thought, 'thanks a lot, but I've had it with this, 'bye'.

Henrik, however, was so keyed up that he said, 'I can't leave this situation, no way.' It was a challenge for him, one that wound him up and kept him going instead of wanting to throw in the towel like me.

Hands thrust in pockets, his breath a cold plume in the frosty air, Henrik said, 'Jane, this is my wife under attack. You're hurting and I can't stand next to you and see this without doing something. I want to fight for your career'.

When people attack me, it hurts, it makes me cringe. But to Henrik it is as if they are physically assaulting me and that makes him angry.

That day, walking around Newmillerdam, we made up our minds: we could give up and go to Florida – or we could stay and fight. We chose the latter. No more complaining, no more talking, positive action was the answer. Henrik said, 'There are more tours, more concerts, there's television, musicals, movies. You can sing, you can act. The world is your oyster, Jane – let's go for it.'

As I looked across the water at the bare wintry trees rising on the far side, to the high moors above Wakefield, I said, 'Do you remember that psychic in Florida that you went to see? He said that within ninety days you would be starting an entirely new career and living far from there near mountains and water?'

Henrik nodded. 'And it was just sixty days later that I finally decided to take on a new partner on the engineering side and dedicate myself almost full-time to being your manager.'

Fired with a new resolve, we returned to the office and started planning a campaign to take us forward. We knew it wouldn't be easy and there would be many pitfalls and a great deal of jealousy along the way, but at least we were standing together in this and never again would we allow enemy action to nearly destroy our precious marriage.

Henrik turned down many offers for my own TV show while we waited for the perfect one. Finally, he signed a three-month exclusive deal with an independent TV production company, to allow us time to thrash out several ideas and develop the right format for me. We had many meetings and I told them I was interested in developing a talent show to give something back. I said, 'There's so much talent out there, I would like to give some other people the chance that I was given.'

At the end of the day, we came up with the format for *Star for a Night* and, with the producers from the production company, we had a meeting with the BBC. I enthused about why I wanted to do this show, and at the end, the BBC people said: 'Right, we can see you are enthusiastic about this. Let's go for it'. It was agreed that we would start off with a pilot and, if the ratings were good, it would be extended to a series. The pilot was aired one Saturday night in the middle of 1999 and had great ratings, with forty-three per cent of total viewers for that hour watching.

The series was commissioned and I started to travel the length and breadth of the country, auditioning literally thousands of aspiring stars. I would get so attached to them and frustrated when they weren't selected. Also, I personally knew of the great pool of brilliant talent that existed in the clubs and desperately wanted to give some of them a chance to shine. Many of them thought I could pull strings and there was some resentment when I didn't. What none of them realised was that while I was there for the auditions, I wasn't there for the final selection; that was done by the show's producers. In a way it was helpful, taking the stress off me – after all, the show was only one hour long once a week, there simply wasn't time for everybody to go on. I wanted them all to win, all to have a boost, and I took it personally when they were criticised by the panel because I know how devastating that can be. But the proof of the pudding, as we say in Yorkshire, is in the eating, and the show did so well in the ratings war (which reminded me of the dreaded points cards on the ships) that it was recommissioned.

In March 1999, we were approached by the Chelmsford Summer Festival committee, which by way of introduction explained that it was arranging a theme concert. It had Lesley Garrett the previous year and very much wanted to be the first to bring me out in association with a big orchestra and would the Royal Philharmonic Orchestra do? I almost fainted on the spot. I recovered, to hear them say that they needed to get everything sorted out for the big August Bank Holiday and when could we let them know?

'As soon as I pick myself up off the floor,' I felt like saying.

Henrik arranged a meeting between us, the committee chairman and the people from the orchestra at the Royal Philharmonic's offices in London to discuss the programme. They said they always did a theme; this year it was to be a tribute to Barbra Streisand and Rogers & Hammerstein. They would split the evening up between me singing and straight orchestral pieces. The chairman said, 'On the Saturday we've got Sister Sledge and Bjorn Again, and for the Sunday we want something just a bit bigger.'

As a professional singer, I rehearse on my own once I have agreed material. Dave Arnold of the Royal Philharmonic and I discussed songs and keys and the meeting wound up with a date to meet in a small piano shop in Soho, where we would run through my material. We were fully confident that the Soho meeting plus an hour from 4–5 p.m. on the night of the concert was enough. The committee chairman, however, gave us the impression he felt that for a big concert such as this, surely we would need to rehearse for at least two weeks? We reassured him that everything was under control but even on the night of the concert, the chairman was nervously flapping about, not sure if it would work out, whether a vast crowd of some six to eight thousand people would really enjoy listening to the combination of a very new populist star and a classical orchestra. I wanted to reassure him – to say, 'yes, of course they will,' – only I was so full of my usual insecurities, that all I could do was stand quaking in the wings.

At first, I was disappointed that the weather was a bit cloudy; but as soon as I went on stage the clouds parted. I could see stars and a sea of people lighting candles all up the hill. To see that from where I stood – candles and stars – was breathtaking. My voice seemed to sail out that night, every single note crystal clear. You wouldn't think that, with it being outdoors, the haunting sound of the violins and the grand piano would flood the hillside and be heard so clearly. It was magnificent; and so were the fans. They carried us through from song to song. I felt they would have stayed until dawn if they could, and watched the sun come up, awash with the beauty of the night and the music.

That summer, on a roasting hot day in July, I also did the Wicked Woman concert in Hyde Park. It was an amazing scene gazing out at that vast expanse of grass as the sun set over London. I looked back at that sickly little girl who couldn't travel on a bike, to the girl who thought she'd arrived when she went down to London the first time to play a club and ended up stuck on the M25, to the wonders I was now faced with every day.

As part of our plan for the future, we looked into co-promoting a tour. We never expected it to be easy, but I had already done a big tour and didn't think it could possibly be any worse than that – and with Henrik's organising skills, we believed it could, and should, be a pleasant experience for everyone concerned. One of the most important things I wanted to ensure this time was that the crew got a good meal every day and a proper bed for the night, something that doesn't always happen. I always think you have to take care of the people who work hard for you.

The first tour had sold out but, even though I would never insult my fans by wearing baggy sweatshirts and jeans with holes in the knees on stage, I thought the first tour could have been more glamorous, more showbiz. During rehearsals for the second tour, I told everyone that I didn't want to cut corners. 'People pay for their night out – we owe it to them to give them a really good show,' I said, determined to work hard towards achieving that extra little bit of glamour and excitement. I was glad I was working this into the show because the bookings were coming in and the tour was getting bigger and bigger.

Henrik was getting some wonderful dates lined up in all the big towns and even in a few arenas. After Chelmsford, I thought I could tackle anything, but when Henrik looked up at me from his desk one day and said, 'I've just booked the Albert Hall,' I had to sit down fast. The words, 'Albert Hall, Albert Hall' spun around my brain. 'I think I need a large drink,' I said.

I knew that it was important to have the right musical director and was delighted when I was introduced to Michael Alexander, someone who had been Shirley Bassey's arranger and MD and done a lot of broadcasting. He invited us to his home at Four Oaks in Sutton Coldfield. It was a little oasis, 'probably closed when most people pass through,' he said when we met.

I took to him at once, and so did Henrik when he discovered that Mike was also into motorbikes. We met his wife, Stephanie, then looked around his very well-equipped garden studio and had lunch with a glass of wine. Over lunch I told him some of the problems we had been experiencing, none of which seemed to surprise him in the least.

He said, 'This business is full of warm, wonderful, sincere

people – always with a smile, nothing gets them down. The public doesn't always get to see the heartache that can lie beneath the surface.'

Henrik asked him bluntly, 'Will you work with Jane? We would expect one hundred per cent commitment. You'll be asked to take on a lot of responsibility for all the music. We're not big yet, so it won't be as fancy as perhaps you are used to.'

Mike nodded. 'Having worked with most people in the light entertainment field, Jane is as good as any. I can see a long career ahead. I believe the key to whole thing is to build a close-knit team around her. One thing is, I arrange scores, write out notes on a piece of paper and I want musicians and backing singers to sing what I write: I have the last word.'

I said, 'That's fine. We have to have a strong direction. But I think I have a sense of what works for me, so I would like to discuss things, have some input. Also, when we do another album, I want to co-produce because I believe that I can do it.' We talked more about all the problems, and I said that whenever I was very stressed, my voice started to seize and I had already lost it completely twice. Mike understood what I was talking about at once because he knew a famous singer who had also lost her voice in an emotional trauma – it was great to meet someone who really understood all the pressures involved in the industry.

Mike arranged rehearsals in a church hall that looked like a dusty scouts' hut in the wilds of Staffordshire, which was central for everybody. I'd asked the two Sues, Sue Ravey and Sue Drake, to be my backing singers. When I told Sue Ravey about Mike, that he had been MD to Shirley Bassey and to the BBC's *Pebble Mill* for some years, she looked alarmed.

'He's very nice – he won't bite your head off!' I said.

Although I'm a stickler for punctuality, I was running late

for rehearsals and wasn't there when the two Sues arrived. Mike handed them the music and, according to them, they were so terrified of Mike's build-up that the notes on the page just blurred, making no sense whatsoever. Mike said, 'Right, we'll start with warm-up exercises.' At that time, neither of them bothered with that kind of thing (they do now!) and they were absolutely shaking while they were singing, unable to read a note, unable to hold the sheets still, both of them thinking, 'Goodbye job'.

Mike came out to meet me when I arrived at the hut. Almost his first words were, 'Where did you get those two from? They're hopeless.'

But by the time Mike and I walked back in, there they were by the piano, singing perfectly. Mike stopped and stared. 'Good lord, what happened?' he said. We all laughed about it later, but the problem had been that, professional and experienced though they were, Mike's reputation had been so good that their nerves had failed them.

At the end of that first day of rehersals, Mike handed them a stack of notated song sheets and said, 'See you next week girls, and you'd better know this lot'.

Cheekily, Sue Ravey said, 'Well if we don't know it, I'll show my arse in the Co-op window'. The following week, they knew every part inside out and upside down because they were determined to show him. Apart from which, Sue said, 'No way did we want to expose ourselves in the Co-op window!'

At the end of the rehearsal period, we had done all the songs except one: 'The Hand that Leads Me', which I had written for my mother. Mike said to the two Sues, 'You've got this to learn, so we stood around the piano and I started to sing it. I heard a noise and turned around: the Sues had their song sheets held up high to hide their faces. Mike asked, 'What are you two laughing at?'

For a moment I thought, 'Oh no! Are they laughing?' But when they dropped the song sheets, I saw they were crying. They never did get used to hearing that song. What made it worse was when they stood on stage and saw everyone in the audience weeping. Mothers and daughters would look at each other, it seemed to draw them closer. In the end, Sue Ravey said, 'It's no good, Jane, we're sniffling and can't sing – so could you please make a joke of it and bring us the tissues right upfront on stage?' The more they tried to stop crying, the more they did it – it's like laughing at school, once you start, you can't stop. So after that, I did as they asked and handed out the tissues on stage, and they were fine.

Ever since Blackpool, I was always mindful of the running order and spent a lot of time with Mike, establishing the perfect one. It's vital throughout your show to have constant hills and valleys, making sure it all builds and builds. Whether on one night or a six-week venue, each night is individual to each member of the audience – that's their night and it had better be good. By working hard, we got a standing ovation every time. At the end, I was often given flowers by the audience. At one concert, a young man was so overwhelmed that he ran out to the kiosk and bought me a Mars bar because there were no flowers on sale. I gave it to Mike to hold. He was about to put it in the pocket of his white suit when I said, 'Don't do that, it'll melt'. The audience roared with laughter, although I hadn't meant it to be funny – that was just the housewife in me coming out.

Mike and I do a funny little scene during the show, when he tries to get me to play the piano and I refuse, saying 'No, I can't'. Mike then says, 'Try', and I start off with a few simple bars from 'Chopsticks', then blow him away with arpeggios of 'My Foolish Heart', while he takes over my role and tries to sing. This all came about accidentally during one rehearsal. I'd kept my ability on the piano quiet, but one day Mike spotted me tinkling away. As soon as I saw him, I jumped up guiltily, because he's so brilliant.

Mike was always looking for the artist to do the un-expected. He said, 'Go on, don't stop. We could do something with you playing on stage.'

'I said, 'Leave it out. I'm hopeless.'

But he convinced me and it turned out well and was entertaining, so stayed in as part of the show. I thrive on the feedback from the audience – and the love of the fans. You have to respect them, you can't desert them and go off at a tangent. You've got to be there for them. I've had so many managers at theatres saying what a lovely type of fan I've got: well behaved, so respectful. 'Your fans make an orderly queue,' they'll say. Such compliments are very unusual, so I'm very proud of my fans. And they are so loyal. I see the same faces in the front row, willing me to be good. I always do a signing afterwards, often staying behind for an extra hour. To me, it's wonderful getting that reaction from the public. The fans are all ages, all sexes, right across the board from the gay community to fourteen-year-old girls and seventeen-year-old boys; mums and dads; little girls who come with their auntie, mum and grand-mother; entire families sometimes. Then there's Amy, a little girl who dresses like me in her sequinned 'Jane McDonalds'.

On stage, I wear a headphone pack on a receiver that connects with invisible in-ear monitoring that stops a lot of feedback and lets me listen to whatever instrument I want to sing the melody to. Normally, this pack is attached to the back, under your clothes, causing a little bump – which in a sheath dress can be unsightly, but everyone does it. On a couple of occasions, the wire came out of my pack and I'd get Mike or someone to fiddle with it and stick it back in. At one point Mike said, 'Look, this is not the best place to put this pack, it's in the way and, when you turn sideways, there's a lump in your dress. The best place is the top of your inner thigh where you won't notice it. Use a bandage or tape to strap it securely in place.'

I tried it and he was right. The wire went up behind my bum into the earpiece and you didn't see it. One night, the worst happened in the middle of a concert: on stage, the wires came out mid-song and I couldn't hear a thing. While not missing a note, I frantically indicated to Mike what the problem was, and he offered his assistance. He got up from the piano, walked to the centre of the stage, knelt down behind me and put one hand up my frock, fiddling around my inner thigh trying to get this lead back in while the audience roared with laughter.

After about thirty seconds of fiddling Mike said, 'No, no, no – this is far too personal for me to deal with. You'll have to go off and get it seen to. Get your husband to do it.'

I smiled at the audience and walked off to the wings, where Henrik carried on where Mike had left off. That night, giving me a wink, Mike dined out on the story: 'There was this famous superstar performing in front of the stage, trying to sing while laughing, the audience is laughing, I'm knelt down behind her with my hand up her frock, one eye on the wings, where I'm expecting a mad Viking to come at me with an axe at any moment!'

Everything was building towards the Albert Hall on November 22nd. I have said that I don't suffer from stage fright; just pure panic. I don't enjoy anything until it's over, but then I am exhilarated and wish the moment would never end. As with the Palladium, I arrived earlier to do a sound check and, when I walked out on the stage, I was petrified. I looked at the great vaulted dome miles above, at the distant empty seats vanishing almost into the horizon and I thought, 'Flipping heck, am I going to fill it? Are all these people going to want to come and see Jane McDonald?'

By now, my fears were just fleeting – the professional side of me always kicked in and took over. But, as an extra boost to my performance, I invited the family down. I always work harder when I'm trying to please Mum. They all came down in a minibus, stayed overnight and had a fab time touring London the next day.

On stage, I was to wear a fabulous dress by Jacques Azagury, the designer who Nick had found for me – a cerise diva dress smothered with sequins and split almost up to my navel. It put me in mind of a music teacher I once had who'd say, 'Sing with your crotch, Jane, sing with your crotch'. When I tried the gown on, I said, 'Blimey, the front row will *see* my crotch in this!'

We wanted to make a very casual, short first half, with a girl-next-door, intimate feel. I'd be saying to the audience, 'You can talk to me, let's chat'. In contrast, the second half was to be very grand, with me saying, 'This is me performing now – this is the show'. For the encores on tour, I would go off and return in a flowing matching cerise chiffon coat that floated behind me as I walked, very Diva McDonald, that had my followers whooping in the aisles.

The thing that I remembered the most was the warmth of the audience reaching out to me and Mum sitting in the front row with Gran as I looked down and said, 'My mother is everything to me. She's my mentor, my best friend. Some day I hope I'll be like her. All through my life, my mother has been there to love, comfort and guide, her hand always there when I was a little girl to reach up to hold. I wrote this song for her: "You are the one that leads me… guides me… loves me – Thank you for it all – but thank you most of all for the hand that leads me…".'

Even though the lights were shining in my eyes, I could see daughters and mothers all over the auditorium smile and glance at each other. Mum later told me that, yes, the words did move her but, she said, 'I have a very nice mother, too – I felt that the words were reaching out from me to her'. I think that this was more praise than I could ever have hoped for.

I felt as if the rest of the tour had been leading up to the Albert Hall. But it's really up to the audience to determine what kind of a show it is. If you walk out on stage and they go POW, like a rocket going off, then you know you're in for a sensational night, it's pure electricity, it's phenomenal. As soon as I walked out on to that huge stage it exploded with a great roar that really did seem to lift the roof off.

I wasn't expecting it. I'd had that at the Palladium – but I thought perhaps it was because the cameras were there and I was all very new from *The Cruise*. But with the Albert Hall, I'd been off television for a year – and sometimes people forget, think you're a one-hit wonder, and don't bother. I walked out on that stage and they were still there: it was complete love from that audience. I thought, 'I love you all back!' and they all knew that. The audience knows I adore them and thank them for everything and they feel special, at least I hope they do, because that's how I feel.

Later, when we unwound on tour, Sue would tell me what she saw from behind me. I would talk about my mother and my father and sing the songs I'd written for them. People would start to cry, but while they were wiping their eyes, they'd start to laugh because, being me, I'd change the whole atmosphere and say something funny. The men would be trying to wipe a tear away without anybody seeing it, you would start to see the light reflected from everybody's glasses lifting up, tissues coming out. Ladies didn't mind, they'd all fumble about, wiping away tears and while they were doing that, they'd be laughing. I'd want to take them by the hand on a real rollercoaster of emotion because we all enjoy a good laugh and a good cry – I should know, I'm always either sobbing my heart out or splitting my sides.

That night at the Albert Hall, all my friends were there. Chris Terrill had slipped in and was sitting far up in the Circle. He said it was the first time he had ever just sat and enjoyed my show without working with a camera glued to his shoulder. I had hoped he'd be there. When he heard me thank him and sing 'The Best Thing That Ever Happened to Me' just for him, he admitted later that he wept unashamedly. Jacques Azagury was there with his family; Barbara Windsor, who was on the panel of *Star for a Night*, was there; and Bobby Crush. At one point I was doing that piano sketch with Mike, when I said, 'Where is Bobby Crush when you need him?' and he shouted, 'I'm here!' Everyone started laughing – it was that intimate; it was like being in your front room. The Albert Hall is awe-inspiring – but I no longer felt awed. When you see that vast audience and see people hanging out of the boxes screaming, waving and shouting out to you, you are a bit in awe. But then it just went into the show and it was me fulfilling my dreams, bringing all that glitter to life.

Afterwards, I was on a high for quite some time. Even after the end of tour party, I couldn't go straight to bed. On every other tour night, Henrik would usually be tucked up in bed by eleven because he had to work the next day. However, I would make cocoa, wake him up and talk him to death. He didn't mind, because that was my coming-down time. I'd then have a bath, be in my own space and unwind.

After so much hard work on the tour, I decided to have a break and took Sue Ravey for company to a health spa in Shropshire. When we arrived we had to fill forms in and they gave us cheap plastic pens with the name of the place. I was thrilled. 'Oh, can we keep these?' I asked.

The receptionist looked so surprised, I'm sure that most of the clients there must carry diamond-studded Mont Blancs. She said, 'If you like.'

'Oh, ta,' Sue and I said in unison. Sue said, 'These must have cost all of tuppence, anybody'd think we'd won the lucky dip!' We both started giggling.

I said, 'I do like that about you Sue, you get such a thrill out of little things.'

Sue said, 'What about you? When I was round at your mum's house at six o'clock the other evening, who was in dressing gown and slippers, cup of tea in hand, saying, "Oh this is total comfort, it's so nice to take me clothes off"?'

We were both pampered beautifully the first day. The next morning, I went into Sue's room to find her putting the finishing touches to making her bed. She fluffed up the pillows and pulled the counterpane over. 'There, you can't tell I've slept in it,' she said with satisfaction.

I said, 'Sue, you're just like my mum, tidying up for the maids. You shouldn't make your bed, you've come to relax. And anyway, they'll be thinking that you've slept with me in my room, and that will be the next thing in the papers.'

Sue's eyes grew round. 'Ooh heck, I never thought!'

We unmade the bed and, just for good measure, threw some towels on the floor so the room would have that lived in look – you can't be too careful.

When I was younger, I used to have this dream about skiing – me and my ideal man on the piste. I knew I was destined to be like the Maid of the Mountains, I didn't know where or when, so going on the ski slopes with Henrik in Aspen in the January of the new millennium was a dream come true. We were trying to snatch a holiday before starting work on my second album and filming in New York for the programme *OK! TV*. We didn't know if we would be able to ski, or would even enjoy it. We bought our outfits in Florida and flew to the Rockies. Right from the word go, it was fantastic. The first day, Henrik was on top of the mountain, skiing straight down, past the baby class where he'd left me standing. Mr Olympic Team, was so instantly addicted that we didn't meet up again until three days later in the bar of the ski lodge.

I walked in and saw a vision of this blond hunk, white polo neck and a red jacket. I could see a lot of women looking at him and thought I'd better get over there quick. I fell in love all over again on the spot – which was wonderful, after all the trials and tribulations we'd been through. I recommend a skiing vacation to any couple in need of putting a bit of romance back in their lives.

Henrik negotiated really hard for me with my new record label, Universal Music. It was a wonderful deal that allowed me complete artistic control and the final say on everything as well as co-producer credits. It was such a pleasure to be with a company that allowed me to move on, that gave me freedom to stretch my wings. From the time the deal was confirmed in January, we had less than three months to deliver the album. I told Ted Carfrae (who's the producer with me) that I wanted to go back to R.G. Jones to record the new album, because I loved the sound there. From the start, I was treated with the utmost respect, and I gained in confidence. Nick Fiveash also had some input into the way I sang. We discussed it quite a lot. When I sang 'This is the Moment' on the *Des O'Connor Show*, he said, 'Listen to those lyrics, Jane. Relate them to your life, all you're going through at the moment.'

It was that period when it had all gone wrong, everything was breaking down, I was going through so much. Des O'Connor was the first big telly that we did that wasn't actively promoting the first album. It was a one-off, to promote the second tour. I listened to the words that spoke of succeeding despite setbacks with a new intensity, and suddenly I twigged what Nick was talking about. At the moment when I sang that line, I looked straight into the camera and held my finger up, 'Listen to me, I will make it!'

That continued into the new album, 'Inspiration'. I sat and really thought about the lyrics and put the words to a moment in my life or situation. When he heard the finished mix, Nick said, 'That's great! You're singing in a more thoughtful mature way'. I am a sponge for knowledge, always ready to listen. If somebody's giving me constructive criticism, I will take it. I don't get offended, I don't say, 'Don't you dare speak to me like that'. If I think it's a valid comment, I will take it on board, and I think this has only helped me.

OK! TV, a gossipy celebrity-led programme, asked if I would make a film in New York with Nigel Havers. I flew to the States, with Nick accompanying me, to help take care of business. The magazine had booked us into a brand new hotel, very Philip Starke, very minimalist. Nick adored it but I craved big soft couches, a soft bed and thick drapes – in other words, pure luxury. I was supposed to get a suite but when we walked into my room, I stared at a single narrow bed like a board in a monk's cell – or a prison. You could have bounced a silver dollar on the rigidly tucked in cover and made a hole in the ceiling. I walked along the corridor to see Nick's room which, while still very stark, was a double suite.

He said to the porter, 'This is wrong.'

'No, that's how it was booked, sir.'

Leaving me to start unpacking, Nick shot off down to reception where he demanded a bigger room for me. They said I was in a de luxe suite. Nick said, 'But my room is bigger!' – They said, 'Yours faces into the building, Miss McDonald's faces out onto Broadway. Those rooms are at a premium.'

Nick said, 'It might face on to Broadway, but it's tiny. You can barely put a suitcase in the room.'

They asked Nick if I minded facing into the building. He said no, all I wanted was a bigger bed and more space. He was given the keys to another room and came rushing back upstairs. 'Pack your bags, you're moving,' he said. I had what felt like a hundred cases because of the filming, and not knowing what would be needed. After all, the subject of the film was a blind date with Mr Havers, so I had to look good. By then, the porter had vanished, as porters tend to in New York. Nick and I lugged my loads of bags out of my room, along the corridor, up the lift, to the new room. We walked in to be confronted by every piece of furniture piled high like a pyramid on the bed.

'My God,' I said, 'is it supposed to be installation art or what?'

Nick phoned down to the lobby. 'The furniture is on the bed.'

'Goddammit, we steam-cleaned the apartments this morning! We'll give her another room.'

So we had to drag all the bags back to another lift, along another mile of corridor, into another room. True, this one was very big, but there was a bench for a sofa, the bed was still very crisp and flat, empty of cushions and any hint of comfort or luxury – just a bolster at the head which I knew as soon as I looked at it, would give me a stiff neck.

Trying to cheer me up, Nick said, 'This is N.Y. modern, seen as the best.'

In the spirit of my father, I said, 'I'm tired and I've got a bed, *it'll do*.' The next day, we had a 6 o'clock wake-up call. The make-up artist was there in my room doing my make-up, I was yawning after a dreadful night, my back so stiff I was like that bent old woman in *Babes in the Wood*, when the producer – who'd arrived at the hotel at 2 a.m. – came running into the room, gasped, 'I'm so sorry! Can you believe the hotel? We thought you would have moved. Pack! We're booking you into the Athena'.

I said, 'Oh my God, I'm too tired to crawl there.'

We packed all the bags yet again, but ended up in a beautiful hotel on 5th Avenue. It was gorgeous, all satin covers, feather cushions and big drapes. Nick said, 'Diva McDonald has found Nirvana at last.'

We were up at 6 a.m. each day and filmed until nine at night, totally exhausted by the schedule. On the Sunday, our one day off, Nick said, 'We're going shopping'. The night before, he had sat in his room half the night with a New York guide and done a plan: Bloomingdale's, Macey's, the Village and back, 'Lunch here, we do this there.' Next morning, with a flourish, he presented me with this itinerary, which was why when we got halfway through the day, we were even more exhausted and why in Bloomingdale's, I couldn't stop giggling hysterically over something Nick said.

Bloomingdale's was on the itinerary because, when in New York, Nick always shops there for Ralph Lauren shirts. We'd been to other departments in the store, in fact we'd been to other stores, I'd bought a coat and God knows what else, so we had piles and piles of shopping. It was getting to be lunchtime and I was hungry. Nick's shirts had been paid for and bagged, it was now my turn at the cash desk. While I waited, I said, 'Right, what do we do now?'

Nick was standing there like a mule, laden down with all my bags as well as his. He said, 'We'll go back to the hotel, *dump*, and then carry on down to Greenwich Village.'

I couldn't help it: it must be my schoolgirl sense of humour. I couldn't speak for laughing, or sign the credit card slip. The assistant didn't know what was going on with these mad English people. I laughed all the way out of the store, all the way back to the hotel and didn't stop. We'd be in the back of the cab going to down to the Village, chatting away, then I'd look out of the window, see the word 'dump' floating before my eyes and my shoulders would heave. All through lunch, I was almost in hysterics. I laughed all the way to the airport. It was just as well that I had Nick with me – anyone else would have had me committed.

With things going well, I decided to buy a house on the outskirts of Wakefield near our favourite spot, Newmiller-dam, somewhere a bit bigger than Silcoates Street, where Mum could finally have that garden of her own where she could grow flowers and sit on a real patio in the sun. We started to box up everything in the old house, but Henrik finally persuaded me to thin out my wardrobe. TV eats clothes; and I needed so many new outfits for the tours, for all the TV shows and interviews, that even with five bedrooms and a massive dressing room of my own, there wouldn't be enough room for everything.

Sue is the same size as me (in fact, I've asked her to go shopping for me on tour – all she has to do is try things on and they'll fit), so she was the first person I thought of when I was emptying my cupboards. I telephoned her to come over and help herself to whatever she wanted, knowing that she still worked in the clubs and could use them. She went off with armfuls of my sequinned outfits, matching shoes, the lot, so much stuff that she told me later she'd had a grand clear-out of her own wardrobe in order to make enough room. One thing she took was the famous silver dress and matching heels that launched my career. Sue and I share songs that we hear the other sing and, even though they are not 'our' songs, we do each other the courtesy of asking 'Do you mind if I use it in my act?' The first night Sue sang in a club after the great clothes haul, she told me she walked out in the silver dress, the shoes, a diamanté necklace I'd given her in Blackpool, and sang 'You're My World'.

She said, 'It was a bit spooky. Standing there in the spotlight, I thought, oh heck, tonight I'm Jane McDonald.' Sue even has my silver sequinned dress, plus a framed signed photograph of me wearing it that I gave to the backing singers as a memento of the second tour. She said, 'I'll be there in my living room, ready to go out in the silver lamé, and look at the wall and there you are. Sometimes, I don't know who I am any more.'

One night, when Sue popped around for a cosy chat, it made me laugh when she told me how she had gone shopping in a big department store for an outfit to wear at my wedding. She had been looking in the section where they've got all the nice clothes and sequinny stuff, when she heard a mother and daughter shopping. The younger one said, 'Oh look, there's a Jane McDonald dress here!' Sue said, 'It made me realise just how famous you had become.'

'Oh yes,' I said in my dressing gown and slippers, feet up on the sofa, cold cream smothered on my face, 'very famous.'

Still, being well known means you get to write your story. At a very posh buffet lunch thrown for me by my publishers when we were talking about me writing a book, I was walking around with Henrik and Nick, being introduced to all the bigwigs, the various editors, the PR people; secretaries were coming up for my autograph, the place was packed and I was enjoying seeing a world I knew so little about, though, as an addicted reader, I was thrilled to be let in behind the scenes. The lunch was all laid out on long tables: salads and cold cuts, little pastry things and then great bowls of strawberries and big pots of cream. While talking to the senior publishing director, I helped myself to a bowl of strawberries and went to take a dollop of cream – then I stopped because I'm not keen on crème fraîche, and asked, 'Is this real cream?'

'Yes, double cream,' said the director.

'I said, 'Oh great, because I don't want any of that femme fresh stuff.'

Nick nearly spat his strawberries across the room. I immediately realised what I'd said and, just as in New York, I was gone.

EPILOGUE

Some years earlier, when Steve Holbrook came to see me perform at Torre Road Working Men's Club in Leeds, he had told me that the song, 'Papa, Can You Hear Me?' from *Yentl* would have great significance in my life. That was the same night when Steve had been seated in the audience watching me, and the backdrop behind me had faded to be replaced by the Stars and Stripes rippling in an invisible wind, telling Steve that I would be linked to America.

Some time later, Steve telephoned me, as he does from time to time. He said, 'My mum's just stood in the kitchen watching you on telly singing "Somewhere". You're going to be in a musical, with a French connection. You're going to get a major offer around February 14th.'

It wasn't on the 14th but shortly afterwards, on February 17th this year, that a fax came in from Michel Legrand's London office. It was very short: 'I am the manager for Michel Legrand, and we would very much like to discuss a collaboration between Michel Legrand and Jane.' Henrik sent a fax back very quickly to say, 'Jane is away, we'll get in touch when she returns.' A meeting was set up for the following month, when Michel came to meet me in London, the day after I'd finished 'Inspiration', my new album. We met in the basement of the Steinway shop in Soho, where a grand piano was set up for his use. He shook my hand and said, 'Jane, I would be delighted if you would consider singing Marguerite, the lead in my new musical.'

I almost died. This was a man who had written the music for over two hundred classic films, from *The Umbrellas of Cherbourg* to *The Thomas Crown Affair*; who won an Oscar for 'The Windmills of Your Mind'; who writes for people like Streisand – and he wanted to work with *me*!

Michel sat down and played the libretto. I had to tell myself: just stand back for a moment and listen to what is happening, absorb the whole atmosphere because you will never forget this moment. I looked at Henrik and I looked at Philippe, Michel's manager, and I looked at Michel, with his lion's mane of flowing white hair, the strong features. I could smell the aroma of old wood and varnish: it was like going back in time.

Michel said, 'Your part is going to be played by harp.' My heart jumped because the harp is my favourite instrument and I'd just used two of them all the way through 'Inspiration'. As he played, he said, 'There's no such thing as coincidence. This is how it's meant to be. I've been looking for you for a long time. You are a very spiritual person, Jane, it's all linked.'

His musical is about seven ghosts in a castle. Marguerite is the first ghost, who has been there since the fourteenth century. She's still so in love with her husband that she has not been able to leave. He has never returned; she's still waiting for him...

We discussed the provinces, the West End, Europe, the Far East – and then Broadway. He said, 'We could work on an album of the musical, like Streisand did with *Yentl*.'

☆　☆　☆

Last night I flew to Lanzarote. I needed the space away from the world to finish this book in peace and quiet. We thought we were getting a wonderful villa, but when we arrived late, we were given a really small apartment in the New Town that smelled of rats and musty damp furnishings. I was so disappointed. Henrik turned to the villa agent and said, 'We can't stay here. We didn't book this.'

The agent shrugged and spread out his hands expressively. 'Sorry, it's a mistake. But tonight, it's late. Tomorrow we will find you the perfect villa.'

Angry and upset, we went out to dinner. When we returned and switched the weak light on in the living room, it illuminated the bookshelves, on which there was nothing else but a single video cassette. I picked it up. It was *Yentl*, starring Barbra Streisand. Something made us sit and watch it. As the credits rolled, three things leaped out from the screen and, each time, I asked Henrik to press the 'freeze' button. One was the dedication to 'My father and all our fathers'; the second was the name of the camera supervisor: Peter McDonald; and the third was the name of the composer, Michel Legrand. 'Oh, my God,' I said, holding the tape out to Henrik. 'This has to be a sign – why else are we here, in this nightmare of a place?'

Today, I am sitting on the terrace by the swimming pool of a fairy-tale villa high above the sea that is so deep a blue you could drown in it. Beyond, are the jagged chocolate-black volcanic peaks that I remember from the *Black Prince*. When I was on the ship I used to look at the white-plastered millionaires' villas sprinkled on the cliffs and imagine the kind of people who lived up there, far beyond my reach in their magical eyries.

I stretch out my hand for a long cool drink and lazily suck

through a straw while thinking of the final chapter of the book I am here to finish writing. I can smell the hibiscus and the bougainvillea vines that fall in a riot of deep purples and reds down the walls. Palm trees and jagged cacti, transplanted from the island's interior moonscape, fill raised beds of black volcanic clinker around the pool.

I have a certain philosophy, the jigsaw pattern of each day and each week and each month and each year of our lives make together a big picture. I don't think it's until we go over to the next world that we can see the full picture, when we see why each piece has to be there.

It's enough to be here in the sun with Henrik. I feel that I have been searching for him all my life. Perhaps like Marguerite's story, Henrik and I met five hundred years ago. Five hundred years from now, will I still be looking for him?

CAREER HIGHLIGHTS

January 1998
The Cruise starts a 12-week broadcast on BBC1.

July 1998
Jane's first album, 'Jane McDonald' goes straight into No.1 in the
  UK charts for 3 weeks and remains in the charts for 26 weeks.
  Jane is listed in the *Guinness Book of Hit Records* as the first ever
  UK female artist to enter the album charts at No.1 without a
  prior release.
The Cruise Wedding Special. Jane's May 26 wedding to Henrik is
  aired on BBC1.

September 1998
HRH The Prince of Wales asks Jane to perform at a Prince's Trust
  benefit.

October 1998
Jane is voted 'Yorkshire Woman of the Year'.
Start of a 30-date concert tour of the UK, with a mid-tour
  performance at the London Palladium.

December 1998
Jane sings at the 1998 Royal Variety Show before HRH The Prince
  of Wales.
Jane's debut single, 'Cruise Into Christmas', enters the charts at
  No.10.

The end-of-tour concert at the London Palladium is broadcast as *Jane's Cruise to the Stars* by BBC1 on New Year's Eve.

May 1999
Jane hosts *Mr Gay UK* in Leeds for Channel 5.

June 1999
The *Star For A Night* special is hosted by Jane for BBC1.

July 1999
Jane sings at the 'Wicked Woman' concert in Hyde Park, London.

August 1999
As part of the 'Midsummer Magic '99' series of open-air concerts, Jane sings at The Lawn, Lincoln.
Jane sings at the 'Chelmsford Spectacular' open-air concert with the Royal Philharmonic Orchestra, conducted by Dave Arnold.

October 1999
Start of a 27-date UK tour, culminating at the Royal Albert Hall.

November 1999
Jane McDonald In Concert enters the Top 5 UK video charts.

January 2000
Star For A Night, the BBC1 series hosted by Jane, begins broadcast.

May 2000
'Inspiration', Jane's second album goes into the UK album charts at No. 6.

July 2000
The 'Jane McDonald Summer Spectacular' 7-week season begins at the Bournemouth International Centre.

September 2000
The second series of *Star For A Night*, hosted by Jane, begins broadcast on BBC1.